Cuba's Attacks

By Ed Prida II and Edward Prida II

Ed II y Edward Prida III

VOLUMEN 3
COLECCION: INTELIGENCIA POLITICA

© *Eduardo Ramon Pri   da*
    The attacks of Cuba
"My dream is to drop three nuclear bombs about New York ".
Raul Castro

© *Eduardo Ramon Prida and Edward Prida III*
Registration Number: TXu -1-713-911
January 10, 2011
West Palm Beach, Fl. VOLUME 2
COLLECTION: POLITICAL INTELLIGENCE

This book is part of "The Sovietization of Cuba and its Consequences" of the author
© *Eduardo Ramon Prida*
Cuba threatens and attacks…
"My dream is to drop three nuclear bombs on New York" Raúl Castro
© *Eduardo Ramon Prida and Edward Prida III*
Registration Number: TXu -1-713-
911 January 10, 2011 West Palm
Beach, Fl.

Gratitude:

To the enemies, always their evil behaviors push me to the confrontation, to those who encourage me or discourage me, equally thank you very much.

But to the one who has taken me by the hand to be a knowing witness, with pains, combats, tortures; Yes, thanks GOD for choosing me for this mission, I do not resign, and I just hope to do better.

Thank to my sons, and Edward for being who he is and being where he should be.

¡Eternal Thanks!
AN ANASHA!
Ed II and Edward Prida III

Dedicatory:

Dedicated to the Americans who have fought to save Cuba, first mixed with the Mambises fighting successfully against colonial Spain with General Thomas Jordan, General in Chief of the Mambí Army and his group of Command, who for many years fought in the fields of Cuba, to Lieutenant Colonel Teddy Roosevelt, who in a humanitarian spirit promoted the need for this war and personally recruited the volunteers to form the liberation troops known as Rough Ryder and fought in front of them, they saved them from death in the concentration camps thousands of Cubans and for that reason they paid a high price for altruistic and courageous lives.

To the formation of altruistic soldiers who have left their lives in dozens of countries without desire for conquest, with no other motive than Love of neighbor.

Especially grateful to the Army, Air Force and the Navy that have educated and instructed my children to defend the United States of America.

Ed II & Ed Prida III

Note to the reader:

The information in this book could give us some light. It is important to know that the method of "doing" them is very planned, when we prepare an operation, we will see scenes, after scenes, like a movie. We are observers unable to suspect that everything has been prepared, all are active measures.

If we already know that everything has been planned, you get an advantage to identify and perform accurate analyzes. They project a certain shadow, but this shadow is our ignorance of the objectives they pursue, that until the last act, you will never know.

These twelve forms of aggression of Russia using its colony Cuba, many do not have appearance of aggressions, but they turn out as such, creating deaths and terror, others absolutely unknown and others we could classify them elegantly as "science fiction" as the call of sharks to the beaches, the creation of hurricanes, the rare attack on diplomats, chemical, biological, cybernetic and electronic warfare. For the average citizen this does not seem true, much less possible.

The book is a tablet, extract of many information that we should all know, so that the enemy has less space to cheat us with his neo language and its color changes.

To cover the Sun with a finger is to affirm that the Cold War is 'History' and that Communism no longer exists, for others, Cuba is a small and poor country incapable of harming the first power of the Planet, for the "evil megalomaniacs" "Cuba is a beacon of Freedom for America and its Revolution is an example of fighting against the" American Empire "and they are conspiring with it. but there are still others that the subversion has bitten them as much as the first and are anesthetized, constantly appealing to the State Department, the CIA, or the New World Order to impose Castro on the Power and still maintain it.

The objectively true, is that today the enemy has not only advanced in our terrain and many specialists believe that we are much closer to a conflict on a world scale than before, it is estimated that enemy activity today is 600% higher than in years 50 and 60. If that was called the Cold War, with what name to baptize this one that we are living. I would dare to baptize her as the "Krio War" is much more what the ´Cold War, because she anesthetized before slaving and killing us slowly ¨

If we read the goals of the United States Communist Party in 1962, we will see that its goals are met. They show us that we have been deceived, but we have time to seize them with force and reason, everything they have stolen from us.

Knowing the truth of their malign actions, delegitimizes the regime and decomposes on its own, as did perestroika and glasnost with the Soviet regime.

Raúl Castro declared to NBC in 1959, his intention was to destroy the United States, his motivation reflected the vivid plans of Nikita Khrushchev in which they involved Cuba, since 1953, when Víctor Pina and Raúl Castro met in the Kremlin with Nikita Khrushchev , to receive the orders and objectives of the attack on the Moncada barracks of Santiago de Cuba, and on what form the USSR was going to participate.

I hope that sharing this information is good for all.
With immeasurable love:
        Ed II and Edward Prida III

To: Honorable President Donald Trump
From: Prof. Ed Prida
Report: Cuba Attacks to the United States of America

Dear Honorable President Donald Trump:

We're supporting your effort to Clean the Swamp and the finish with the Deep States, like you are doing now. Also, we keep in our heart to defend our country, who we swear loyalty and defense bring our sons and our blood.

Our enemies consider the Isle of Cuba like the "Advanced Post" or a "Bridge Head" to be used by the Russian Armed Forces to attack the United States of America like Nikita Khrushchev planed his Subversive Plan against Cuba in 1953.

This is a resume and, we send a book with the evidence and proof of every kind of aggression and the high cost in death, financial and demoralization of the United States for the knowledge the Cubans in the Isle and in the World. We think "Enough is Enough".

1.- Cuba is the base of submarines, nuclear strategic bombers Tu-195 and the nuclear fuel depot in Cienfuegos Russian Navy Base.

2. - The Mariel Container is not a Merchant Terminal is a Medium-Range Missile Base that violates the INF treaty. The missile class CLUB Russia already has several missile types capable of operating in the "intermediate" range with any kinds of military load. They hide the missiles inside the container and able to hit targets at 1,400 – 2,600 km.

3.- Cuba has been the headquarters since 1962 of a Radio Electronic System for Meteorological Modification, codified by the DAAFAR as "Pronto Auxilio" in Quivican. Cuba

4.- Cuba attacks with ultrasound power the brain of the US and Canadian diplomatic personnel rapture the arteries inside the brain arterial system. 5.- Cuba maintains electronic gadget what special frequency frequencies in the United States beaches to call the thousands

of sharks to our beaches that have produced 641 deaths in recent years and this equipment gets maintenance by the Cuban military enterprise known as CARISUB, headquartered in Hialeah, Fl.

6.- Cuba are using the modern system of Intelligence Imaginary Satellite Networks covering the whole territory of the United States, based in Rincon and Bejucal in the South of Havana: Capable of hindering the highways traffic, the electric power, air, and maritime traffic, besides making arson in our forest from by the satellites.

7.- Cuba is the largest producer of cocaine in paste in the world, the largest global cartel conducted by an officer of the CIM (Military Counter Intelligent) of Cuba named Jester Garrido, who has helicopters, airplanes, and submarines in Europe, America, and Africa.

8.-Cuba was the head of the operations of the attack on JFK, the photos and documents of 19 Cubans High Ranking in Dallas on Nov. 22, 1963, at 12:30 pm. We researched and found undeniable pieces of evidence.

9.- Cuba is a source of Subversive and Coup d'état in Africa, Asia, and America.

10.- Cuba encourage and direct Mass Immigration against the United States.

11. Cuba is a source of corruption in the local governments around the USA and the States of Florida using the Multi-Culturalism is to destroy our Education System through the School Board against Pure American Historical Heritage and in favor of the Homosexual deviations.

12. Cuba is the most powerful and nearest base of the Cybernetic War from the Command Center of Ramiro Valdes located beside of the Novia del Medio Día Highway. They are stealing the bank accounts, electronic on the Internet and introducing thousands of subversion and Intelligence agents, the list I have published is of over 2000 agents recognized by the DIA. Cuba research and produce Chemical and Biological Weapons, the tested in Venezuela, Angola, Brazil, Cuba, United States, Honduras, Puerto Rico, etc.

Dear President and Americans, I have the proof of every evidence and I will pay with my honor and my life about it.

Eduardo R Prida 1475 West 29 Street Apt 3 Hialeah, Fl 33010

CONTENT

Chapter 1
Cuba, the Russian Navy Base in the Caribbean

The General Rafael del Pino, my old friend, a Cuban jet fighter pilot jokingly said that the largest aircraft carrier in the world was Soviet. At that time, they did not have this type of ship. Ironically, he was referring to Cuba is an aircraft carrier of the USSR.

For the current Russia, militarily Cuba is still necessary. The geographical position near and to the South of the United States is the ideal place as a point of concentration of forces for a preventive nuclear strike and logistical base for naval and air patrols.

Cuba is an Air Base of Bombers and Patrols of Naval Recognition and Electronic Intelligence, which have been publicly known since 1961. Nor is it fresh news that Russian cyber-attacks have their base of operations in Cuba.

The Russians have an aerial fleet of ridiculous bombers, the announced range of the 12,000 km bombers, is not enough for the radius of action and necessary range of return, and rather I consider it a half-truth, empty maybe , when the Russians talk about range of action and reach, they are referring to the ability to transport the plane, without a payload. These data and concepts in the Russian conceptual style, very different from the Western, these concepts have been manipulated historically in the

International Aeronautical Federation to speculate with the records, which are always granted to the Russians as the best.

From Cuba the Russian missiles can reach 100% of the American territory and privileged position for the early detection of any movement of missiles that leave the terrestrial atmosphere for the anti-missile defense of Imperial Russia ... it is not important that this war system is in the hands of Cubans or Russian, the important thing is that they are in accordance with the interests of Russia, which also works to hold Cubans on the island hostage within the
"Castro

Nikita, Castro, Aragones, Leonov en Moscu, Mayo de 1962 amenazando con golpear fuerte a los EU

The bellicosity of Moscow presaged that they were looking for a first surprise nuclear strike. Everything seemed unsuccessful for JFK, in fact he was only receiving the inheritance from other administrations and his lack of knowledge about the USSR. Among the inheritance was a CIA penetrated by the enemy, linked to domestic enemies, known to the mafia, with malignancy mixed with the CIA, when in fact they were infiltrated enemies like the Cuban American Bernard Barker and part of the system of Counter Intelligence.

The Subversive Program of the Frankfort School is advancing and all the light that McCarthy projects on communist enemies, in the Senate and Congress, is being extinguished. The liberal approach prevailing after the defeat in domestic politics of the struggle against communism and all its collaterals in the Senate that Senator McCarthy very clearly of who they were and what the Communists wanted to do, however, the USSR was gaining ground in his plans for psychological warfare with the surprise of an artificial satellite in orbit, even though the United States could not compete in the space race.

The industrial and military espionage with the massive infiltration of Jewish communists in the teaching and scientific activity had facilitated the propaganda success of the USSR, just on April 12, 1961, another blow as the first Sputnik, the cosmonaut Yuri Gagarin, the first man in the space was a Soviet. The arguments about the superiority of communism over capitalism was the theme of the day, the liberals felt comfortable with the sickle and the hammer.

Today it is easy to know that the Soviets did not have strategic bombers able to reach the American territory because they never had the supply of fuel in the air, much less airborne troops because they had no transport aircraft, the Ilushin-12, "The Ukrainian" a very simple copy of the Hercules C-130, but it was inoperative, the Soviets had no means to transport fuels by air or sea, only by rail; Attempts to make refueling in mid-air have been very impossible for the Soviets, they tried for years to use the wing tips as a connection point and the typical instability of the Soviet aircraft made it impossible, accidents after accident were harvests, operational standard is a tanker for every two bombers, it has never been possible for the Soviets and Russians to reach that step.

The increase in the radius of action has not been enough to reach strategic targets within the American continent and return, they have not achieved the metallurgy and chemistry necessary to achieve lightness, strength and flexibility of the materials that make up a high-performance aircraft.

According to the objective navigation calculations this could not have been possible, since if with optimal navigation routes and meteorological status, the return to the area where they will take back fuel is not possible.

The air navigation for them was radio beacon radio beacon, over the continent, for interoceanic flights, rested only by the millennial "astronomical navigation and its sextants", with more than 150 years of delay. In Cuba, the sextants who, as an emergency, had Bristol Britannia 318 of Cuban Airline were robbed by the Soviet advisors, one of them named Andrussa, and Spanish' Soviet who was translator, pirigochi in Russian).

The use of ballistic missiles or teleguided launched from the bomber Tu-104 or TU-16 did not have enough in that time, much less had the electronic technology of guidance of the missiles to achieve the proposed objectives.

The long-range missiles reach the so-called ICBM (Inter Continental Ballistic Missile), according to the tests conducted did not have precision in the guidance and the nuclear detonations did not reach the necessary power, if these came to explode, a high percentage of them, did not detonate, this is the report that the Soviet nuclear physicist offers to the Kremlin.

It's conditioning this situation the refusal of the Soviets to accept the cancellation of nuclear tests, because it left them at a disadvantage of 10 or 15 years behind the United States, this problem arises two new conditions from the side of the Soviets, not to accept internationally a treaty to stop the nuclear tests and to become strong In a military plaza near the United States, this role was based on retaining the island of Cuba at all costs.

The Soviets and their colony in the Caribbean, always repeat that nuclear missiles of intermediate range, bombers with nuclear bombs, tactical land-to surface missiles and land-sea missiles with nuclear charges and a troop of 60,000 troops were on the Island to that the United States did not attack the
Castro regime, this is not true, since 1953 they began their plans to take Cuba for strictly military use and in February 1960, they sent the first military contingent of 1,000 troops to the island

"Advanced Post" KGB Subversive Operation

*This was the great deception play, prepared 10 years before or more through the Subversive Plan "Jovenzuelo" with the facade (maskirovka) of Komsomolsk (young communists) peasants with a donation of a thousand tractors to teach Cubans the agricultural techniques, these supposed masters of agriculture came under the command of the Marshal Ignagtiev,   Head of the Strategic **Missiles** Troops of the USSR with the very secret mission of the study of the terrain and prepare the grown of the* *weapons that would later be sent in June, July, August and September of 1962, where the conditions for that location were already ready.*

The ship carrying such a strange cargo was received by students and workers with the coverage of the radio and television press, according to Ignagtiev's book.

Fidel Castro was unaware until that moment of the real purpose of the "farmers" detachment.   This was the debut of the Soviet strategic troops to create the Missile Bases in Cuba.

This was an operation masquerades unprecedented as an internal movement of troops within the Soviet territory, from South to North, an Army Corps with all its arsenal and logistics for two months. They received the order to change course in the middle of the route to the Arctic.

The simplistic and superficial interpretation of this historical event usually begins with the discovery of the missiles by the CIA. However, this interpretation distances us from knowing in depth that this was part of an operation that had its roots in 1923 when 200 communist Jews arrived in Cuba, sent by Josef Stalin and then the assault on the Moncada Barracks, the expedition of Granma and the overthrow of the government of Cuba in January 1959.

All these steps of the Subversive Plan led to the location of the nuclear missiles to defend the position that the Soviets had conquered in America. They did not defend the people of Cuba and their revolution 90 miles from Imperialism as proclaimed, the KGB's influence agent Fidel Castro.

In 1962, it is time for the USSR to decide regarding its fighting ability in relation to its invented opponent the United States. Despite their efforts it was not possible to achieve a parity of forces without a point of support, the ballistic missiles, because the vulnerability of the Soviet territory to the US air attack was absolute. The Plan of taking the position had been sponsored by Nikita Khrushchev since 1953 with the attack on Moncada.

Then Khrushchev quickly abandoned a costly and desperate effort to equalize US air power and the power of intercontinental missiles and their nuclear devices was very slow and costly to develop: the solution was in Cuba.

In October 1962, the <u>USSR had only six huge and vulnerable platforms</u> for the ICBM R-7 near Tyuratam and Plesetsk and deployed around it 20 ICBM R-16. The estimates of the United States put an amount of Soviet ICBM operating at 50.

On May 24, 1962, the USSR made the decision to deploy R-12 and R-14 missiles in its new Cuba colony. The range of flight of the R-12 and R-14 missiles could reach the majority of the United States, except in the extreme northwest of the country. The commander of the strategic missile forces, Marshal Sergei Biryuzov supported the idea. On June 13, Minister of Defense Rodin Malinovsky ordered the preparations for the deployment of Soviet troops in Cuba.

The General Directorate of Operations of the Chief of Staff, led by Colonel General SP Ivanov, started Operation Anadyr , name of a river in the far north of Russia. Due to the top secret of the plan, even the classified military documents referred to the operation as a "strategic exercise", intended to test the movements of weapons and units around the Soviet Union.

In June, the Chief of Staff of RVSN, Colonel General MA Mikulski , issued a directive that ordered the following steps in the preparations for the "exercise": Customize all participating units with an assigned number of personnel; Prepare all classified documents of units for transportation; Prepare provisions for 60 days and rocket propellant deposit at 1.75 for a quantity of fuel required for each R-12 missile and 1.5 for each R-14 missile; Prepares, reviews and packages personal weapons and ammunition; Prepare documents about armaments (The amount greater than the need is that Eloy liquid oxygen is consumed over time)

Also, in June, the Chief of Staff of RVSN began drafting an organizational structure for the rocket division to be deployed in Cuba. In mid-month, the Chief of Staff of the Soviet armed forces approved the new structure of the division and gave the green light to the formation of its units, including new units that had not been part of its original composition, for example, a Bread factory and an engineering unit and sappers.

Although the directive of the Chief of Staff of RVSN instructed to employ soldiers and officers available from missile regiments for a Cuban expedition, it also established strict selection criteria, based mainly on strict health requirements. In addition, the KGB security service evaluated all personnel traveling to Cuba. As a result, a considerable percentage of the regular staff of the units had to be replaced by new members.

Later, it would create considerable problems during the deployment of missiles in Cuba. Bombers Ilyushin Il-28 equipped with nuclear weapons to achieve territory of South America ... This photo shows us three fuselages aboard a Soviet ship, these aircraft were assigned to the Air Base of San Julian, at the western end of Cuba. This base was built by the United States during the Second World War for the purpose of training flights of the B-29 bombers, which flew between Corpus Christi and San Julián, as a practice of the bombings on Japan.

It has been said that 42 of them came to be assembled and operational in October 1962. They estimate that about 96 nuclear bombs were only at the San Julián Air Base in west of Pinar del Rio City.

Contrary to the widespread and repeated opinion more than the Our Father ... there is no evidence that a non-aggression treaty existed between Kennedy and Khrushchev in 1962.

As a summary of agreement, the consulted Soviet and American literature, supposed leader of the democratic and patriotic revolution, was never consulted for the deployment of troops and nuclear weapons and the high risk that it represented for the Cuban population, all under the command and in absolute interest of the Soviet Empire.

There was no inspection of the Security Council of the UN Cuban territory to validate the complete withdrawal of nuclear weapons, given the show of flaunting independence of Fidel Castro, which was the opposite, dependent until his breathing Soviets, that they had put him in power and kept it to maintain Cuba as a nuclear weapons site against the United States.

Years have passed and everything is known, many Soviet generals have written in their memoirs the dozens of nuclear-loaded missiles left in the area of Cascorro, Camagüey. Medium-range missiles R-12 and R-14 that they are still polluting the surrounding areas spreading cancer in the population. In Guira de Melena there were the Lunik and the Saturn in Managua military unit, among those known only for me.

Ballistic self-propelled nuclear tactical missile with a range of 250 miles with 1.6 megatons of expansive force.

These were replaced years later by the SS-22. At present, Cuba, as a sort of mockery, exposes the Soviet missiles that it kept secretly for many years,

they are doing it because they are now inside containers.

Russia tracks the United States Airspace from Cuba

A Russian agency specializing in space technologies let you know about the "deployment of a mobile reception and transmission complex in its Caribbean colony Cuba".
The reception and control station of surveillance and reconnaissance satellites will be operational by April 30, 2019.

These Advanced Intelligence systems will receive the data of the optical observation spacecraft Resurs -P and Kanopus -V, these have infrared cameras, and will transmit them in coded mode to Moscow through the Luch- type transmitting satellites, it is expected that **this** *system can reproduce high resolution images of 0.7 meters in the visible and infrared bands*

Installation in Cuba makes it easier for the Russian armed forces information on routes of land, sea and air communication, control of pollution and agricultural natural resources of US territory, as well as all air movement and missile launches.

Kanopus -V remote sensing satellites were designed to monitor any type of explosives or new armaments experiment.

With the detection system located in Cuba by Russia, the four Kanopus satellites in geostationary orbit will be able to detect and create foci for forest fires, the launching of missiles, destruction of missiles in their takeoff stages, movements of all kinds within the territory of the United States. United.

For its part, the pro-Russian regime in Cuba is very pleased to have one of the subsidiaries of Roscosmos of the Russian Intelligence on its soil in collaboration with the "Scientific and Technical Center of Geocuba and Tecnoimport ".

Cuba, and his narcotraffic ...

We will never know the extent of the damage to US national security interests. Aldrich Ames could have caused. However, we can safely assume that one of the vital interests harmed by the espionage of Ames is the ability of the United States to stop the flow of illegal drugs to the United States.

Mr. Ames not only had access to the most sensitive CIA information on Russia and the former Soviet Union, but also had access to the most sensitive information about the war on drugs. At the time of his arrest, Ames was a senior official in the CIA's narcotic intelligence office.

The possibility that Ames passed sensitive information to the KGB In relation to the war on drugs, the Wall Street Journal published on March 10 an interesting article entitled "The KGB and the war of the United States against drugs". The article said what many of us have held for years: that the KGB used moles like Aldrich Ames to sabotage the battle of the United States against international drug trafficking.

It will not surprise anyone that the KGB tried to undermine the US war on drugs. The KGB was institutionally dedicated to the destruction of the United States of America; therefore, the KGB's involvement in drug trafficking makes a lot of sense. Drugs have been an increasingly destructive force in our society for decades, poisoning our youth and stoking the flames of violence in our cities. Increase the consumption of drugs and alcohol is one of the points of the Subversive Plan against the United States

The counter-intelligence activity of the United States has always been very weak and the facts show, James Angleton, very likely that through his mistress Phillbee was in contact with the Soviets and even the State Department for 60 years, almost You can affirm that you work for the enemy, the last one was John Kerry.

Sharing any kind of intelligence with Fidel Castro is absurd. Castro must be laughing at the State Department and everyone.
Aldrich Ames was a key figure in the new US effort to thwart the entry of narcotics into the United States and prevent the corrupting influence of drug lords.

In the 1980s, the intelligence community of the United States learned that it was on the defensive that it was being attacked with drug trafficking and a new form of organized crime without precedent.

Today we know that the President George Bush made a mistake in thinking that the enemy could cooperate in the fight against drug trafficking and terrorism, he did not think that they were the main instigators of everything that hurts humanity, he was short-sighted and perhaps a little ill-intentioned With horror we can see, that it is routine for the FBI and the CIA to discard the information about the activity of the Cuban Intelligence against the United States.
The KGB paid very well to Ames and his travels to Colombia perhaps could have other reasons beyond greet the family of his wife Maria.

The venality of Aldrich Ames contrasts sharply with the intense, ultra-twisted ideological betrayal of a Kim Philbee . How many other Western intelligence officials, unhappily salaried, cooperate with the former KGB? in the war on drugs have also been tempted by the rich findings of betrayal in the post ideological era?

Cuba remains silent about 'new Russian bases' 24 July 2008, the " former Cuban leader" Fidel Castro, has urged his country to take a firm stand against Washington over the possible restoration of Russian military bases on the island. Castro says that Cuba should refrain from apologizing or giving explanations and excuses. In a statement posted online, Castro praised his brother's handling of the issue. Fidel's younger brother, Raúl, is the acting Cuban president.

"Raúl did very well in his dignified silence on the bases of the Russian strategic bombers in our country." Castro, 81, said. The strategic bombers mentioned are Tu-160, bomb Cap 1 Union Sov Russian long-range strategic supersonic bombers, nicknamed "White Swans". It has been said that they could refuel in Cuba during flights over the Caribbean. The possibility of restoring permanent Russian military bases on the island has also been raised.

The Tupolev Tu-160 is a supersonic bomber capable of carrying 12 nuclearloaded cruise missiles.

However, they only have 16 units in operation, which in practice in maintenance and training are only about 9-10 high or perhaps less, which is ridiculous the amount for the territory they must cover. Castro's comment comes after Izvestia published an article citing an anonymous military officer of the Russian Air Force. He said that Russia was considering using Cuban airfields to replenish nuclear-capable bombers patrolling areas near the US borders.

However, the permanent deployment of the Tupolev Tu-160 and Tu95 strategic bombers in Cuba would be meaningless from the military point of view. see, the source in the Russian Ministry of Defense told Interfax. The development could be a response to the moves of Washington in Eastern Europe. The United States seems determined to build an anti-missile defense shield near the borders of Russia.

Russia considers that this ABM system is a direct threat to its security, since the proposed radar will allow the United States to track all of Europe and Russia at least. In addition, Moscow says it is unacceptable that silos for missiles in Poland can be used to launch other weapons.

Washington reacted to the news that Russian military bases could once again become a reality in Cuba. Memories of the Cuban missile crisis of 1962 still haunt the United States. At that time, the United States and the Soviet Union clashed after the discovery of Soviet missiles on the island, only 144 km south of Florida.

The man nominated to be the next Chief of Staff of the US Air Force. UU., General Norton Schwartz, has responded to the article in Izvestia . He told the United States Senate that, if Russia continued with the Cuban proposals, Moscow would have crossed a "red line", a step that would be unacceptable for the security of the United States. UU

What's kind of mission they are doing around USA?
For years, the Tupolev TU-16, TU-95 and TU-195 flying for the purpose of collecting Electronic Intelligence and tracking the position of American Submarines in the Gulf of Mexico and Central Atlantic Ocean. Twice on July 4, Russian Tu-95 Bear bombers on long-range patrol missions were intercepted by scrambled US jets from airbases located on the west coast. According the American Scientific experts: **Today Russia operates three main types of the Bear family: the Tupolev Tu-95 Bear-H strategic bomber, the Tupolev Tu-142 Bear-F maritime patrol aircraft and the Beriev Tu-142MR strategic communications aircraft. Both the Bear-H and the Bear-F have multiple variants. The Tu-95MS Bear-H is a strategic intercontinental-range cruise missile carrier and these were built between 1982 and 1992.**

There are two current variants of the Tu-95MS flying today. Older aircraft have the Osina missile system that only allows the employment of the Kh-55 (NATO calls it the AS-15 Kent) armed with a 200 kiloton nuclear warhead. Six missiles were carried on an internal rotary launcher, but newer aircraft use the Sprut system to deliver the Kh-55 and can carry sixteen missiles, adding ten under the wings.

From 2003 the Bear-H was modified to carry six Kh-555 cruise missiles that are conventionally armed versions of the nuclear Kh-55.

The Sprut version of the Tu-95MS has also been modified to carry the conventional Kh-101 long-range stealth cruise missile and the Kh-102 nuclear version. These weapons are longer than the Kh-55 and will not fit in the rotary launcher and must be carried under the Bear's wings with a maximum carry of eight. With a full load of Kh-101/-102 the range of the Bear is quite reduced to around 4,300 miles.

The Tu-95 MSM looks to be a final upgrade program that was launched in late 2009 to update the bomber's capabilities. Some of the upgraded equipment will include a new radar, modernization of the navigation system, a "glass" cockpit, enhanced defensive measures and improved engines, which will provide better fuel efficiency to help counter the loss of range accompanied with the external carriage of the Kh-101/-102. At least one Tu-95MSM made its combat debut by launching missiles at Syria in November 2015.

The least recognized of the Bear family is the Beriev Tu-142MR Bear-J strategic radio-relay aircraft. Designed to ensure that Moscow can maintain contact with its ballistic missile submarines, the aircraft is externally very similar to the Tu-142MK Bear F with a few notable differences including a forward-facing pod atop the tail. The mission of the Bear-J is similar to the U.S. Navy's E-6B Mercury TACAMO (TAke Charge And Move Out), which provides the ability to communicate with submerged submarines, specifically the ballistic missile submarine fleet.

Operated by a crew of nine, they are protected against electromagnetic radiation by a special window coating, as they may have to conduct their mission during a nuclear exchange. Rather than carrying weapons in the bomb bay, the Bear-J carries the trailing wire antenna that will be deployed via an external ventral pod. The complicated and humoristic 25,187-foot wire antenna takes 37 minutes to be fully extend, and 48 minutes to retract. While deployed, the Bear-J will fly an extended series of tight turns to ensure the wire is as close to vertical as possible ensuring the best situation to conduct VLF communications with submerged SSBNs. Approximately 10 Bear-J airframes remain and are based primarily at two airfields. One is at Kipelovo (formerly Fedotovo), and is about 400 kilometers north of Moscow, and these aircraft serve the ballistic missile subs of the Northern Fleet on the Kola Peninsula. The other base is in the far east at <u>Mongokhto</u> and serves the Russian Pacific Fleet from the base on the <u>Strait of Tartary</u>.

According to Fox News, the first safety alert occurred at 10:30 am ET when bombers with Russian nuclear capability flew off the coast of Alaska and two US Air Force F-22 Raptor jet planes left their base at the Joint Base Elmendorf-Richardson. in Alaska to intercept the Tu-95.

The second fight was ordered at 11.00 when the F-15 of 144 Wing of Fresno, California, were forced to intercept what has been described as "another pair of Tu-95 Bear bombers flying from California".

The intercepting missions of Russian bombers that fly not far from the continental United States (sometimes a few hundred miles away). In fact, American (or Canadian) fighter aircraft are not always launched to intercept these "zombies": in 2014, only 6 out of 10 "raids" saw American or Canadian aircraft fighting the long-range attack aircraft of Moscow .

For example, during the first incidents of this type, on April 22, when two Russian bombers Tu-95 Bear H flew to the US Air Defense Identification Zone. UU (ADIZ), no US aircraft were sent to identify and escort the strategic bombers most likely investigating the response times of the North American Aerospace Defense Command (NORAD).

Interestingly, the Tu-95s were launched over the Pacific Ocean on a longrange flight a few days after the flight ban (after the accident that saw a TU95 slip off the runway and catch fire at the Ukrainka airfield that caused the death of a member of the crew.

In the Gulf of Mexico:

Russia's decision to send long-range strategic bombers on regular patrol missions in the Gulf of Mexico is unprecedented, a senior US military official said on Wednesday. UU., Claiming that the country had never done it before, even during the Cold War.

The official, who spoke with The Associated Press on condition of anonymity because it was not authorized to publicly discuss the flights, also said that the pace of Russian flights in North America, including the Arctic, has remained largely stable, with about five incidents. by year.

Long-range bombers have been in the area before, but only to participate in several visits to the region when the plane stopped overnight at locations in South or Central America. During the Cold War, other types of Russian aircraft flew patrols there, including surveillance flights and anti-submarine aircraft.

Colonel Steve Warren, a Pentagon spokesman, refused to call this a Russian provocation.

"The Russians have patrolled in the Gulf [of Mexico] in the past and we have seen the Russian Navy operate in the Gulf of Mexico," he said on Wednesday. "These are international waters." It is important that the Russians conduct their operations safely and in accordance with international standards. "

The announcement by Russian Defense Minister Sergei Shoigu , who also claimed that patrols would be carried out in other parts of the world, came when the NATO chief accused Russia of sending new troops and tanks to eastern Ukraine.

"In recent days, we have seen multiple reports of large convoys moving to eastern Ukraine," said NATO Secretary General Jens Stoltenberg . "We assess that this important military concentration includes artillery, tanks, air defense systems and Russian troops." His statement described the situation as a "serious threat to the ceasefire."

Moscow denied the accusation as unfounded, but Shoigu also said that the dispute with the West over Ukraine would require Russia to reinforce its forces in the Crimea, the Black Sea Peninsula that Russia annexed in March. Shoigu said that Russian long-range bombers will make flights along Russian borders and over the Arctic Ocean.

He said: "In the current situation, we have to maintain a military presence in the western Atlantic and the eastern Pacific, as well as in the Caribbean and the Gulf of Mexico."

Shoigu did not say how frequent the patrol missions would be or offer any other details but noted that the increasing pace and duration of flights would require greater maintenance efforts and that relevant directives for the industry have been issued.

He said that long-range aircraft of the Russian air force will also carry out "reconnaissance missions to monitor the military activities and maritime communications of foreign powers."

Strategic Russian bombers with nuclear capability regularly conducted patrols across the Atlantic and Pacific oceans during Cold War times,

Even more worrisome was the growth of the Soviet strategic nuclear arsenal. The United States had enjoyed a decisive lead in nuclear weapons since the beginning of the arms race, but the Soviets sought to close the gap following the Cuban Missile Crisis. During the 1970s, the Soviets began augmenting their nuclear forces by adding multiple independently targetable reentry vehicles to their existing launch platforms, something the United States had already begun doing a few years earlier.

Most of the increase in the USSR's arsenal occurred in its ICBMs, which were becoming accurate enough to destroy U.S. missiles in their underground silos. A 1977 study by the Congressional Research Service forecast that by the end of the decade the USSR would possess nearly 4,600 nuclear warheads on its fleet of ICBMs, more than twice the U.S. number.

The hardline anti-Soviet sentiment as a political force in the United States leaders dated back to the beginning of the Cold War and was embodied by individuals such as Arizona senator and 1964 GOP presidential candidate Barry Goldwater, a man who once called for the United States to completely withdraw diplomatic recognition of the USSR, probably the best option to broke the subversion and espionage from them, but the liberal subversive campaign stopped the Senator Goldwater's political force.

But the right wing, crippled by Goldwater's defeat and, even more significantly, by the Vietnam experience, found themselves exiled from mainstream American politics for a time, but the enemy every moment stronger politically facilitated the emergence of a new, post-Vietnam strain of right wing foreign policy point of view.

The American politician learned to watch naked the Soviet Union in the objectives that they were reaching to destroy USA. The USSR's goal, in their minds, was in short time the global conquest. It was not a normal nation-state led by rational leaders, they claimed, but a moral evil that the United States had to confront anywhere and everywhere in order to protect itself and other free nations from destruction.

By the 1976, the USSR grew more and more powerful. the CIA's assessments of the Soviet Union was a mistake of underestimate the size of the Soviet buildup and the scope of its ambitions.

 One American, emerged with the clear thinking, Richard Pipes, a professor of Russian history at Harvard University. It concluded that "all the evidence points to an undeviating Soviet commitment to what is euphemistically called 'the worldwide triumph of socialism' but in fact connotes global Soviet hegemony."
 The assessment against the CIA's report was completed, and its contents ended up serving as a blueprint to grow number of critics who argued that the U.S. was destined to lose the Cold War if it did not adopt a more adversarial approach to the Soviet Union. They pointed to the Soviet buildup and the USSR and Cuba's increasing involvement in Third World countries such as Angola, Yemen and Ethiopia as evidence of its expansionism.

In truth, the alarmism of the right overlooked a number of important facts. It was true that the Soviets were strengthening their military and political forces against the United States . Still the U.S. intelligence follow in the same direction when indicated that morale was poor among Soviet troops was struggling to address widespread drunkenness among its soldiers.

By the late 1970s it was also clear that the Soviet economy, lack of oil, gas and low productivity industry, was in a state of long-term decline, but they continue with the offensive around the planet.

The Soviet argument about the Total defense spending by the NATO alliance exceeded that of the Warsaw Pact nations, many of which Moscow considered politically and militarily unreliable. While Soviet strategic nuclear forces were growing more powerful, they remained numerically and technologically inferior to those of the United States, most of which were carried by invulnerable ballistic missile submarines. The United States had also begun to develop an array of new, advanced weapons such as the MX missile, the M-1 tank and precision-guided munitions whose sophistication the Soviets could not match. Nevertheless, these two factors, the Soviet buildup and the reemergence of anti-Soviet hardliners, had the effect of shifting the U.S. foreign policy debate significantly to the right. By the second half of the 1970s, the hawks had all but taken control of the Republican party, at least in terms of its approach to international affairs. The moderate and conservative Democrats were also agreeing for greater U.S. military spending and a strong opposition tougher toward the USSR.

Politically, the Carter administration, taking office in January 1977, Carter quickly developed a reputation as an indecisive leader whose foreign policy was disjointed at best. He had greatly upset conservatives by persuading the Senate to ratify a treaty turning control of the Panama Canal over to the Panamanian government and then canceling production of both the neutron bomb and the new B-1 strategic bomber.

In May 1978, all 38 members of the Senate Republican caucus released a public statement that criticized Carter for "compromising America's ability to defend itself." In 15 short months of incoherence, inconsistency and ineptitude, our foreign policy and national security objectives are confused and we are being challenged around the globe by Soviet arrogance, real offensive Subversive Plan from Cuba with a passive invasion of 128,000 Cuban refugee and between them intelligent agents, delinquents, sex offenders, and the biological attacks with HIV, in the back of this action was Yuri Andropov and his KGB.

The national Republican leaders issued a subsequent statement that stated that "the Carter administration is responsible for and presiding over the decay of American influence and the decline of American military power."

Efforts to negotiate a follow-on agreement to SALT I had been underway for years, and details of the new accord were finalized in the spring of 1979. The United States and USSR each to a total of 2,250 nuclear delivery vehicles – ICBMs, SLBMs and strategic bombers.

Those on the right expressed opposition to the treaty even before negotiations were completed. Some opponents of SALT II voiced specific criticisms of the agreement, such as its failure to limit the size of the Soviet fleet of medium-range Backfire bombers. The military expert opposed it because they saw it as a form of appeasement, they was comparing it to Neville Chamberlain's 1938 Munich agreement with Hitler. Like an "act of phased surrender" to the Soviet Union.

It was against this backdrop that the 1979 imbroglio over the Soviet brigade in Cuba took place. When its presence was made public, conservatives pounced. They argued that the USSR's decision to deploy troops so close to American shores was further evidence, if any was needed, of the Soviet Union's aggressive intentions.

Sen. Henry "Scoop" Jackson, a Democrat from Washington state hawks, charged that the brigade's deployment to Cuba "is not an isolated event." It represented "a most dramatic example of a pattern of Soviet and Cuban behavior which is hostile to the interests of the United States, its friends and allies."

Conservatives also blamed the situation on Carter's weak leadership, even though the evidence indicated that the brigade was already there when he took office. "There is no doubt in my mind [that] this administration and its policies have been instrumental in placing us in the situation we find ourselves today,"

Republican senator Strom T en. Russell Long, a key moderate Democrat from Louisiana, announced a few days later that he would vote against ratification, citing the Soviet troops in Cuba as evidence that the USSR was acting in bad faith. A number of senators who were undecided about SALT II indicated that it would be hard for them to support the treaty unless the Cuba issue was satisfactorily resolved.

Through September, concerns about the Soviet troop presence in Cuba among members of Congress and the general public grew increasingly pronounced. U.S. Secretary of State Cyrus Vance met five times with Soviet ambassador Anatoly F. Dobrynin and twice with Soviet Foreign Minister Andrei Gromyko in an effort to persuade the Soviets to withdraw the troops, but Moscow made it clear that it was unwilling to do so, insisting that the brigade was there only to train Cuban military personnel.

The Soviet refusal left the White House in a political bind, since Carter had publicly stated that "this status quo is not acceptable." Dogged throughout his presidency by criticisms that he was an unsteady leader who lacked the backbone to stand up to the Soviets, Carter faced enormous pressure to act firmly in order to shore up support for SALT II. At the same time, the president understood that there was nothing he could do to force the Soviets to remove the brigade without causing U.S.Soviet relations to deteriorate further – a development that also would have undermined support for the treaty in the Senate.

On Oct. 1, Carter spoke to the American people about the situation in a nationally televised address. Seeking to walk a fine line between appearing too concerned and too unconcerned, he told the public that while the Soviet unit "presents no direct threat to us," its presence in Cuba was nonetheless "a serious matter."

How we can see, the American Intelligence and the politician never understand the real reason for the Soviet Union and Castro's regimen need the Soviet troops in Cuba. The reason was in relation with Bravo Operation of the KGB, this operation needed create a wave of the internal repression and man and women in prisons to reach 120000 Cuban ready to send to Florida in May,1980 like a real refugee.

Potentially the excess of repression can became in a civil rebellion, and the Soviet need to defend, at last his citizens and hidden weapons residents in Cuba. Those kinds of Soviet troops never been in contact with native armed forces in maneuvers, training or any other activity. The Soviet military personnel never were in contact with Cuban military, except the advice technician and the professors in a few places like anti air missile and aviation.

 He listed several steps the United States would take in response. These included the resumption of aerial surveillance flights over Cuba, the creation of a joint military task force responsible for the Caribbean, increased U.S. military exercises in the region, and expanded U.S. economic assistance to impoverished countries in Central America.

Carter also told the nation that Soviet officials had made "certain statements" to their American counterparts that the U.S. interpreted to mean that "they do not intend to enlarge the unit or to give it additional capabilities." This was the closest thing that Carter could point to as a concession by Moscow.

None of the actions announced by Carter were particularly substantive – but, then again, neither was the supposed crisis they were intended to resolve. The president's speech did little to change many minds about SALT II or U.S.-USSR relations generally, but the controversy began to slowly fade from view in the weeks following his address.

Political conditions in the U.S. in the fall of 1979 were such that the discovery of the brigade in Cuba was bound to set off a firestorm. AntiSoviet hardliners who saw the USSR as an imminent, existential threat had succeeded in pushing American public opinion on foreign policy further and further to the right over the preceding years. The News of the Soviet forces in Cuba reached the public just a few weeks after Carter had submitted SALT II to the Senate for ratification. That the controversy unfolded shortly before the onset of the 1980 presidential campaign only added to the situation's combustibility. Had the Soviet troops been detected a year or two earlier, it's unlikely that it would have caused the furor that it did.

In the end, SALT II was never got a vote. The brigade issue delayed Senate action on the agreement until late 1979, by which time its fate was overtaken by events. The Soviets invaded Afghanistan at the end of

December, and in response Carter officially asked the Senate to postpone its consideration of the treaty indefinitely.

His administration had planned to mount a renewed push for ratification at the start of his second term, but he lost his 1980 bid for reelection to Ronald Reagan, the favorite son of anti-Soviet hardliners and an expressed opponent of the treaty. Had the Soviet troops controversy not arisen, it is quite possible that SALT II would have been approved.

The uproar in the United States over the troops in Cuba was a strong indication that the era of détente was over. In his speech to the nation, Carter stated that "the brigade issue is certainly no reason for a return to the Cold War." But it had never really ended, just diminished in intensity.

The improvements in superpower relations during the 1970s were real, but they were not enduring. Although it is little remembered today, this controversy in 1979 served as an unfortunate prelude to the dangerous tensions that existed between the United States and USSR in the early 1980s, a period during which the risk of nuclear war was as high as at any other moment in the Cold War.

CIA's Report for years 1980-1990

Director of Central Intelligence Agency

CIA •HISTORICAL REVIEW PROGRAM
RBASEAS SANITIZED
Soviet Policies and Activities in Latin America and the Caribbean
Special National Intelligence Estimate

     NIE 11/80/90-82 25 June 1982
     Copy

DISSEMINATION CONTROL ABBREVIATIONS
    NOFORN-   Not Releasable to Foreign Nationals
NO CONTRACT— Not Releasable to Contractors or Contractor/Consultants

PROPIN-Caution—Proprietary Information Involved NFIBONLY-NFIB
Departments Only
ORCON-Dissemination and Extraction of Information
Controlled by Originator
This Information Has Been Authorized for Release to n
A microfiche copy Of this document is available from OCR/DLB (351-7177); printed
copies from CPAS/IMC (351-5203). Regular receipt of DDI reports in either
microfiche or printed form can also be arranged through CPAS/tMC.
SNIE 11/80/90-82
SOVIET POLICIES AND ACTIVITIES
IN LATIN AMERICA AND THE CARIBBEAN
Information available as of 15 June 1982 was used in the preparation of this Estimate
has been 202 release through the HISTORICAL REVIEW PROGRAM of the
Central Intelligence Agency.

**THIS ESTIMATE ISSUED BY THE DIRECTOR OF CENTRAL
INTELLIGENCE. THE NATIONAL FOREIGN INTELLIGENCE
BOARD CONCURS. The following intelligence organizations
participated in the preparation of the Estimate: The Central Intelligence
Agency, the Defense Intelligence Agency, the National Security Agency,
and the intelligence organization of the Department of State. Also
Participating: The Assistant Chief of Staff for Intelligence, Department
of the Army: The Director of Naval Intelligence, Department of the
Navy The Assistant Chief of Staff, Intelligence, Department of the Air
Force**

The Director of Intelligence, Headquarters, Marine Corps

CONTENTS

Soviet activity and interest in Latin America have increased significantly in the past few years, and in the aftermath of the battle for the Falklands the Soviets and their Cuban allies will be probing for new opportunities. Since 1979, Moscow has moved more aggressively to exploit opportunities presented by pressures for revolutionary change in Central America and the Caribbean and by the willingness of Latin American states to deal with the USSR and its allies. The Soviet Union has helped to consolidate revolutionary regimes in Nicaragua and Grenada, has provided considerable aid—mainly through proxies and other third parties—to revolutionaries else" 'here in Latin America, and has intensified its efforts to develop favorable political and economic ties with such countries as Argentina, Brazil, and Mexico. Despite this intensified interest, geographic remoteness has tended to relegate Latin America—except for Cuba—to. the periphery of Soviet security concerns.

Cuba plays a central role in Soviet relations with Latin America not only as a dependent client serving Moscow's interests but also as an independent actor influencing Soviet policies and tactics. Fidel Castro's vigorous support of Nicaraguan revolutionaries, for example, was originally a Cuban initiative and had a marked impact on Soviet attitudes and policy toward the region. Soviet leaders came to share Castro's assessment that the prospects for the success of revolutionary forces in Central America were brighter than they had earlier calculated. The Soviets have been working closely with the Cubans to consolidate the Sandinista regime in Nicaragua, which both view as central to promoting leftist gains in the region.

The Soviets have by and large successfully implemented a policy of encouraging unrest in various Central American states, gaining a foothold in Nicaragua, and improving their relations with the governments of the more important South American countries. From the Soviet perspective, such a policy has potential for distracting American attention from other regions; is relatively cheap in economic terms; has not required major commitments to local allies; and has not raised confrontation with the United States to an unmanageable level. The Soviets are thus likely to persist with this strategy.

Soviet support and guidance for Latin American revolutionary movements now focus on:

— Encouragement of broad revolutionary coalitions, uniting pro Soviet Communist parties with their traditional leftwing rivals. — Creation of loyal military components.

— Use of hemispheric and extra hemispheric intermediaries.

— Training of revolutionaries.

In El Salvador the Soviets have facilitated the flow of arms and military equipment to the Salvadoran insurgents from Cuba and other third parties. Although Moscow does not appear sanguine about the insurgents' short-term military prospects, it probably still believes that they can seize power through a prolonged armed struggle.

In Guatemala and Honduras, the USSR and its allies have been pressuring the local Communists to join broad revolutionary fronts and participate in armed struggle. The Soviets and Cubans have provided financial assistance and training.

Moscow undoubtedly sees potential opportunities for the left in Colombia, the Dominican Republic, and Chile.

In Argentina, Brazil, Mexico, and Peru, Moscow's policy has aimed largely at cultivating positive state-to-state relations. This approach has emphasized trade expansion and—in some cases—readiness to sell military hardware. Although these efforts have not usually been translated into increased Soviet influence, they have given some Latin American countries additional opportunities to assert their independence of the United States. By building on bilateral ties, the USSR also seeks to achieve specific economic objectives and hopes to gain broader political support for its policy initiatives in the hemisphere and elsewhere in the world.

Since 1980, Soviet economic interest and activity in Latin America have intensified. The USSR has become Argentina's largest grain buyer, incurring large trade deficits. Despite the Falklands crisis, this year's purchases are still expected to be 11-12 million tons, or about one-fourth of the USSR's total grain imports.

In pursuit of major arms clients over the last decade, the USSR has secured only Peru—where it is now the primary supplier of air and ground equipment. Moscow's military relationship with Lima, however, has given the Soviets little leverage over Peruvian policies.

Despite Soviet success in Peru, most of the Latin American military establishments have preferred Western-made arms and have been suspicious of the Soviets. Moscow surely hopes, however, that its support for Argentina in the Falklands dispute and interruptions in the supply of arms from some Western sources will make at least the Argentine military more receptive to Soviet offers.

Even in countries where the USSR's policy is keyed to developing bilateral state-to-state ties, as in Mexico, Moscow continues to conduct a variety of covert activities and other "active measures" to improve its position and play upon domestic vulnerabilities over the longer term. These activities include:

— Funding local Communist parties and front organizations. <u>Disseminating disinformation and forgeries aimed at the United States.</u>

<u>— Drumming up support for hemispheric revolutionaries.</u>

<u>— Infiltrating military and security services as well as other important sectors of Latin American bureaucracies.</u>

<u>— Manipulating the media and mass organizations.</u>

<u>— Developing and using agents of influence, mainly through the Cubans.</u>

The Soviets are also educating numerous Latin American and Caribbean students in the USSR, cultivating organized labor, and profiting from the growth of pro-Marxist sentiments among religious activists.

Despite increased Soviet optimism about trends in Latin America, Moscow recognizes that there are major constraints on its ability to influence developments there. Foremost is US political, economic, and military strength; but pervasive Latin American antipathy to Soviet Communism and a Soviet desire not to alarm regional governments through too blatant backing of leftist insurgencies also inhibit Moscow's actions. Moscow has therefore moved in ways designed to avoid directly provoking the United States. In contrast to the USSR's overt and direct bilateral dealings with the larger states, its support for revolutionary

movements has been low-key and indirect, often employing
intermediaries and surrogates.

Moscow's long-term objectives of eroding and supplanting US influence
in Latin America are unlikely to be affected, however, by its recognition
of these obstacles to its ambitions. Over the next few years, Soviet efforts
to gain influence are likely to increase. Washington's response to this
challenge will be complicated by the fact that its own deep concern about
Soviet troublemaking in the area is not shared by many regional
governments. Sympathy with revolutionary causes will persist in
countries such as Mexico and Panama. Even countries less sympathetic
to leftist causes, such as Brazil and Venezuela, would be opposed to US
military intervention to check revolutionary gains in Central America
and the Caribbean.

The persistent strain of anti-US sentiment in the region, which has been
accentuated by the Falklands crisis, offers the Soviets some new
opportunities to expand their influence. However, Soviet initiatives are
of less intrinsic significance than US policies and actions. US efforts to
build hemispheric solidarity with the current Salvadoran Government
and to gain Latin American support for countering Soviet-supported
leftist insurgency elsewhere in Central America have been damaged. The
Soviets are certain to attempt to exploit what they perceive as a US
setback.

The large and growing quantity of military hardware in the hands of
Soviet clients has major implications for the region. In addition to
defending both Cuba and Nicaragua against attack, such military
power--especially in Nicaragua—facilitates support to the Salvadoran
insurgents and provides shelter for the guerrilla infrastructure. Within
the term of this Estimate, other objectives behind arms supply from the
USSR and various intermediaries probably include:

— Intimidating Nicaragua's neighbors, thus disposing them toward
acquiescence in the Soviet-Cuban foothold in Central America.

Supporting insurgents in Guatemala.

— Laying the groundwork for support of possible future insurgencies in Honduras, Costa Rica, and elsewhere in the hemisphere.

The recent US warning of the consequences of delivering Soviet supplied MIG aircraft to Nicaragua may have prompted the deferral of such deliveries. Nevertheless, preparations for their arrival are continuing.

Over the longer term, there is also a possibility that the Soviets may seek access to naval and air facilities in Nicaragua and Grenada. Such access would have a significant impact on US security interests, especially with regard to the Panama Canal and other lines of communication.

DISCUSSION

Soviet Objectives

l. Soviet activity and interest in Latin America have increased significantly in the past few years. Moscow has moved to exploit new opportunities presented by pressures for revolutionary change in Central America and the Caribbean and by the willingness of Latin American states to deal with the USSR and its• allies. Since 1979 the Soviet Union has helped to consolidate the revolutionary regime in Nicaragua, has provided considerable aid—mainly through proxies and other third parties—to revolutionaries elsewhere in Latin America, and has intensified its efforts to develop favorable political and economic ties with such countries as Argentina, Brazil, and Mexico.

2.   Despite this intensified interest, Latin America •s geographical remoteness from the USSR has tended to relegate it to the periphery of Soviet security concerns, except when Soviet involvement with Cuba or Cuban activities have threatened to provoke a serious crisis in Soviet-US relations. Over the years Latin America has been less important in the USSR's rivalry with

the United States than other Third World areas such as Asia and the Middle East, where Soviet stakes are greater and Soviet power less constrained.

3.   Soviet interest in Latin America is to a substantial degree motivated by the USSR's global competition with the United States and its ideological and pragmatic commitment to support revolutionary causes worldwide. Moscow's basic aim in the region is to undermine US influence, which it seeks to achieve

For purposes of this Estimate, Latin America is defined as at mainland countries/territories/dependencies from Mexico south to Argentina. Central America refers to Belize, Guatemala. El Salvador, Honduras, Nicaragua, Costa Rica, and Panama. The Caribbean includes those island state"/territories/dependencies with a coast on the Sea.

The Estimate considers Soviet prospects in Latin America and the Caribbean over approximately the next two yean t This estimate examines the Moscow • Havana connection as it bears upon the formulation and implementation of Soviet policy toward Latin America and the Caribbean. Analysis of the overall bilateral Soviet-Cuban relationship does not fall within the scope of the paper. The both by strengthening Soviet diplomatic. economic, and military ties with governments of the region and by promoting radical change. This approach is in line with Moscow a forward strategy in the Third World, which has the long-term aim of changing the international correlation of forces in favor of the USSR.

4.   The Soviet leadership understands that growing instability in Central America creates serious policy dilemmas for Washington. In Moscow's view, if the United States does not respond effectively in Central America during the next few years. revolutionary momentum will accelerate there and elsewhere in Latin America. If Washington intervenes directly, however, Moscow perceives that it will be able to stimulate international criticism of VS action. In either case. Moscow anticipates that revolutionary ferment in America's own backyard will

divert US attention and resources from more distant problems. sow
divisions between the United States and its allies and undercut
Washington's credibility in the Third World.

5.   Moscow's current support for revolutionary causes should not
        obscure its other important priorities and interests in the area,
        which it promotes simultaneously and sometimes in contradiction
        to its backing for revolution. The level of Soviet economic,
        military, and political activity with the larger countries indicates
        that they are major targets in Soviet strategy toward Latin
        America. A substantial share of the USSR's agricultural imports
        comes from Argentina and Brazil, and Moscow has a major arms
        supply relationship with Peru. Such state-to-state relations give the
        Soviet Union an opportunity to expand its presence and influence
        in specific countries. The Soviets, of course, also seek to encourage
        those states—such as Mexico—to adopt policies independent of the
        United States.

6.   Moscow regards the Falklands situation as a significant
        opportunity to intensify Latin American alienation from the
        United States and expand its own influence in the region. It is
        trying to stiffen Latin American resentment of US support for
        Britain and to stimulate distrust of the US commitment to regional

 It almost certainly sees the crisis as opening the possibility of
Argentina's turning to the USSR to reequip its armed forces. Moreover,
it probably also views the crisis as weakening the US ability to mobilize
Latin American nations against Soviet, Cuban. and other leftist
advances in the area.

Strategic Background

7.   The Soviets have had ties with some Latin American Communist
        parties since the 1920s, but until the 1960s they expended little
        effort to expand their influence in the hemisphere. Soviet

involvement was limited largely to providing some financial assist*
ance to the local
Communist parties, which in return—by and large—were expected
mainly to support Moscow's position at Communist international
gatherings. while seeking to broaden their influence over events in their
own countries. Moscow's expectations in the area remained modest until
the advent of Fidel Castro.

8.   Castro's alignment of Cuba with the USSR by 1961 marked the
      turning point in Soviet involvement in Latin America. Castro's
      move handed Moscow an opportunity to establish an ideological,
      political. and military foothold in the hemisphere. and a potential
      to gain in the strategic competition with the United States. The
      outcome of the Cuban missile crisis and the containment of
      Castroism to Cuba in the early 1960s nevertheless punctured
      Moscow's hopes of quickly altering the strategic balance and
      forcing the pace of change in the region.

9.   In the 1960s in Latin America and the Caribbean the USSR did
      not—except for Cuba— frontally challenge US dominance. The
      Soviets did vigorously undertake "active measures" intended to
      undercut US influence.' The Soviets use the term "active measure"
      to refer to a broad range of overt and covert intended to provoke
      policy effects. These measures. which represent an unconventional
      adjunct to traditional diplomacy. are deigned to influence the
      decisions of foreign governments, relations between other nations,
      undermine confidence in foreign leaders and institutions, and
      discredit opponents. They include such actions as manipulation of
      the media. disinformation and forgery, use of foreign Communist
      parties and fronts, sub rose economic activities. and various
      political influence operations. Operational Intelligence
      Memorandum

82. Trends and Development" in Soviet Active Measures (April 1982),
assesses Soviet "active measure" more broadly and in greater detail,
military or any significant economic assistance to any non-Communist
Central American or Caribbean country.

It emphasized in its policy the more pragmatic concerns of building diplomatic, commercial, and even military relations with the existing governments, as in Peru. Moscow apparently hoped that stronger bilateral ties would place it in a better position to profit from growing nationalism and its accompanying anti-Americanism. Correspondingly. the Soviets also discouraged the small orthodox Communist party from engaging in violence and were reluctant to support leftist groups advocating revolution. Although the Soviets did try from time to time to cultivate some local leftist leaders—such as Jamaica's Michael Manley, who was quite eager to curry favor with them—their efforts were limited, and they were content to let the Cuban; take the lead. In fact, they encouraged Manley to maintain correct relations with the United States in order to qualify for economic assistance which they were unwilling to extend.

10. In the case of Chile's Salvador Allende, Moscow's reluctance wholly to embrace his regime reflected a wide range of considerations beyond its concern with the US reaction: his political opportunism, conflict with members of his own Socialist party as well as the Communist Party, inability to co-opt groups of the extreme left, and lack of a loyal military force to defend his regime. In their reflections on the Chilean experience, Soviet leaders have noted the possibility of a "peaceful road to socialism." while warning revolutionaries of the need for a broad left coalition and their own military formation.

ll. This measured approach by the Soviets yielded both political and economic benefits. The number of regional states with which Moscow established relations expanded (see map), and the USSR's 1970s imports were 10 times those of the previous decade, largely because of grain purchases from Argentina.

Role of Cuba

12. Cuba plays a central role in Soviet relations with Latin America both as a dependent client serving Moscow's interests and as an independent actor influencing Soviet policies and tactics. Cuba's dependence on the

USSR for economic and military assistance has been a tender point for Castro, who vehemently denies any linkage between Soviet largess and Cuban actions in support of the USSR's foreign policy objectives. Soviet Diplomatic Relations in Latin America and the Caribbean, in fact, he has enjoyed greater freedom in his policies in
Latin America than he has elsewhere in the Third World. Nevertheless, Castro pays close heed to Soviet interests and to the limits of Moscow's tolerance on tactical matters.

13. Soviet and Cuban approaches to the region have not always been harmonious. Initially Moscow was convinced that a "march toward socialism" in Latin America would be slow and disapproved of Castro's indiscriminate aid to hemispheric revolutionaries as "adventurist. By 1968, however, Soviet political pressure and economic incentives, combined with Cuban foreign policy reverses, began to bit the two countries' goals and interests back into convergence and culminated in their joint intervention in Angola and Ethiopia in the mid. 1970s. By 1979 the two had expanded their collaboration to include support of violent revolutionary parties and groups, particularly in Central America.

14. Castro's vigorous support of Nicaraguan revolutionaries beginning in 1978 was essentially a Cuban initiative. and it has had a marked impact on Soviet attitudes and policy toward the region. Moscow was impressed by Havana •s success in exploiting the revolutionary situation in Nicaragua. Not only did the Cubans supplant US influence there, but, in a country in which Moscow had previously had no official representation, it soon enjoyed diplomatic, military, economic, and even formal party links with the Sandinista National Liberation Front (FSLN). Soviet leaders apparently came to share Castro's revised assessment that the prospects for the success of revolutionary forces in Central America were brighter than they had earlier calculated and felt that the United States was irresolute in countering leftist gains.

15. The Soviets have been working closely with the Cubans to consolidate the Sandinista regime; both share the view that Nicaragua is central to promoting leftist gains elsewhere in Central America. The

Cubans have also served as intermediaries with insurgent groups elsewhere in Central America and with the radical Bishop regime in Grenada. Moscow prefers that Havana take the lead in advancing regional revolutionary causes—in deference to Castro's understanding of local political dynamics and longstanding involvement with revolution in Latin America; because Cuba is a hemispheric, Spanish-speaking power; and to shield the USSR against any backlash from the United States and from the larger Latin American countries where it has a bilateral stake.

16. Despite the efficacy of Havana's role so far, Moscow is no doubt alert to the potential for damage to its broader interests arising from its Cuban connection. Potential for friction between Moscow and Havana exists in their conflicting preferences for different factions within some Latin American revolutionary movements. Partly to monitor Cuba's activity and check those they judge too provocative to the United States, the Soviets will continue their efforts to expand their own influence and leverage—particularly in Nicaragua.

Soviet Policies and Tactics

17. Moscow employs diverse means to exploit differing local conditions and to serve multiple Soviet interests. It is helping to consolidate the revolutionary regime in Nicaragua and is supporting the regime in Grenada. In some Latin American countries—particularly El Salvador, Guatemala, and Honduras—it is advocating and supporting violent revolution. In others, it is employing a mix of diplomacy and "active measures. " This pattern is likely to persist for at least the twoyear period of the Estimate.

Consolidation of Revolutionary Regimes

18. Moscow places a high value on consolidating and ensuring the survival of revolutionary regimes in the hemisphere. The new radical regime in Nicaragua and, to a lesser extent, that in Grenada are politically and symbolically significant for the USSR, especially after its

experience with Allende's Chile. The Soviets hope that the leftist, proSoviet, anti-American governments in Managua and Saint Georges will contribute to the emergence of other similarly oriented regimes in Central America and the Caribbean and serve as a conduit for revolution elsewhere in the hemisphere.

19. Nicaragua. Moscow, whose involvement in Central America was low before the Sandinista victory, is assiduously cultivating the new revolutionary regime in Nicaragua. It has subordinated its ti$ to the minuscule local Communist party and established formal party links with the Sandinistas. A Soviet diplomatic mission was established in January 1980, . and the total number of Soviets now in Nicaragua, including military advisers and technicians, is probably between 150 and 175.

20. The trend toward closer relations has accelerated over the last year or so. Recent high-level Nicaraguan visitors to Moscow have included Defense Minister Humberto Ortega. Sandinista Political Commission Chairman Arce, and Foreign Minister D'Escoto. Junta leader Daniel Ortega's visit to Moscow and meeting with President Brezhnev in May 1982 have put Soviet ties with Nicaragua on the same level as those with many important Soviet clients elsewhere in the Third World.

21. Even at a time in which the Soviets are being tightfisted with economic assistance, Moscow and its allies are meeting some of Nicaragua's economic needs. Moscow's economic assistance program is governed by a 1980 "framework" agreement—a form usually reserved for major aid recipients such as Afghanistan and Cuba—that calls for assistance to all major economic sectors. To date, Moscow, its East European allies, and Cuba claim to have committed about $480 million in nonconvertible currency credits to finance agricultural, roadbuilding, and communications equipment and other machinery. The claims may involve some double counting and could there. fore be inflated; nevertheless, some of the equipment financed by these credits has already been delivered.

Evidenced by the visits of Defense Minister Ortega to Moscow in the last year or so. military consultations are becoming more frequent and direct. Moscow no doubt hopes that its military assistance will forestall efforts to topple the regime and strengthen pro-Soviet elements in the Sandinista establishment.

24. The bulk of Nicaragua's military equipment and assistance has come from the USSR and its Communist allies. with other third parties providing modest levels of assistance (ee table l). Soviet military agreements are estimated to be worth at least $100 million through 1981. Some equipment has been sent from the USSR to Cuba and Algeria and transshipped to the Sandinistas. Growing East European military cooperation with Nicaragua is almost certainly undertaken at Soviet behest. The Soviets also appear to be encouraging such parties as Libya and the Palestine Liberation Organization (PLO) to provide military assistance and training to the Nicaraguans. The PLO apparently views its role in Nicaragua and its aid to revolutionaries elsewhere in the region at least partly as a guarantee of continued Soviet military and political support.

 Military Equipment and Assistance Supplied by Communist Countries to Nicaragua a In addition, Libya has provided a $100 million cash loan, and may have promised considerably more than that (although the Libyans are notorious for not honoring such commitments).

22. Moscow has also tried to blunt US economic pressure on Managua. The countries of the Soviet Bloc's Council for Mutual Economic Assistance (CEMA) gave Nicaragua 80,000 metric tons of grain to offset the cancellation of the 1981 US grain deliveries. Nevertheless, the Soviets appear reluctant to commit the substantial hard currency assistance most needed by Managua and have privately advised the regime to be cautious in disrupting economic ties with Nicaragua's most important Western economic partners.

23. In the area of military relations, Moscow continues to work largely through Cuba and other third parties to help build up the Sandinista military eastbound direct role is as it USSR   Tanks. heavy

amphibious carrier are more personnel carriers. artillery. multiple
rocket launchers, trucks. transport aircraft. helicopters, patrol craft.
and training.

Table I

Military Equipment and Assistance Supplied by Communist Countries to Nicaragua [a]	
USSR	Tanks, heavy amphibious ferries, armored personnel carriers, artillery, multiple rocket launchers, trucks, transport aircraft, helicopters, patrol craft, and training
Bulgaria	Pilot training
Czechoslovakia	Small arms
East Germany	Trucks and military equipment
Poland	Pilot training
Cuba	Machineguns, artillery, mortars, small arms, ammunition, and training
Vietnam	Small arms

[a] Among major items in this inventory are about 25 T-55 tanks, about 800 trucks, 12 BTR-60 armored personnel carriers, six GSP heavy amphibious ferries, two MI-8 Hip helicopters, six AN-2 aircraft, one Zhuk-class patrol craft, 12 D-20 152-mm gun-howitzers, 48 ZIS-2 57-mm antitank guns, 12 BM-21 multiple rocket launchers, and more than 100 antiaircraft guns.

Among mayor items in this inventory are about 25 T-55 tanks. about
800 trucks. 12 BTR-60 armored personnel carriers, six GSP new
amphibious. two MI-8 Hip helicopters, six AN-2 aircraft. 12 D-20
152mm gun-howitzers, 48 SUS-2 57 mm antitank guns, 12 BM•21
multiple rocket launchers. and more than 100 antiaircraft guns.

25.   In contrast to at least 2.000 Cuban military and security personnel,
the number of Soviet military personnel in Nicaragua is relatively
modest—between 50 and 75. The Soviet contingent thus appears to
be roughly equal in size to that from Eastern Europe (mainly East

Germany), the Middle East (the PLO and Libya), or Asia (Vietnam and North Korea). However, many of the Soviets. along with their Cuban counter• parts, seem to be acting as advisers to key members of the armed forces. Soviet military advisers are attached to the Nicaraguan General Staff, are assisting in the preparation of defensive contingency plans. and are probably providing intelligence support.

Soviet military aides are also closely involved in plans to reorganize and improve various Nicaraguan military services, particularly the Air Force—where they have largely displaced the Cubans. Moreover, Soviet pilots and technicians who accompanied deliveries of several AN-2 air transport planes and two Ml-8 helicopters last summer apparently are still there and have used this equipment to transport Nicaraguan military personnel.

26.   The Soviets also plan to provide several AN-26 transport aircraft soon, and a group of Nicaraguan pilots reportedly are scheduled to go to the USSR for appropriate training. In addition, efforts to expand and upgrade some Nicaraguan airfields, coupled with reported training of Nicaraguan Air Force personnel in Cuba, Bulgaria. and probably elsewhere in Eastern Europe to fly MIGs, suggest that Moscow may have been planning future deliveries of fighter aircraft, including some already in Cuba. The recent US warning of the consequences of such a move, however, may have prompted deferral of such deliveries. Nevertheless, preparations for their arrival are continuing.

27.   Moscow's apparent interest in avoiding highvisibility involvement in Nicaragua is derived partly from its desire not to provoke US countermeasures against either Nicaragua or the USSR. In working through intermediaries, especially in military matters, Moscow has sought to ensure that its prestige is not tied directly to the fate of the current regime in Managua. A more conspicuous Soviet role would also risk alienating Mexico. Panama, and other regional countries that are showing some signs of unease over the Nicaraguan military buildup. For these reasons, the Soviets

probably will be content to continue to rely on allies and nonregional intermediaries to provide the bulk of military assistance to Nicaragua. However. Moscow will continue to build more direct channels of influence and make occasional direct deliveries of military equipment to test US reactions to expanding Soviet involvement.

28. **Grenada. Moscow has appeared less certain about the long-term prospects of the leftist government in the small island state of Grenada and has been somewhat more circumspect in supporting it. Although the** Soviets welcomed the leftist coup and have come to regard it as an authentic "anti-imperialist revolution," they have been reluctant thus far to open an embassy on the island. Their economic assistance to the Bishop government so far has also been modest, amounting to a little more than $1 million in agricultural and construction aid and some limited technical assistance for the island's new television facility and two new radio transmitters far more powerful than the island requires for local broadcast needs.

29. In the area of military assistance, the Soviets have provided about three dozen military trucks and reportedly have offered military training in the USSR to about a dozen Grenadians. Moscow presumably also plays an indirect role through Cuban military assistance efforts, and has encouraged its East European allies to provide aid. Of importance is the 3,000-meter runway being built. principally by the Cubans, that will be capable of accommodating all known types of Cuban and Soviet aircraft.

30. There are signs that the USSR and Grenada may be moving to upgrade their relations. The Bishop government has established a diplomatic mission in Moscow——the first Grenadian embassy in the USSR— which could prompt a reciprocal move by Moscow. In recent months, key Grenadian military and political aides have also visited Moscow. presumably to seek additional Soviet economic and military aid.

31.   **Suriname.** Recent developments in Suriname have given Moscow a new opportunity to develop relations with another regime with revolutionary/ socialist pretensions in the Caribbean. The abortive March coup attempt against the government dominated by army commander Bouterse has been a major factor in the regime's decision to look for support from Cuba. Havana has responded with a small shipment of arms. and promises of full military and economic support. Although the Soviets will probably let Cuba take the lead, they have already signaled their interest in exploiting the new situation by announcing that they will open a resident embassy in the near future.

32.   **Guyana.** Soviet efforts to cultivate the leftist leaning government of Forbe Burnham and his Peoples National Congress (PNC) in Guyana have been constrained by Moscow's longstanding relationship with the pro soviet People's Progressive Party (PPP)' led by Cheddi Jagan. Although in the last year or two Moscow has moved somewhat away from the PPP, relations between Moscow and Burnham continue to be characterized by mistrust. Although the Soviets seem reluctant to extend economic aid to the financially hard-pressed government, they have sought to take advantage of the regime's economic problems by continuing to encourage a PPP-PNC coalition.

Support for Insurgencies and Revolution

33.   **Much of Moscow's support for insurgent and revolutionary movements in the hemisphere is covert, opportunistic. and flexible. Accordingly, the Soviets are expanding their links with leftists— particularly in El Salvador, Guatemala, and Honduras—where growing revolutionary activity promises opportunities to install anti-US and potentially pro-Soviet regimes. Elsewhere, they have encouraged the several small orthodox Communist parties in the Caribbean to prepare or violent revolution and have called on the Chilean left to initiate armed struggle against the Pinochet regime.**

34. **Soviet support and guidance for Latin American revolutionary movements now focus upon:**

— **Encouragement of broad revolutionary coalitions, uniting pro-Soviet Communist parties with their traditional leftwing rivals.**

— **Creation of military components loyal to the revolutionary coalitions.**

— **Use of hemispheric and extra hemispheric intermediaries.**

— **Training of revolutionary cadres.**

35. **In El Salvador. Moscow has continued to support Communist participation in the Unified Revolutionary Directorate, the umbrella organization conducting the insurgency. and has endorsed armed struggle as the left's best alternative. Moscow has facilitated the flow of arms and military equipment to the Salvadoran insurgents from Cuba and other third parties and has contributed logistic support to the operation. While generally supporting the entire revolutionary front, Moscow has strengthened the position of the Communist Party of El Salvador (PCES) within it by funneling some of its assistance to the insurgents through the PCES. This has endowed the Salvadoran Communists with a degree of influence much greater than their numerical strength would warrant. In bole steering the position of the**
PCES. **Moscow hopes to ensure that the party—and through it the USSR—will be well positioned to exert influence on events in El Salvador, especially if the leftist insurgency should succeed.**

36. **Despite this involvement, Moscow has tried to soft-pedal its role in El Salvador, partly to avoid provoking strong US countermeasures there that could spill over into Nicaragua and lead to further deterioration in relations with Washington. Moscow seemed to have been impressed by the Reagan administration's reaction to the situation in El Salvador and appears concerned that the**

outcome of the election in March 1982 may have significantly lessened the immediate prospects of the revolutionary left. However, the Soviets have taken comfort in the West European reluctance to endorse the elections. The Soviets also hope that actions by the political right in El Salvador will further complicate the US administration's efforts to mobilize Congressional support for additional military and economic support for that country, and, over the long term, assist the left. Although the Soviets appear less sanguine about the insurgents' short-term military prospects, they probably still believe that the insurgents can seize power through a prolonged armed struggle.

37.   In Guatemala and Honduras, Moscow and its allies have also been pressuring the local Communists to join broad revolutionary fronts and participate in armed struggle. Cuba, probably supported by Moscow, has promised arms to Communists and other radical leftists if they unify. The Soviets have provided financial assistance and training and have encouraged various third parties to do the same. In the last few years, for the first time since the mid-1960s, the Soviets have even resumed giving paramilitary training in the USSR to Honduran Communists. Moreover, in the last year or so, Soviet personnel in Cuba reportedly have participated in political training of Guatemalan Communists and have been more directly involved in giving tactical advice to the Guatemalan insurgents.

38.   The Soviets and the Cubans have also pressured the Dominican Communist Party intensify a grudging. agreement to prepare for eventual armed struggle in the Dominican Republic. Recently, how-ever, they urged the party to join a united front with the leftist Dominican Liberation Party for the May 1982 national elections—a coalition that the local Communists nevertheless avoided. Moscow is also using the
Dominican Communists to channel funds to the United Party of Haitian Communists, which reportedly is trying to organize a movement of Haitian exiles for the eventual ouster of President Duvalier. In addition, the USSR sponsors propaganda activities to enlist support for

hemispheric revolutionaries through Soviet front organizations such as the World Federation of Democratic Youth and the World Peace Council.

39.   In the case of Chile, the Soviets have •adopted an openly militant line aimed at promoting a united armed struggle against the Pinochet regime. Moscow provided the chief of the Chilean Communist Party with a forum at the 26th CPSU Congress to call for armed revolution, and subsequently has broadcast similar messages to Chile by other Chilean and even Salvadoran Communists. Despite increasing calls to overthrow Pinochet, Moscow does not believe his demise is imminent and has not committed significant material resources to assist the Chilean Communists.

40.   Moscow undoubtedly sees potential opportunities for the left in the political and social flux in Colombia. but has also been seeking good relations with the government in power. Its involvement with Colombian revolutionary groups, therefore, is more ambivalent. The Soviets have longstanding close ties with the Colombian Communist Party (PCC) but
the extent of their dealings with, and influence on, the party's paramilitary arm, the Revolutionary Armed Forces of Colombia (FARC), which is one of the country's most effective guerrilla groups, is uncertain. Since the mid-1970s, FARC has as. summed a more independent and radical line than the PCC. which has publicly renounced violence to gain power? Some top FARC leaders reportedly have received training in the USSR, and Moscow maintains some contact with the group through the PCC.

41.   Nevertheless, the Soviets are not known to have opposed active Cuban support for insurgency in Colombia. Following the seizure of the Dominican Embassy in Bogota in 1980 by the M-19 guerrillas, the Cubans assumed responsibility for their training and subsequent infiltration into Colombia. These Cuban-directed efforts have caused some diplomatic embarrassment to the Soviets— for example, the

cancellation of a visit by the President of Colombia that had long been sought by Moscow.

42.   One of Moscow is newest and most effective tactics for the support of Latin American revolutionary movements involves the use of proxies and other third parties. Within the region, Cuba has recently been joined by Nicaragua in playing this instrumental role. Nicaragua maintains training camps for Latin American insurgents and acts as a funnel for transporting externally supplied arms into El Salvador. Guatemala, and—to a lesser extent—Honduras. Some Nicaraguan personnel reportedly have been functioning as advisers to the Salvadoran and Guatemalan guerrillas, and Nicaragua serves as a base for the Salvadoran guerrilla command structure. Extra hemispheric actors include most prominently the PLO, but Libya, Vietnam, and several East European countries have also participated. Latin Americans are sent for paramilitary and political training to sites in Cuba, Eastern Europe, Libya, and else where in the Middle East. as well as the USSR itself. Arms and other support are shipped from or through a number of countries as a means of distancing the USSR from what would be seen as especially provocative acts.

Bilateral State-to-State Relations

43.   In Argentina, Brazil. Mexico. and Peru, Moscow •s policy has aimed largely at cultivating positive state-to-state relations. This approach has emphasized trade expansion and—in some cases— readiness to sell military hardware. Although these Soviet efforts have not usually been translated into increased Soviet influence. they have given some Latin American countries additional opportunities to assert their independence of the United States. By building on bilateral ties, the USR also seeks to achieve specific economic objectives and hopes to gain broader political support for its policy initiatives in the hemisphere and elsewhere in the world.

44.   Economic. The US-sponsored partial grain embargo following the invasion of Afghanistan, combined with Soviet agricultural problems, has intensified South Viet economic interest and activity in Latin

America. It has led to a significant growth in grain purchases from Argentina as well as Brazil. Since 1980 the USSR has become Argentina's largest grain buyer, account* ing for about 80 percent of that country's 1981 grain exports. Despite the Falklands crisis, this year's sales are still expected to be 11-12 million metric tons, or about one. Fourth of the USSR's total grain imports— although the ultimate volume will depend upon the results of the Soviet grain harvest. The USSR and Argentina also have concluded a five-year agreement which calls for annual Soviet purchase of 60,000 to 100,000 metric tons of Argentine beef; 1981 purchases totaled 87,000 metric tons.

45.   Such economic dealings with the USSR so far have paid handsome dividends for Latin American countries. Moscow has imported on a cash basis and has run massive trade deficits. (See chart.) According to the latest Soviet figures, Moscow's trade deficit with Argentina reached $3.3 billion in 1981. Brazilian exports to the USSR have also from 1980 by more than 100 percent to $744 million in 1981—while imports totaled only some $23 million. Such highly favorable trade arrangements are of great benefit to Argentina, and of more modest benefit to Brazil, in helping to offset their balance-of-payments deficits with other regions. Before the outbreak of the Falklands conflict, the Soviets—in response to their own hard currency stringencies—sought short-term credits from Argentina to cover grain purchases, but they did not appear to use the conflict to press this Soviet

Trade with Latin America and the Caribbean (Excluding Cuba)

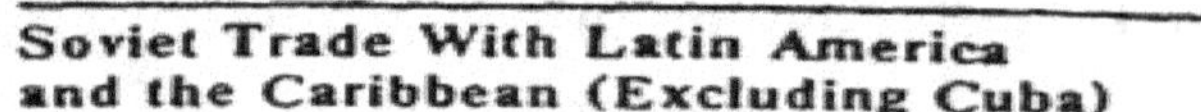

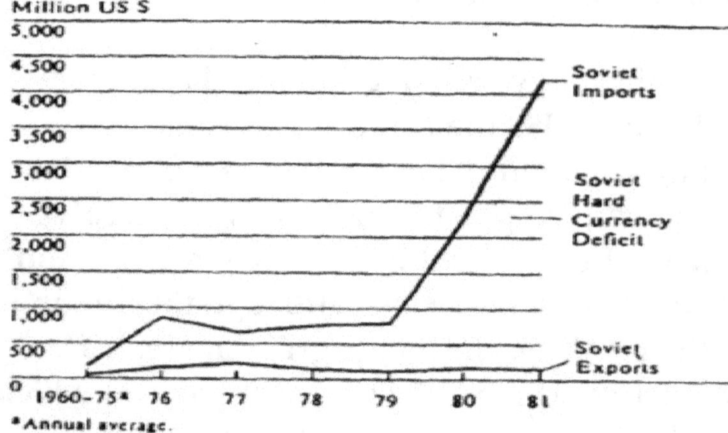

Unclassified

 The demand. Argentina, badly in need of hard currency from grain sales to finance its military activities, has been unwilling and unable to offer any short-term credits and, in fact, has requested advance hard currency payments from the USSR for impending grain deliveries. In the absence of an agreement on the wissue, the USSR has obtained West European financing for its purchases.

46. Despite these deficits, the Soviets have derived certain benefits of their own from this trade. In addition to meeting urgent economic needs, the USSR was able to undercut the 1980 US grain embargo and blunt its potential for future use. The Soviets are pressing to develop the bigger Latin American countries—particularly Argentina and Brazil—into important markets for Soviet finished goods, especially equipment for hydropower projects. There are now almost 1,000 Soviet and East European civilian technicians in the region. (See table 2.)

47. The nuclear field is another important area in the growing relationship between the USSR and Argentina. In an attempt to diversify its sources of supply, Buenos Aires has turned to Moscow for zircaloy production equipment. Earlier this year, the two

parties signed a nuclear supply contract that calls for the Soviets to provide enrichment services and I ton of heavy water. Consistent with Moscow's opposition to nuclear weapons proliferation, this contract requires safeguard measures. By expanding a relation. ship with the most advanced nuclear development program in Latin America, Moscow probably hopes to become a welcomed supplier of highly lucrative nuclear materials to other regional states, such as Brazil.

48.   The Soviets are also making an economic push in Brazil. Moscow's decision last year to sell oil there when it was reducing deliveries to its allies and other Third World countries reflected a desire to court the Brazilian Government as well as a pressing need for hard currency. Soviet oil exports to Brazil through 1982 will be 20,000 to 24,000 barrels per day, or about 3 percent of Brazil's oil requirements. Long-term trade agreements initiated by the two countries last year envision a trade turnover of $5 billion over the next five years. According to the terms of the agreements, Brazil will supply agricultural products under long term contracts while the Soviets will continue sales of crude and provide turbines for Brazilian hydroelectric projects.

49.   Moscow has also expanded technical exchanges with Brazil. Attracted by Moscow's willingness to

provide advanced technology on attractive financial terms, Brasilia has signed a technical service and financing agreement for the installation of Soviet ethanol manufacturing plants. The protocol calls for the construction of 15 facilities, with the USSR supplying equipment and nonconvertible commercial credits of up to 25 percent of total costs. Additionally, a Sao Paulo oil exploration company has agreed to Soviet assistance in evaluating the oil potential of the Parana basin. Moreover, Brasilia has also agreed to expanded Soviet participation in hydroelectric development and has contracted for assistance in evaluating coal deposits and assessing the feasibility of advanced coal gasification techniques.

50. The Soviets are also increasing their economic and commercial activity in Mexico, albeit not rapidly. For the last seven years, Mexico has had observer status with CEMA. Despite a gradual expansion during this period, Mexican trade with the USSR still accounts for less than I percent of Mexico's foreign commerce. Discussions with the USSR on a quadrilateral oil swap underscore Mexico's openness to dealings with the Soviet Union, but Mexico's insistence on commercially viable arrangements may continue to restrict trade expansion. Moscow wants Mexico to ship oil to Cuba. In turn, the USSR would supply Mexican customers in Europe. In addition to gaining substantial transportation savings. Moscow may think that the United States would be less likely to interrupt Mexican than Soviet shipments of oil if Washington resorted to an oil blockade of Cuba. The Soviets may also seek to obtain advanced US technology in Mexico, but Mexican efforts to avoid violating US export controls could limit Soviet opportunities.

51. **Military Sales and Training.** The Soviets' efforts to enter into military sales relationships have not kept pace with the growth of their economic relation Over the last decade, the USSR has secured only Peru—where it is now the primary supplier of air and ground equipment—as a major arms client. In the wake of the US refusal since the early 1960s to sell Peru sophisticated aircraft, a newly installed leftist military regime turned to the USSR in 1968 for military equipment. To date, Soviet military sales to Peru have amounted to more than $1 billion. While some of this equipment is dated, it more than meets Peruvian requirements and has included sophisticated jet aircraft, helicopters, surface-to-air and air-to-sur• face missile systems, and tanks. The Soviets have also been able to introduce their own military advisers for the first time into South America, and there are currently 125 to 150 Soviet military advisers and technicians in Peru. In addition. 2,000 to 3,000 Peruvians. including military and intelligence personnel, have been trained in the USSR, and Peruvian intelligence has a liaison relationship with the KGB.

52.	Peru has sometimes taken pro-Soviet or at least anti-US positions, but Lima's military relationship has given the Soviets little leverage over Peruvian policies. While the Peruvian Army and Air Force continue to seek new and more advanced military equipment from the USSR, key civilian members of the current Belaunde government—including the President himself—are expressing a desire to reduce the degree of Peru's military dependence on Moscow, although the likelihood of this is low. Not only do the Peruvian Army and Air Force appear to value the Soviet tie, but the Falklands crisis has made the USSR more attractive as an arms supplier. The local Communist party remains an insignificant political force and Moscow has shied away from supporting more radical elements. The Soviets are conscious that promotion of violent struggle could cause the military to sever the Soviet arms relationship and thereby severely set back Soviet interests. Moscow seems satisfied, at least for now. that the arms relationship represents its best entree. and hopes that over the longer-term leftist and pro-Soviet elements will become stronger.

53.	Despite Soviet arms sales to Peru, most of the Latin American military establishments, including those in Argentina. Brazil, and Mexico. have preferred Western-made arms, been suspicious of the Soviets, and repeatedly declined Moscow's offer of military equipment and joint training programs. These countries' officers corps are by and large staunchly anti-Communist, and their increasing concern over leftist gains in Central America will complicate Soviet efforts to make inroads in the military sales area.

54.	Undoubtedly. Moscow hopes that its political support for Argentina in the Falklands dispute and interruptions in the supply of arms from some West* ern sources will make at least the Argentine military more receptive to Soviet offers. Such a move would be a difficult one for the Western• and US-trained Argentine military leadership, which has been particularly outspoken in its antiCommunism. Nevertheless, if Western

restrictions on arms continue, Buenos Aires may seriously consider
purchasing selected military equipment from the USSR to replace
its losses and demonstrate disenchantment with the West. It is
possible that Argentina might be more open to the acquisition of
Soviet arms if they were supplied through an intermediary such as
Peru. Moscow may believe that its chances of establishing arms
supply relationships with some other governments in the region
will be enhanced.

55. **Political.** On the political front, the Soviets have consistently
sought to discredit US policy. They are prepared at every turn to
capitalize on the Latin perception of US political and economic
pressure. Moscow has applauded demonstrations of independence
from the United
States, such as the refusal of Argentina, Brazil, and Peru to join in the
US-sponsored trade sanctions against the USSR following the
Afghanistan invasion. The Soviets have sought to exploit Mexico's
opposition to US initiatives in El Salvador and to play on the differences
between Mexico and the United States over how best to restore stability
in Central America. Moscow is especially pleased to see differences
between the United States and Latin American countries regarding
policy toward the USSR. and probably views such disagreements as
signs of a further weakening of US influence and increase in its own

56. The Soviets have tried to use the Falkland Islands dispute between
Argentina and Great Britain to further ingratiate themselves with
the government in Buenos Aires and elsewhere in the region. After
initial hesitation, Moscow publicly supported Argentina and
apparently passed limited intelligence information to Buenos
Aires. Nevertheless, Moscow did not approve the invasion. nor has
it formally endorsed Argentina's claim to sovereignty over the
Falklands, although it has depicted Argentine policy in positive
terms as a continuation of the process of decolonization.

57. Moscow has intensified its diplomatic and political efforts to
improve its capabilities and demonstrate the importance it
attaches to bilateral ties With the states in the area. In the last year

or so, the Latin American section of the Soviet Foreign Ministry has been expanded and a new department created to emphasize more narrow regional expertise in handling the growing volume of contacts. During this period. the Soviets also have begun to send higher level visitors to Latin America. In the spring of 1981, for example, Politburo candidate member Rashidov visited Brazil.

More recently, in April 1982, Politburo candidate member Aliyev, accompanied by Brezhnev's personal senior foreign policy aide, paid a visit to Mexico City. Moscow, for its part, has played host to visits by Mexican President Lopez Portillo in 1978 and subsequently his foreign and defense ministers. While these visits have not resulted in any significant agreements between Mexico and the USSR, the publicity accorded to them by the two countries reflects the symbolic importance that both attach to their bilateral ties.

58.   Even in countries where the USSR's policy is keyed to developing bilateral state-to-state ties, Moscow continues to conduct a variety of covert activities and other "active measures" to improve its position and play upon domestic vulnerabilities over the longer term. These activities include:

— Funding local Communist parties and • front organizations.

— Disseminating disinformation and forgeries aimed at the United States.

— Drumming up support for hemispheric revolutionaries.

— Infiltrating military and security services as well as other important sectors of governmental bureaucracies.

— Manipulating the media and mass organizations.

— Cultivating pro-Soviet sentiments among academics and students.

— Developing and using agents of influence, mainly through the Cubans.

59.   To Moscow, the local orthodox Communist parties are essentially instrument50f Soviet policy (for sizes of parties, see table 3). The USSR provides funds to most Latin American Communist parties and is encouraging them to become more active, particularly in organizing broad coalitions of the left. In Mexico. for example, in keeping with Moscow's long-standing desire to forge greater unity among the local leftists. top-level Soviet party officials took part in negotiations preceding last year's fusion of the Mexican Communist Party with four smaller leftist parties. The Soviets also tried to pressure other Mexican leftist groups—including two parties that have adopted by the government—into joining the new leftist coalition. Their subsequent decision to ease such pressure presumably reflects their awareness of the limits of Soviet influence with some local leftists and a desire not to antagonize the Mexican government. Nevertheless, the Soviets probably calculate that such low-key involvement in strengthening Communist parties in the existing political systems poses little immediate risk to their state-to-state relations. The Soviets and Cubans employ their statestate and covert leftist contacts in Mexico to undermine US influence within the region. They are using Mexico as a base from which to conduct "active measures' against other countries.

Pro-Soviet Communist Parties in Latin America and the Caribbean

Country	Estimated Population, Mid-1981	Communist Party	
		Estimated Membership	Status
Argentina	28,130,000	45,000	Proscribed
Bolivia	5,490,000	500	Proscribed
Brazil	124,800,000	6,000	Proscribed
Chile	11,162,000	20,000	Proscribed
Colombia	25,217,000	12,000	Legal
Costa Rica	2,332,000	3,200 (PVP)	Legal
Dominican Republic	5,855,000	6,000	Legal
Ecuador	8,275,000	1,000	Legal
El Salvador	4,610,000	800	Proscribed
Guadeloupe	304,000	3,000	Legal
Guatemala	7,310,000	750 (PGT)	Proscribed
Guyana	857,000	Unknown (PPP)	Legal
Haiti	5,923,000	350 (PUCH)	Proscribed
Honduras	3,940,000	1,500	Proscribed
Jamaica	2,268,000	Unknown (WPJ)	Legal
Martinique	302,000	1,000	Legal
Mexico	69,100,000	112,000 *	Legal
Nicaragua	2,559,000	250 (PSN)	Legal
Panama	1,928,000	550 (PPP)	Legal
Paraguay	3,268,000	3,500	Proscribed
Peru	18,119,000	3,000	Legal
Uruguay	2,944,000	7,000	Proscribed
Venezuela	17,913,000	4,500	Legal

* This figure is the total membership claimed for a Communist-dominated coalition called the Unified Party of Mexico (PSUM), which is somewhat more independent in orientation than the other parties listed in the table.

T Table 3 Pro-Soviet Communist Parties in Latin America and the Caribbean

• This figure is the total membership claimed for a Communistdominated coalition called the Unified Party of Mexico (BUM). which is somewhat more independent in orientation than the other listed in the table.

60. The Soviets have also stepped up their propaganda activities in the area over the last several years. These efforts aim both to discredit US policy in the hemisphere and to strengthen leftist elements. Moscow. for example, has directed its representatives in Latin America to spread false accusations about the

reasons for Washington's tilt toward Britain on the Falklands dispute. The Soviets have also used front organizations such as the World Peace Council, the World Federation of Democratic Youth, and the World Federation of Trade Unions to mobilize support for Central American and Caribbean revolutionary groups. Moreover, through its greatly expanded English-language, medium-wave coverage (relayed from Cuba), Radio Moscow now blankets the Caribbean.

61. In keeping with the pattern elsewhere in the Third World, the Soviets try to infiltrate the bureaucracy of the host government. In the case of Jamaica under Michael Manley, for example, the KGB developed contacts with a wide range of Jamaican political figures—including Manley and government ministers—and helped Manley to organize a special intelligence unit to monitor his political opponents and US Unclassified

activities. The KGB was also in close contact with some of Manley's radical supporters who employed violence against the opposition. Yet, at the same time, the Soviets regarded the regime as unstable and proved unwilling to provide significant economic assistance, which might have helped to ensure its survival. Moscow is now apparently seeking to pursue correct and businesslike relations with the current government of Edward Seaga, if only to retain a Soviet presence in Jamaica, while continuing to maintain contacts with local leftist groups.

62. The Soviets are also educating numerous Latin American and Caribbean students in the USSR to improve Moscow's image, establish a cadre of local sympathizers, and spot and evaluate potential agents for the Soviet intelligence services. Moscow reportedly offers hundreds of scholarships per year to students from countries such as Brazil, Colombia, Costa Rica, Cuba may have received more Latin American students than all other Communist countries combined. Students from virtually every country in the region have been noted at various schools in Cuba since Fidel Castro came to power in 1959. and many of them have received paramilitary training. Panama, Nicaragua. the Dominican Republic, Jamaicat Mexico, and Venezuela to study in the USSR at Lumumba University (see table 4). The Soviet interest in cultivating organized labor in the area has also increased. For example. the USSR now has formal ties with the Nicaraguan trade union organization and maintains an educational exchange program with trade unionists from Colombia.

Table 4

Academic Students From Latin America and the Caribbean in the USSR and
Eastern Europe, [a] 1956–81 [b]

| | Departures to the USSR and Eastern Europe | | | | | | Being Trained as of December 1981 | | |
| | 1956-81 | | | 1981 | | | | | |
	Total	USSR	Eastern Europe	Total	USSR	Eastern Europe	Total	USSR	Eastern Europe
Total	13,955	8,785	5,170	1,390	945	445	6,800	4,360	2,440
Argentina	450	235	215	10	5	5	35	25	10
Belize	20	20	—	5	5	—	20	20	—
Bolivia	910	520	390	20	10	10	105	65	40
Brazil	560	290	270	20	5	15	45	30	15
Chile	730	530	200	10	5	5	70	40	30
Colombia	1,565	975	590	110	100	10	1,015	555	460
Costa Rica	910	560	350	100	50	50	670	385	285
Dominica	10	5	5	10	5	5	10	5	5
Dominican Republic	925	700	225	150	125	25	800	700	100
Ecuador	1,805	1,070	735	190	140	50	835	355	480
El Salvador	305	160	145	10	5	5	85	30	55
French West Indies	155	100	55	15	10	5	75	45	30
Grenada	40	40	—	20	20	—	40	40	—
Guatemala	145	120	25	20	15	5	80	55	25
Guyana	350	140	210	20	5	15	95	20	75
Haiti	170	85	85	10	5	5	40	25	15
Honduras	470	295	175	50	25	25	230	125	105
Jamaica	65	35	30	10	5	5	55	25	30
Mexico	735	460	275	35	25	10	140	80	60
Nicaragua	725	450	275	250	150	100	425	260	165
Panama	1,000	650	350	175	100	75	1,000	650	350
Paraguay	20	10	10	—	—	—	—	—	—
Peru	1,315	1,005	310	145	125	20	795	770	25
Uruguay	65	35	30	—	—	—	—	—	—
Venezuela	510	295	215	5	5	—	135	55	80

[a] Excludes Yugoslavia.

[b] Cuba may have received more Latin American students than all other Communist countries combined. Students from virtually every country in the region have been noted at various schools in Cuba since Fidel Castro came to power in 1959, and many of them have received paramilitary training.

63. The Soviets have profited from the growth of pro-Marxist sentiments among •religious activists. They have been especially impressed with the direct support such activists have provided the Sandinista regime and other revolutionary causes elsewhere in Central America. Crowing resistance among church leaders to this de facto partnership between religion and revolution notwithstanding, Moscow and Havana probably will seek to benefit from the sympathies of many church activists for leftist revolution in the region.

Constraints

64. Despite its increased optimism about trends in Latin America, Moscow recognizes that there are major constraints on its ability to influence developments there. Foremost is the attitude and role of the United States. Moscow believes that US political, economic, and military strength still gives Washington potential for considerable leverage in the hemisphere.

65. Moscow has therefore moved in ways designed to avoid directly provoking the United States. In contrast to the USSR's overt and direct bilateral dealings with the larger states. its support for revolutionary movements has been low-key, often employing intermediaries and surrogates. This pattern of indirect support also reflects Soviet uncertainty about the long-term prospects of revolutionary movements and unwillingness to commit the USSR irretrievably to respond to possible US actions against them. Furthermore, Moscow has been careful to play down its direct commitment to the Sandinista regime and has apparently not sought a "friendship" treaty with Nicaragua as it has with some Third World clients outside the Western Hemisphere.

66. More important, the Soviets have displayed concern about the application of US political and military leverage in response to the crisis in Central America. The Reagan administration's frank warnings have emphasized that Washington is indeed sensitive to Moscow's efforts to exploit political instability in its own backyard and that such activities there might' well trigger a strong US reaction. The level of arms deliveries to Cuba in 1981 —the second-highest annual total on record— and the Soviet efforts to build up Nicaragua's military forces are to a degree indicative of this anxiety. At the same time these measures provide Cuban and Nicaraguan armed forces with increased offensive capabilities and with further means to intimidate neighbors and provide haven for leftist insurgents.

67. Antipathy to the Soviets is another constraint on Moscow. Even those governments that have developed important bilateral ties with the USSR. such as Argentina and Brazil. remain strongly anti-Communist and distrustful of Soviet motives with respect to their domestic politics. Brazil. for example, out of fear of Soviet intelligence penetration, has even refused to accept Soviet military attaches. The Brazilians have also kept the USSR out of areas that they consider of strategic importance, such as the nuclear program and uranium exploration efforts. In addition, the Brazilian Communist Party remains outlawed and is

closely monitored by the security •authorities. Thus, in the near-term Moscow recognizes that more extensive and open backing for leftist insurgencies in Central America would risk a backlash against the USSR by regional governments and reinforce their suspicions of Soviet inspired interference in their internal politics. Such backing would also stimulate anti-Communist elements among important social groups, especially the various churches.

68. Moreover, economic considerations also impose some constraints on Soviet activism in the region. Foremost are the poor quality. technological backwardness, and narrow range of Soviet industrial goods, which are compounded by the area's historical preference for Western goods. Taken together, these factors severely limit Soviet export prospects. In cases where Moscow might hope to make political inroads through imports from Latin American or Caribbean countries, its severe shortage of hard currency is a major constraint. Finally. the USSR's record of tightfistedness about economic assistance deprives it of further opportunities to assist pro-Soviet regimes or otherwise gain influence in the region.

69. Another constraint on Moscow is the unstable nature of new leftist regimes and its recognition that its influence is dependent on local political trends that it may be unable to control. The electoral ouster of Manley in Jamaica was a key case in point, and the Bishop regime in Grenada faces economic problems that could generate political discontent. The Soviets probably are still uncertain whether the new revolutionary regimes in Nicaragua and Grenada can survive. The Soviets see Nicaragua's Sandinistas under considerable pressure from the United States and formerly sympathetic European socialists. They also see Nicaragua increasingly beset by a wide variety of political opponents, armed counterrevolutionaries, and mounting economic problems.

Prospects and Implications for the United States

70. Moscow's long-term objectives of eroding and supplanting US
influence in Latin America are unlikely to be affected by its recognition
of the obstacles to its ambitions under present power realities and the
political climate in the hemisphere. In fact, over the next few years,
Soviet efforts to gain influence in the region are likely to increase and
will probably present more serious problems for the United States.
Washington's response to this growing Soviet challenge will be
complicated by the fact that its own deep concern about Soviet
troublemaking in the area is not shared by many regional governments.
Sympathy with revolutionary causes will persist in countries such as
Mexico and Panama. Even countries less sympathetic to leftist causes
such as Brazil and Venezuela would be opposed to US military
intervention to check revolutionary gains in Central America and the
Caribbean.

71. The Soviets will continue to use both state to state and revolutionary
approaches, depending on the situation. Moscow probably will continue
to judge that in the long term it has a great deal to gain by continuing to
develop positions of influence ih the more politically significant countries
such as Argentina, Brazil. Mexico, and Peru. It will couple this interest
with its exploitation of ferment in countries embroiled in insurgencies or
ruled by unstable regimes.

72. Uncertainty about US intentions is the dominant consideration in
Soviet thinking about risks and gains in exploiting regional
opportunities. Without abandoning its support for revolution, Moscow is
likely at present to minimize risk by recommending tactical prudence to
its regional clients Cuba and Nicaragua. Moscow's recent endorsement
of calls for talks between Nicaragua and the United States, for example,
probably reflects its interest in easing US pressure and buying time for
the beleaguered Sandinista regime, as well as in cutting its own costs.

73. So far, the Soviets have been reluctant to provide Nicaragua with
massive economic aid. Nonetheless, if the Sandinista regime falters for
economic reasons. Moscow and its allies probably would be somewhat
more forthcoming with economic support. Because Nicaragua's
population is much smaller than Cuba's, and because Managua seems at

this time to enjoy broader international economic backing than did Havana in the 1960s, in the near term at least the Soviets would almost certainly not have to assume the kind of economic burden that they have been carrying in Cuba for two decades.

74. Intensified pressure on Managua by Nicaraguan dissident armed elements may be seen by Moscow as posing a potential long-term threat to the Sandinista regime. yet as also offering an opportunity to draw Nicaragua still closer to the Soviet Bloc. Moscow will probably counsel Managua to avoid countermeasures provocative to the United States— such as armed forays deep into Honduras—but may assume a more active role in planning Nicaragua's counterinsurgency measures, and might expand its military assistance.

75. In the event Nicaragua were subject to direct conventional attack. it would have to rely primarily on Havana rather than Moscow for immediate assistance. The Cubans concluded a secret defense agreement with Managua in late 1979 and almost certainly would commit their personnel stationed in Nicaragua. as well as additional Cuban forces, to resist any such attack short of a direct invasion by US forces. The Soviets have not. so far as we know, promised direct Soviet support in this eventuality, but presumably they would step up military aid to the Cubans. Moscow's other allies and clients could not be expected to provide much more than political support.

76. The large and growing levels of military hardware in the hands of Soviet clients have major implications for the region. In addition to defending both Cuba and Nicaragua against attack. such military power—especially in Nicaragua—facilitates support to the Salvadoran insurgents and provides shelter for the guerrilla infrastructure. Within the term of this Estimate, other objectives behind arms supply from the USSR and various intermediaries probably include Intimidating Nicaragua's neighbors. thus, dispose them toward acquiescence in the Soviet Cuban foothold in Central America.

— Supporting insurgents in Guatemala.

Laying the groundwork for support of possible future insurgencies in Honduras, Costa Rica, and elsewhere in the hemisphere.

77. Over the longer term, there is also a possibility that the Soviets may seek access to naval and air facilities in Nicaragua and Grenada. Such access would have a significant impact on US security interests. especially about the Panama Canal and other lines of communication. The principal constraint on the Soviets in expanding their military presence in Central America and the Caribbean is their uncertainty as to the US response. Nevertheless. they are very likely to continue to probe US resolve during this decade.

78. The persistent strain of anti-US sentiment in the region, which has been accentuated by the Falklands crisis, offers the Soviets some new opportunities to expand their influence. However, Soviet initiatives are of less intrinsic significance than US policies and actions. The Soviets probably have no firm expectation of any dramatic new political payoffs in the near term, although they probably do hope that their support will moderate local suspicions of Moscow and enable them to project an image of the USSR as a distant but powerful supporter of Latin American and anticolonial interests. They may also calculate that the outcome of the crisis could usher in a period of political instability and open prospects for those in Buenos Aires who might be more inclined toward closer relations with the USSR. The Soviets are already seeking to profit from any general deterioration in US influence in the hemisphere arising out of the Falk* lands crisis, but they realize that Washington's losses cannot immediately chalked up as Moscow's gains.

79. US efforts to build hemispheric solidarity with the current Salvadoran Government and to gain Latin American support for countering Soviet-supported leftist insurgency elsewhere in Central America have been damaged. The Soviets are certain to attempt to exploit what they perceive as a US setback. They will continue to conduct many of (heir activities in the region either covertly or through intermediaries. Although generally successful to date, this tactic is vulnerable to public exposure of Soviet support for subversion and revolutionary violence Furthermore, some Soviet intermediaries (such as

Cuba, Algeria, or the PLO) might possibly be led to moderate their policies through a combination of external pressure and internal problems.

80. The Soviets have by and large successfully implemented a of encouraging unrest in various Central American states, gaining a foothold in Nicaragua. and improving their relations with the governments of the more important South American countries. They probably expect their general progress to continue, especially if the United States appears to be inconsistent, or discredits itself through its reactions to events in the region. From the Soviet perspective. such a policy has potential for distracting American attention from other regions; is relatively cheap in eco• nomic terms; has not required major commitments to local allies; and has not raised confrontation with the United States to an unmanageable level. The Soviets are thus likely to persist with this strategy.

DISSEMINATION NOTICE

l . This document was disseminated by the Directorate of Intelligence. This copy is for the information and use of the recipient and of persons under his or her jurisdiction on a need to know basis. Additional essential dissemination may be authorized by the following officials within their respective departments:

a.   Director, Bureau of Intelligence and Research, for the Department of State

b.   Director, Defense Intelligence Agency, for the Office of the Secretary of Defense and the organization of the Joint Chiefs of Staff

c.   Assistant Chief of Staff for Intelligence, for the Deportment of the

Army

d.   Director of Naval Intelligence, for the Department of the Navy

e.   Assistant Chief of Staff, Intelligence, for the Department of the Air Force

f.   Director of Intelligence, for Headquarters, Marine Corps g,
        Deputy Assistant Secretary for International Intelligence Analysis,
        for the Department of Energy

h. Assistant Director, FBI, for the Federal Bureau of Investigation Director of NSA, for the National Security Agency Special Assistant to the Secretary for National Security, for the Department of the Treasure

k. The Deputy Director for Intelligence for any other Department or Agency

2.   This document may be retained, or destroyed in accordance with applicable security regulations. or refurned to the Directorate of Intelligence.

3.   When this document is disseminated overseas, the overseas recipients may retain it for a period not in excess of one year. At the end of this period, the document Should be destroyed or returned to the forwarding agency, or permission should be requested of the forwarding agency to retain it in accordance with IAC-D-69/2, 22 June 1953.

4.   The title of this document when used separately from the text is unclassified.

You can get the conclusion, Cuba have been played the main role to shift South America against the United States, it's reach directly our National

Security because is tied to Russia main military objective to attack the United States.

Strategic Bombers in the Caribbean Sea

In this moment, Bombardier patrol flights resumed under President Vladimir Putin, and have become even more frequent in recent weeks, with NATO reporting an increase in Russian military flights in the Black, Baltic and North Seas, as well as in the Atlantic Ocean.

Earlier this year, Shoigu said Russia plans to expand its global military presence by requesting permission for Navy ships to use ports in Latin America, Asia and elsewhere to replenish supplies and perform maintenance. He said the military was conducting talks with Algeria, Cyprus, Nicaragua, Venezuela, Cuba, Seychelles, Vietnam and Singapore.

Shoigu said Russia is also talking to some of those countries about allowing long-range bombers to use their air bases to refuel.
Ian Kearns, director of European Leadership Network, a group of experts based in London, said the bomber patrols are part of the Kremlin's efforts to make the Russian military "more visible and more assertive in their actions."

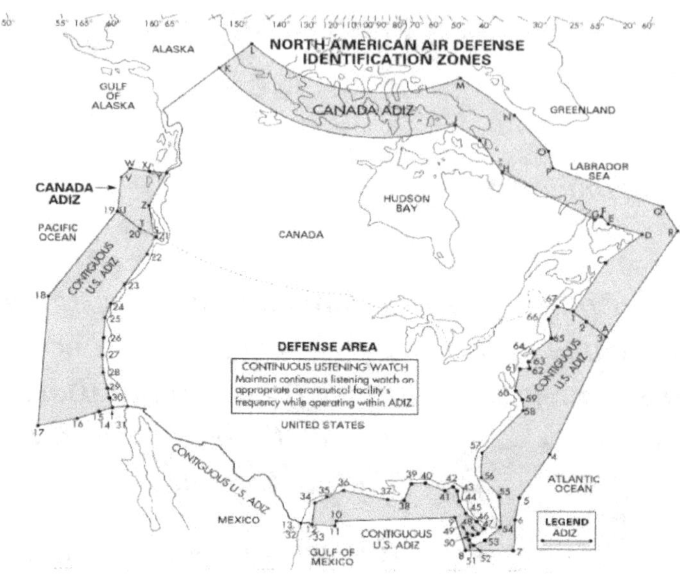

The United States, along with about twenty other nations, have established air defense identification zones (ADIZ) that stretch off their coasts. The ADIZ is a product of the Cold War and the first American ADIZ was established by President Truman in 1950 during the Korean War to reduce the possibility of a surprise attack by the Soviet Union. An ADIZ is a known boundary that extends beyond national territory and is almost always in international airspace. Within the ADIZ, unidentified aircraft are expected to be challenged until their intent can be verified. The U.S. has five ADIZs: East and West Coast, Alaska, Hawaii and Guam.

The new bomber flights "do not necessarily presage a threat," Kearns said. "They are just part of a general increase in activities." However, he added: "The more cases you have that NATO and Russian forces come closer, the more likely it is that something bad will happen, even if it is not intentional."

On Monday, the European Leadership Network published a report that found a sharp increase in Russian-NATO military encounters since the annexation of Crimea into the Kremlin, including violations of national airspace, avoided close air strikes, close encounters in the sea, harassment of reconnaissance aircraft, overflights on warships and Russian missions of mock bombings.

Three of the nearly 40 incidents, the expert committee said, led to a "high probability" of causing casualties or triggering a direct military confrontation: a narrowly avoided collision between a civilian aircraft and a Russian surveillance plane, the hijacking of an Estonian intelligence officer, and a large-scale Swedish and search for a Russian submarine produced no results.

In September, the report said: Russian strategic bombers in the Labrador Sea off Canada practiced cruise missiles against the US.

Earlier this year, in May, the report said that Russian military aircraft were approaching 50 miles off the coast of California, the closest Russian military flight recorded since the end of the Cold War. The ties between Russia and the West have dropped to their lowest point since the Cold War by the annexation of Crimea to the Kremlin and support for pro-Russian insurgents in Ukraine. The West and Ukraine have continually accused Moscow of fueling the rebellion in eastern Ukraine with troops and weapons, claims that Russia has rejected.

The fight has continued in the east, despite the ceasefire agreement signed between Ukraine and the rebels signed in Minsk, Belarus. in September. Stoltenberg, the NATO chief urged Russia to "withdraw its forces and equipment from Ukraine, and fully respect the Minsk agreements." Air Force Gen. Philip Breedlov, Supreme Allied Commander in Europe, said on Wednesday that in the past two days "we have seen columns of Russian equipment, mainly Russian tanks, Russian artillery, Russian air defense systems and Russian combat troops. they enter Ukraine. " Breedlove , who spoke in Sofia, Bulgaria, did not say how many new troops and weapons moved to Ukraine or specified how the alliance obtained the information.

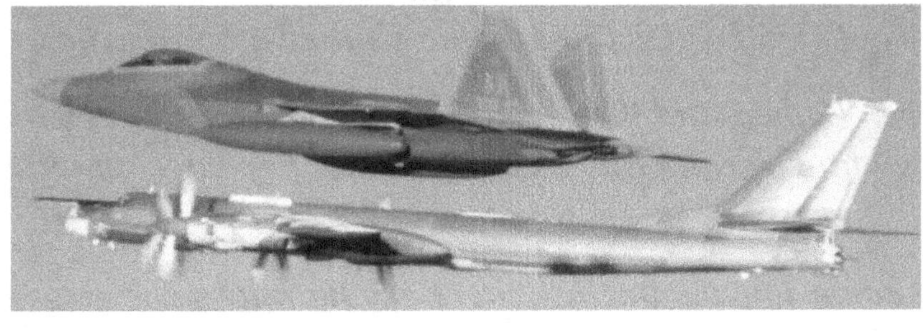

An F-22 of the US Air Force accompanying a Bear Tu-95 (photo / USAF)

These spy planes take off from Cuba with alternate emergency bases in Nicaragua and Venezuela, and soon Mexico will be perhaps another base in Russia.

As a detail to take into account to know the priority of these operations are the visits of the Minister of Defense of Russia to Cuba and those of Colonel Alejandro Castro Espin to Moscow with a group of specialists in Cybernetic War, are unmistakable signs of modernization and activation of the Electronic Intelligence bases and the Russian naval units in the area.

Since 1970 Submarines in Cuba

The silence of Moscow and Havana has been the response to the White House's warning against the construction of a strategic Soviet submarine base in Cuba. On previous occasions, the Soviet government has been quick to deny the much less serious accusations that appear even in obscure publications.

But in this case, when a spokesman for the White House raised the possibility that the Kremlin had secretly started working on strengthening its strength in Cuba.

The pessimists will conclude that this silence confirms Washington's worst fears. Optimists will argue that Soviet leaders are re-analyzing the plans that may be under way for the Cuban port of Cienfuegos or, as suggested in a dispatch published today in The Times, that the whole story has a very dubious factual basis.

The world was probably closer to the thermonuclear war during the Cuban missile crisis of October 1962 than at any time before or after.

However, it has been known that 92 nuclear warheads have existed on Cuban soil protected underground in areas of Camagüey have remained since 1962.

As is customary in communist countries, there are no nuclear protection norms, which increases nuclear pollution and the diseases produced by them. President Kennedy thought about Castro and the Russians made a show to avoid an international inspection to see if the island's nuclear weapons had really been dismantled.

The experience on the Soviet and Russian conduct in these cases is to have planned the operations and the variants of these, under the circumstances of the answers of the United States, they would have simple prepared for the scene of creating the crisis by the location of the nuclear missiles and after negotiating the supposed withdrawal, leaving them in hiding places, without inspection by the Security Council as they did afterwards.

In this situation, any Soviet movement to create a submarine base in Cuba - and we cannot be sure at this moment that such is the Soviet intention - would only increase the tension between the two superpowers and strengthen the retrograde forces in both countries that would intensify the arms race.

In recent years, US spy, aircraft and submarine satellites are tracking Russian ships along the coast to Cuba. The Russian submarines in deep waters have approached the submarine cables that communicate the American continent and have arranged in the same equipment of interception of the communications. The Yantar ship suddenly crossed the Atlantic and began moving around the east coast of the United States last month, sounding alarms within the world of US naval intelligence.

The spy satellites, airplanes and submarines of EE. UU They kept the ship under close surveillance to Cuba, according to two US defense officials. It has been years since the USA. They have seen this type of activity on the part of the Russians, said the authorities.

While that the Russians have insisted that the Yantar is not a spy ship, US naval intelligence believes that it has a significant and disturbing capacity: it is a carrier of small submarine vehicles that can cut and intercept information on vital submarine cables that carry large amounts of data commercial and military, voice communications and Internet service between the United States and Europe. Some of these details were first reported by the New York Times. US officials UU

They told CNN that there were no indications that the Russians intend to cut the cables, but said they are showing their ability to do so. It is about what the United States has observed during the last months of naval operations while Russian submarines in deep waters have approached submarine cables.

A classified network of submarine sensors from the Navy was activated several times as the submarines approached the cables. The officials said that the Russians would be aware in general terms that their actions were detected, on other occasions they have detected devices that collect the communications transmitted by these cables and have been detected by the sensors of the network.

High Level Visits

At the protocol level, the visit of this Minister of Defense must correspond to the visit of the Minister of the FAR to Moscow, but that cannot be because Raúl Castro knows that his Minister of the FAR is mentally retarded and can only say that he loves Fidel and Raúl ... like a parrot and is also unable to understand what cyber warfare consists of.

Re f:
Author's files
Testimonials of the author
Declaraciones del Cmte.. Fidel Castro en la Universidad de La Habana. Oficina de la FEU 8 noviembre 1962
Conversaciones privadas con el Capitán Víctor Pina
Alexander Fursienko, Timothy N. "One Hell of Gamble: Khrushchev, Castro and JFK. 1958-1964 W.W. Norton and Co. New York.1997
Vives, Jose Los nuevos amos de Cuba. Notes del autor.
U.S. Military Jets Intercept Russian Bombers Off Alaskan Coast
https://www.rferl.org/a/u-s-military-jets-interceptrussian...off.../29222731.html
https://foxtrotalpha.jalopnik.com/inside-the-russian-bomber-that-s-beenflying-america-s-1795375146 CIA's File
file:///G:/A%20CUBA%20Attack%20English/CIA%20REPORT%20CUBA%20AND%20SOUTH%20AMERICA.pdf

4:28

***US F-22 Jet Catch a Russian Tu-95 Bomber
Plane in Near Alaska,
Original Update DEFENSE
YouTube - May 12, 2018***

2:04

Two US F-22 jets escort Russia's Tu-95 aircraft - Russian Defense ...

***World Of Weapon YouTube - May
12, 2018***

1:24

*US stealth fighters intercept Russian bombers
CNN.com - May 12, 2018*
*Tu-22M, Tu-95 and Tu-160 Fly past
Zhukovsky, Moscow 2012 | Ty-22M ...*
YouTube - Oct 4, 2008

The Aviationist » Footage From Inside A Russian Tu-95 Bear Strategic ...
*https://theaviationist.com/.../footage-from-inside-a-russian-tu-95-
bearstrategic-bombe...*
*May 18, 2018 - On May 12, two U.S. Air Force F-22 Raptor jets were
launched from Joint ... to intercept and visually identify two Russian
Tu95 Bear bombers ...*
Tupolev Tu-114 · Tupolev Tu-142 · Tupolev Tu-95LAL · Tupolev Tu-85
Russian MoD: US Fighters Escorted Tu-95 Strategic Bombers Over ...
https://sputniknews.com/military/20180512106438421-russia-us-

bombers/ May 12, 2018 - The Russian Defense Ministry earlier said thatTu-95 longrange bombers and long-range Tu-142 antisubmarine planes had flown over neutral ...

Inside The Russian Bomber That's Been Flying America's Coastline https://foxtrotalpha.jalopnik.com/inside-the-russian-bomber-that-s-beenflying-americ...

May 19, 2017 - The Russian Tu-95/-142 Bear has been showing up in a lot of places it ... Russian Bears have pushed close tothe United States, Canada and ...

US stealth fighters intercept Russian bombers off the coast of Alaska ... https://www.cnn.com/2018/05/11/politics/us-stealth-fightersintercept.../index.html

May 12, 2018 - Two Russian TU-95 "Bear" bombers were intercepted by US F-22 stealth fighters in international airspace off the coast of Alaska on Friday, ...

The Bear: Russia's Tu-95 Bomber Is Moscow's Very Own B-52 | The ... https://nationalinterest.org/.../the-bear-russias-tu-95-bomber-moscows-veryown-b-52...

Jan 22, 2018 - Over sixty years later, the Tu-95 remains inservice because few aircraft ... U.S. Air Force Scientists are Working to Arm the B-52 Bomber with ...

U.S. Carrier Intercepts Russian Bombers - The New York Times https://thelede.blogs.nytimes.com/2008/02/12/us-carrier-intercepts-russianbombers/

Feb 12, 2008 - Now, a half-year later, they came in the form of four Tu95 Bears, a type of plane that is somewhat slow and clumsy by American standards but ...

6 Intercepting the Bear - Air Force Magazine
www.airforcemag.com/MagazineArchive/Pages/2018/.../Intercepting-theBear.aspx
https://www.infobae.com/america/mundo/2018/01/26/el-tenebrosobombardero-nuclear-supersonico-de-rusia/

Chapter 2
Base of Meteorological Modification "Pronto Auxilio"

Cuba is in a perfect geographical position for the cyber-attacks against the United States, but also, this is the reason for the increase in the flow of Russian oil to Cuba, which has facilitated the intense activity of the Meteorological Modification Center known as "Pronto Auxilio" that has been able to produce phenomena in meteorology that we have witnessed. This center, codified by the CIA as a "woodpecker", has long been known for its activity.

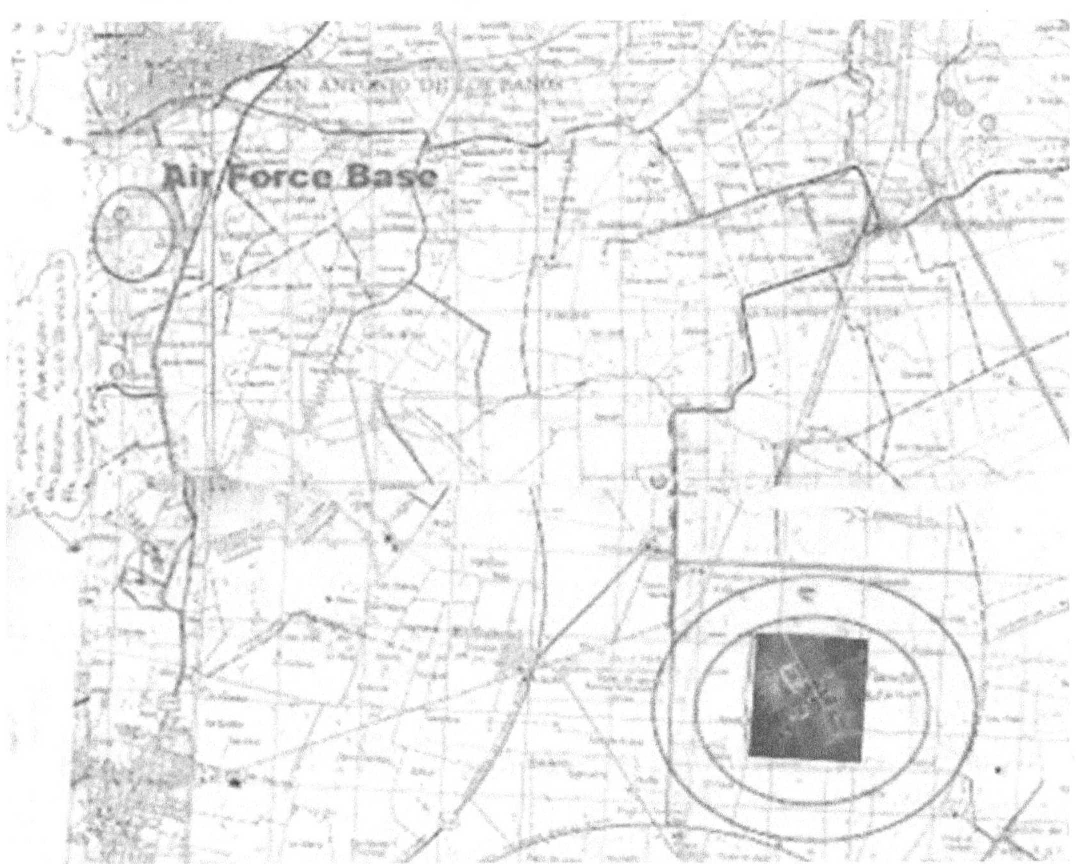

The military map with the exact location and its connection with the coaxial cable of subordination to Military Unit 1779 (Air Base of San Antonio de los Baños), also this same air base serves as the base of operations of the TU195, airplanes that they patrol the south and the Atlantic coast of the United States, from 1967 but during the Obama administration these aircraft repeatedly violated the airspace of the United States, according to the Department of Defense.

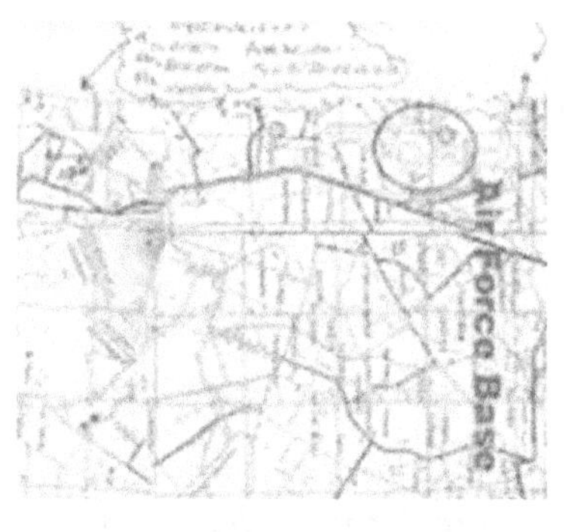

The Military Unit codified by the DAAFAR "Pronto Auxilio" as you will see on the map of the Air Force of Cuba. It is the Meteorological Modification Center, Cuban code "Pronto Auxilio" in Quivican, Cuba, located in: Cuba, Quivican 22.765170, 82.374738 photo: aside this manuscript on the connection of the coaxial cable. Map of the Institute of Cartography of the MinFAR.

The last Chief of Soon Aid I met was Colonel Albo Parra Salina, a Master Air Combat pilot, already retired. In fact, his activity is now engaged in the campaign of disinformation or denying the Russian-Cuban activity in the War of Meteorological Modification or Climate in which he participates.

It cannot be new, Cuba has been characterized by failure to deceive and hinder any act of welfare, only the diabolic can be expected, in recent times Cuba violated many international treaties on weapons, for example, Cuba left in Angola millions of antipersonnel mines installed, masked and without a map so they can not be located and deactivated. Consequences dead, mutilated, waste of resources, misfortunes ... Russian-Cuban heritage in Angola.

Colonel Albo Parra Salina, also head of the Cuban Air Force in Angola, now offers lectures blaming the United States for what Russia and Cuba are doing against Humanity.

An announcement on the Internet about these conferences can be obtained by searching for: Hydrometeorological War or Ecological War by Albo Parra Salinas. Hydrometeorological War or Ecological War
Published by Blanca Gómez Cuenca
http://slideplayer.es/slide/5467237/

Below are the aerial photos of the building from which the Meteorological Modification system operates, according to Colonel Albo Parra.

Carpenter Bird System of the
Soviet Era
(1977)
The Soviet climate modification system is known as the Carpenter Bird system by the CIA. It consists of the transmission of waves with extreme low frequency (ELF) of 10 hertz using transmitters of the Tesla type in Angarsk and Khabarovsk in Siberia, Gomel, Sakhalin island, Nikolayev in Ukraine, Riga in Latvia and also a site 60 miles away. South of Havana, appears on the map and aerial photos. To give you an idea of the magnitude of this system, it is said that the facilities near Havana, Cuba, are maintained and operated by Soviet and Cuban personnel.
These transmitters generate electromagnetic signals that produce an ELF scalar network in the United States. This is done by transmitting these low frequency scalar waves from two different points or pairs so that they

converge at a predetermined point in the atmosphere near the surface of the Earth and cause an interruption of the atmosphere This technology can be used to alter the course of the jet stream or convective and establish longterm weather blockages.

Long Term Climate Block

Evidence shows that California's prolonged drought in the 1980s was caused by a huge high-pressure chain 800 miles off the coast of California that remained motionless for a long time, blocking the usual flow of moist air from the Pacific and pushing storms toward the North. In that occasion the Soviet ships were detected.

The Meteorologists who have analyzed this phenomenon consider it one of the most unusual national patterns ever recorded, unique in the annals of climate records. These durable high-pressure centers were not known until 1977 when Cuba received this technique. (MISTAKE, URSS deployed this equipment in 1962, in Bejucal, Havana)

Evidence suggests that this was possibly caused by the gigantic base ELF waves generated by the weather system "Carpenter Bird" that are transmitted by the Soviets intentionally to block the flow of normal weather patterns.

This phenomenon of long-term high-pressure centers is not limited to producing drought. In 1993, the Midwest region experienced severe flooding as a result of the rainiest period in this area, as the rainfall record began in 1876. This flooding was again the result of what meteorologists called a pattern of blockage from Cuba.

Natural and normal weather systems generally move from west to east through the US. But during the 1993 flood the weather systems stagnated for six weeks in the Upper Midwest.

A high-pressure system over the eastern part of the United States was causing hot, humid air to move up from the Gulf of Mexico and release moisture into the Midwest, where it found the jet stream.

This weather pattern involved an unusual change in the jet stream, which during the summer is usually weak and is usually found much further north in Canada.
This stationary high-pressure front also blocked the path of cold Canadian air, resulting in record low temperatures in the northwest.

According to the September 1993 issue of the specialized magazine of Meteorology "Storm, The World Weather Magazine" I publish:

"It is extremely unusual for weather patterns to persist for so many weeks, which causes heavy rains in the same area almost daily ... The reasons for the weather patterns become fixed, as they did in June and July 1993, they are not clear. "
La Estación de Modificación Meteorológica "Pronto Auxilio" es una base de bloqueo del estado meteorológico creado por una ionización de la atmosfera que bloquea los cambios meteorológicos convirtiéndolos en verdaderas calamidades por sus efectos.

Rare cases:

"It is not usual for Pacific hurricanes to reach the Gulf or the Caribbean Sea, Hurricane Willa will leave rains from Texas to Florida. Presumably Willa is disorganized on Eloy continent and reorganized again when entering Atlantic waters, so it would be renamed. This phenomenon was not known until 2016 with Hurricane Otto, it will be reformed in the northern Gulf. Tropical storm Hermine developed in the Pacific for the first time as Tropical Depression 11E and passed through the mountainous terrain of Oaxaca and Chiapas Mexico to the southern and southern Gulf of Mexico. Then it strengthened until it reached a force close to the hurricane that caused flooding from Guatemala north to Oklahoma in early September 2010. " This version is a summary of the TV news WJXT News4Jax.

"Against the Terrorism Media" euphemistic denomination, Cuba offers us its vision of trajectories of hurricanes considered as rare, but in the list after 1963, year in which the first Soviet devices for the modification of the meteorological state are installed, the hurricanes of trajectory appear

rare with more frequencies than before 1963, a phenomenon that
occurred one every 10 years: Flora 1963
Ginny 1963
Doria 1967
Ginger 1971
Dalon 1972
Gordon 1994
Ivan 2004
Mattew 2016
Then they increase to 5.37 times rare trajectory hurricanes every 10 years.

But the director of Meteorology of Cuba, confesses in TV show, according
to his words, tells us the same thing as Colonel Parra:
"But my point is. I would like to share with you a curiosity. I looked for
hurricanes and tropical storms from the Atlantic with rare trajectories in
the archives since 1851. There are several, and some of them lashed Cuba.
But in all cases, the conditions were different from Matthew. Those rare
and unusual trajectories have always been linked to blocking patterns by
anticyclones or by troughs that become stationary. "

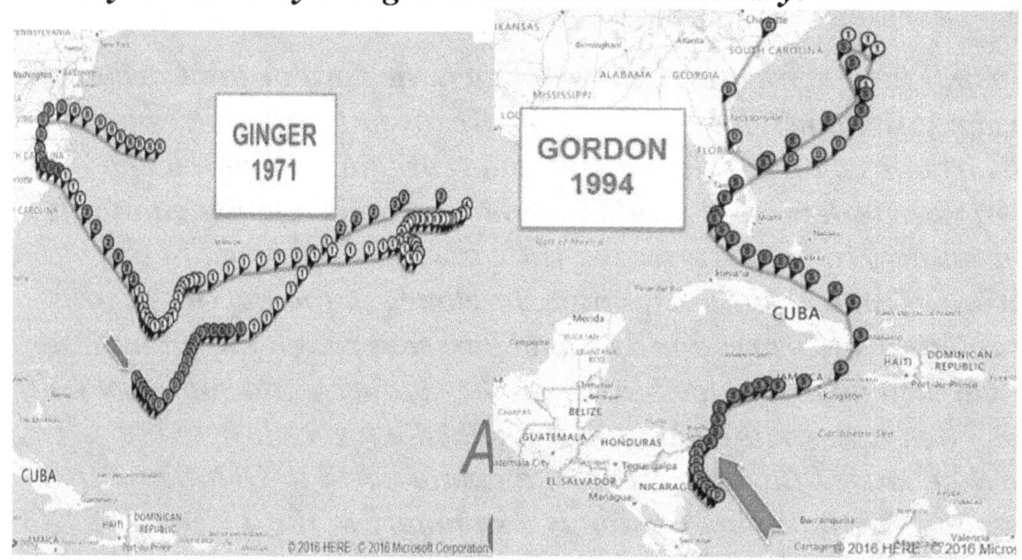

We find the same phenomenon of blockages of the currents, which is
exactly the factor created by the low frequency waves that emit the center
"Pronto Auxilio". Probably Dr. José Rubiera does not know the function
of the
Castro secret weapons named "Pronto Auxilio", Rubiera also changed
Flora's trajectory for Camagüey, his counter marches were in the East ...
Doctor Rubiera with all respect.

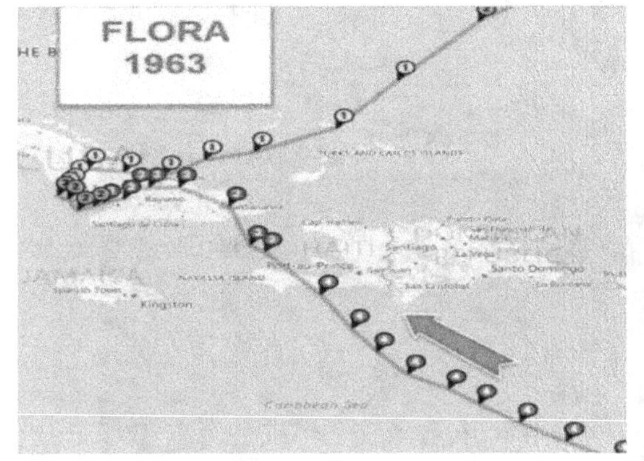

The question is, what interest could it have to destroy your own country ... this is a question that gives a great answer ... to install the totalitarian system, which elegantly call socialism, it is necessary to destroy everything, create artificial crises, dismantle the agricultural and livestock

production industrial, to obtain the most important, the so-called "docility of the population", which are obtained more easily making each individual absolutely dependent on what the State offers, this is the "dependence on the State".

Hurricane, swine, human, phytosanitary epidemics, transport paralysis, expropriation of land, lack of spare parts for manufacturing, no foods,no wears, no housing etc. We need to understand that all of this inconvenience is part to the Communist Subversive to "clean the brain" and the real dependency the people from the State ordenance   Everything destroyed, misery that is socialism. But a lot of promise and propaganda. It also turns out that the rare trajectories occur against the United States territory

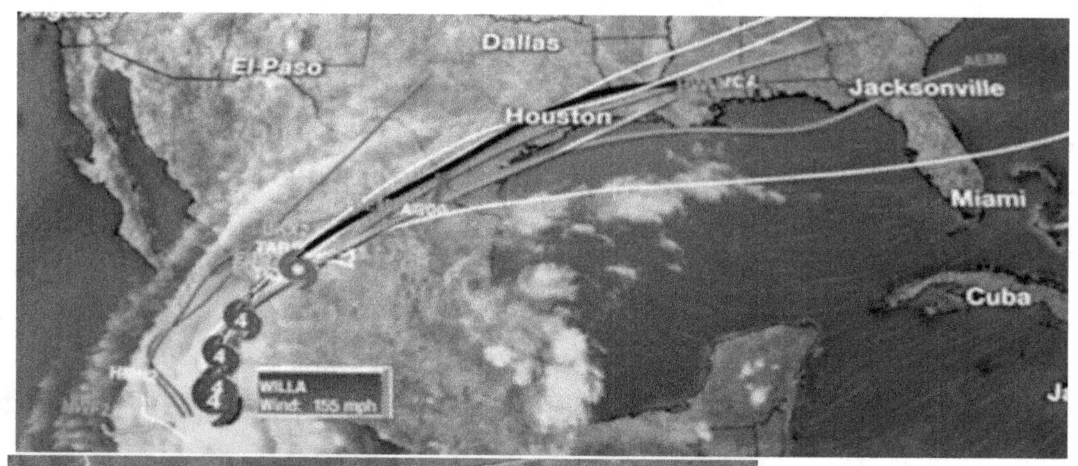

REFERENCE

Author Testimony
Conversation with Col. Albo Parra Salina (1962-1990)
ABC News
KGB files
Associted Press "Chemical, biological Weapons threat growing" by Susanne
Schafer
1997 Global Terrorism: Appendix B State Department (1)
1997 Global Terrorism Appendix B Background Information on Terrorism

Group

Miami Herald text Guillermo Cueto ex Oficial CIA

Presidential Decision Directives PDD 62 PPD 63

PPD Presidential Decision Guidelines June 39, 1995

Foreing Suppliers to Iraq's Biological Weapons by Monterrey Institute of International Studies

UNSCOM-IRAQ exchange on Biological Weapons by Monterrey Institute of International Studies

Letter from the Honorable Congressman R (Fl) Lincoln Díaz Balart to the Honorable William Cohen Secretary of Defense

Text of Transmittal Letter from Honorable William S.Cohen, Defense Secretary to Honorable Strom Thurmond Chairmen of the Armed Service Committee.

Statements by the Honorable Congresswoman R (Fl) Ileana Ross-Lettinen

Iraq jails scientific who developed its germ weapons. The Herald / March 24

1998 / Judith Miller New York Time Service

"Easy to Make, Easy to Hide" by Beau Brendler ABC News

Weapons of Mass Destruction and Capabilities and Program Monterrey Institute International Studies

Editorials of Radio "Caiman" by Juan Jose Jimenez (1990)

Full Text of the Hotline Conversation between US President George Bush and General Secretary of the CPSU Mikhail Gorbachev on April 4, 1990

Chemical Weapons Chronology Monterrey Institute

The China Men in Havana ABIP 1999 Agustin Blazquez Producer / Director

of the documentary COVERING CUBA

A history of Bio Chemical Weapons by Zoltan Grossman e-mail mtn@igc.apc.org

Uncovering Al Hakam by A.J. Venter Jane's Intelligence Review march 98

Information from the Author's Personal File

BioTechnology speeches by Fidel Castro

Other testimonies can be seen in the documentary Red Alert by Eduardo Palmer and Salvador Blanco

** Ed Prida*

Dr. in Psychology served 6 years in the prison of Quivicán of two sentences for crimes against State Security, was extradited when he was on the verge of death for pneumonia and tuberculosis in February 1996 at the behest of the President of the United States.

- *General Coordinator of the "Harold Feeney" Center for the Non*
- *Proliferation of Weapons of Mass Extermination and Terrorism*
- *Former Political Prisoner of the Cause Called to Rebellion and Attack on the President of Cuba*
- *Former Scientific Researcher of Aeronautical Psychology of the Scientific*
- *Research Center of the Air Force of Cuba*
- *Official map of the Air Force of Cuba*
- *File of the author*
- *Conference of the Cor. Albo Parra Salina*
- *The Russian Woodpecker: experiments in global mind control? - Eye ...*
- *https://www.eyeofthepsychic.com/woodpecker/*
- *Posing the question was enough for "the Russian Woodpecker" to become ...*
- *claimed that the signal was responsible for weather modification wars covertly waged upon ... In April 1953, CIA Allen Dulles gave a lecture at Princeton University.*
- *:The Woodpecker Soviet Electromagnetic Attack*
  Duga radar - Wikipedia
- *https://en.wikipedia.org/wiki/Duga_radar*
- *Duga (Russian: Дуга) was a Soviet over-the-horizon (OTH) radar system used as part of the ... The unclaimed signal was a source for much speculation, giving rise to theories such Soviet mind control and weather control experiments.*
- *Stanislav Ilic*
- *The Russian Woodpecker, Chernobyl Meltdown ... - ClimateViewer.com https://climateviewer.com/.../russian-woodpecker-chernobyl-meltdownionospheric-he...*
- *The Russian Woodpeckers (STEEL YARD, STEEL WORK, Duga Radars, &*
- *Krug Ionospheric Probes) MAP: ... 'Woodpecker' Duga Radar Array, Chenobyl, Ukraine .... The CIA,Weather Warfare, and Climate Terrorism.*
- *Images for woodpecker cia meteorological russian*

- *Project Woodpecker*
- *https://www.bibliotecapleyades.net/scalar_tech/esp_scalartech02.htm That's an award from the CIA and National Security Agency. ...*
- *modify weather ... that were dubbed "The Russian Woodpecker" by western ham radio operators.*
- *Was The Chernobyl Disaster a Revenge for The Russian Woodpecker? https://www.bibliotecapleyades.net/scalar_tech/esp_scalartech41.htm Apr 13, 2012 - The Russian Woodpecker was a notoriousSoviet radio signal that could be ... Channel on That's Impossible as a suspected weather control device used by ... aCIA plan to sabotage the Soviet Union's economy through covert ...*
- *The Russian Woodpecker, Chernobyl Meltdown, and Ionospheric ...*
- *https://weathermodificationhistory.com/russian-woodpecker-ionosphericheater-weath...*
- *The Russian Woodpecker, Chernobyl Meltdown, and Ionospheric Heating Over ... Of course, these have not been the only strange weather patterns noted in recent ... .cia.gov/library/readingroom/document/cia-rdp9000965r000100160095-3 ...*
- *The Russian Woodpecker: experiments in global mind control? (March ... educate-yourself.org/cn/russianwoodpecker2008.shtml*
- *Mar 6, 2013 - The Russian Woodpecker was a Soviet signal that could be heard on the ... signal was responsible forweather modification wars covertly waged upon ... In April 1953, CIA Allen Dulles gave a lecture at Princeton University, ...*
- *Duga OTH Radars - Numbers Stations*
- *https://www.numbers-stations.com/military/russia/duga-3-oth-radar/ Over time, claims of it being used for mind control and weather experiments emerged, ... CIA first became aware of Sovietplans to build the radar on 1970 and made ... So the "woodpecker" sound created by it interfered with many other.*
- *Annex A*
- *Weather Modification: Another Asymmetric Terrorist Weapon (this was copied from an article written by me and faxed to the FIU laboratory,*

and published previously in Harold Fenney, Non Proliferation Mass Destruction

- *Weapons Website by Prof. Ed Prida in 1996 -2002 and later appeared like by*
- *Prof. Manuel Cereijo SEPTEMBER 2004*

Russia, China and Cuba use climate modification technology. The project involves the manipulation of the ionosphere and the alteration of the magnetic fields of the earth. This technology has localized and global capabilities. Scientific evidence indicates that this technology also has the ability to manipulate human behavior and the patterns of distribution of care to create negligence and premises of catastrophic accidents by involuntary disintegration of the attention of any operator, be it a boat, a train , a car or an airplane.

All this technology apparently like Star Trek originated in a Serbian immigrant named Nicolas Tesla who came to the United States at the end of the 19th century. During his research he discovered that ionization of the atmosphere would be altered when charged by radio wave transmissions in the low frequency range of 10 to 80 Hz. Studies indicated that with positive ionization, people and animals became tired and they were lethargic and with negative ionization the effect was to feel active and energetic.

Another aspect of this technology is the effect that harmonious radio frequencies produce when they impact the air molecules. The molecules are excited and emit negatively charged electrons that combine easily with hydrogen and oxygen to produce water molecules. But even more profound is the fact that this type of radio waves also transports positively charged ions through the ionosphere to the magnetosphere.

The positively charged ions get trapped in the Van Allen belts, traveling between Aurora Borealis and Aurora Australis, right where we have holes in the ozone layers. Freon, the killer of ozone, by its nature quickly dissipates. This inherent quality is a contradiction to the concept that a freon concentration is creating holes in the ozone layers at the north and south poles. However, when radio waves hit unstable freon precipitates,

they are so reactive that they cannot advance and dissipate in the magnetosphere.

Confirmation of climate modification technology was first revealed in an article that appeared in the September 11, 1989 issue of the Washington Post.

Systems

The project to modify the Russian climate is known as the Carpenter Bird system. It consists of the transmission of extremely low frequency waves (ELF) at approximately 10 Hz using Tesla transmitters in Angarsk and Khabarovsk in Siberia, Gomel, Sakhalin Island, and another in Riga, Latvia, which moved to Cuba, 20 miles south of Havana, between Quivican, Guira de Melena. At one point, this installation in Cuba was operated by less than 200 Soviet soldiers, currently less Russian and more Cuban military. This installation now belongs to the Cuban government, with the cooperation of Russian personnel.

These facilities in Cuba can be easily seen from a distance, since they have many antennas of 300 feet or more in height. These transmitters from Cuba generate electromagnetic transmissions that produce an ELF scalar network over the United States. This is done by transmitting these low frequency scalar waves in pairs so that they converge at a predetermined point on the surface of the earth and cause an interruption of the normal dynamics of the Earth's atmosphere. This technology can be used to alter the course of air currents in the horizontal plane and establish a kind of barrier capable of making a kind of barrier to stop or prolong the weather of weather phenomena.

The system of Cuba has the potential to alter the magnetic field within a radius of 450 miles around it, although it can be multiplied with Eloy using naval units, satellites or aircraft.

Known examples

The prolonged drought in California in the late 1980s was caused by a huge high-pressure chain 800 miles off the coast of California that remained motionless for long periods of time, blocking the usual flow of moist air from the Pacific and pushing the storms northward . Evidence suggests that this was possibly caused by the woodpecker that generates

ELF waves on foot from Siberia and Cuba to block the flow of normal weather patterns.

This phenomenon of long-term high pressure centers is not limited to producing drought. In 1993, the Midwest region experienced severe flooding as a result of the rainiest period in this particular area.

Cuba

18. [illegible faded text]

19. [illegible faded text]

Problem in Cuba

20. [illegible faded text]

— [illegible faded text]

— [illegible faded text]

Chapter 3
Russia deploys missiles in the port of Mariel

"If there's smoke, it's because there's fire." Unfortunately, the facts clearly show that the enemy subversion has reached such a high level that we are inoculated with so many legends and myths, that we already believe them to be true, we are unable to perceive what is happening in our intimate environment, as in our family, in the school of our children, in our churches, in the mass media, in our Congress, in the candidates for public service, in our counterintelligence. Let's wake up now, it's getting late. If we delve into the thinking of Ronald Reagan and Margaret Thatcher and become important today because it is the same threat, "Mexico will be our next Iran." Ronald Reagan said and today is also a bitter reality. For some this is no surprise, but for these "some" there is no space, no attention and we keep running towards the abyss.
The Container Base of Mariel.

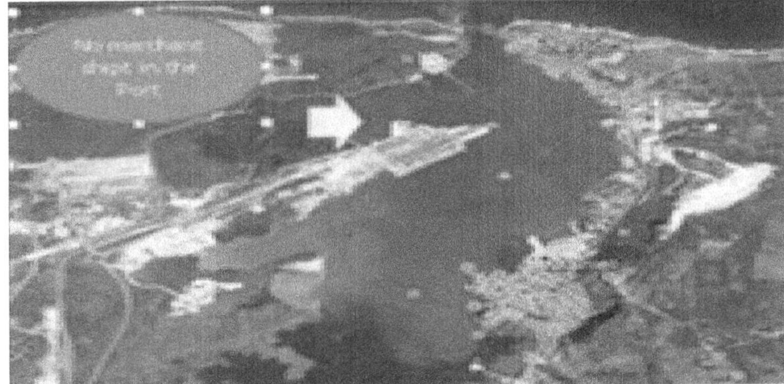

Cuba, with "alleged fraudulent investments from Brazil," built the container base in the port of Mariel that has no commercial use, tracking the movement of merchant ships imposes ridiculous results, which shows that its main function is not commercial.

As a "most sacred mantle", we were inspired by the image of cranes, merchandise containers and merchant ships. A propaganda campaign of the economic advantages that would bring to Cuba and the ruin of the port of Miami that would go bankrupt by competition.

However, during and after the Missile Crisis in October 1962, Cuba has

kept nuclear weapons of different types and this shield has allowed it to survive the regime, therefore, it is not a surprise that given the strategic value of the position and the permanent tendency of the Russians to maintain hegemony not only on the island, but above all the European continent, Cuba represents a high exchange value in future negotiations and always with the legends of "sovereignty" and the impugning leadership of Castro, has prevailed the denial of international inspection "in situ" of the territory, which should never have been accepted.

To detect levels of radioactive contamination due to the danger of contamination for the Cuban population and as an unequivocal sign of the very existence of the different types of weapons that exist and that for more than 50 years have developed subterranean concealment or masking techniques.

The absence of boats in the port of Mariel is typical ... it is not only a reflection of the economic stagnation, knowing the motivations of the system, its purely offensive objective is not strange. Putin recently exposed hypothetical images of the nuclear destruction of the Florida coast. It alerts us and the signal of the enemy has not been taken into account to impose a total blockade of the island, of temporary, economic immigration with stopping the sending of money, communications, etc.

Every day this deadly question for the whole planet is the existence of nuclear weapons in Cuba, it is a reality that has become an anesthetized pain, said

William Casey, Director of the CIA, in his speech at the World Business Council in San Antonio Texas and published in the Washington Post. Reproduction of the speech.

OFFENSIVE MISSILE READINESS (Figure 2)

<u>General</u>

    1. The available evidence clearly indicates that the field-type MRBM sites are for the SS-4 (SANDAL) 1020 nautical mile ballistic missile system. All of the essential elements of this system have been identified: canvas covered missile transporters, launch stands, erectors, oxidizer and fuel trucks, cabling, theodolite stations, power generators, and communication equipment.

    2. The evidence also clearly indicates that the Guanajay and Remedios sites are for a different missile system than that employed at the field-type MRBM sites. The pad design, size, and separation are compatible with what are believed to be IRBM installations in the USSR.

<u>MRBM (1020-nm) Sites</u>

"Today, I wanted to tell you about the war of subversion that the USSR and its satellites have waged against the United States and its interests around the world for a quarter of a century or more. This aggressive subversive campaign has deprived us of many allies and friendly governments and our security is threatened in the neighborhood, as it is in Europe, Asia, Africa and Latin America. This is not an undeclared war. In 1961 Nikita, then leader of the Soviet Union, told us clearly that communism would win not only through nuclear weapons, but, if through the "national liberation movements" around the world. We were refusing to believe him. But also in 1930, we were refusing to believe a Hitler seriously when he put us in "My Struggle" (Mein Kampt) that he could take Europe.

The Soviet Union and Cuba have established a beachhead to subvert the rest of the continent, as they are doing, Nicaragua has subverted the rest of Central America, as it does in Venezuela, Mexico, Colombia, Chile, Brazil, Angola, Ethiopia, Mozambique, etc. "

Everything seems to indicate that the enemy subversion, has so deep that the officials of the State Department who think that the citizens of the United States, its people, is a public charity institution and with traumas of "feelings of guilt to create chaos and genocides "As our enemies paint us, the assimilation of these precepts has become almost unanimous.

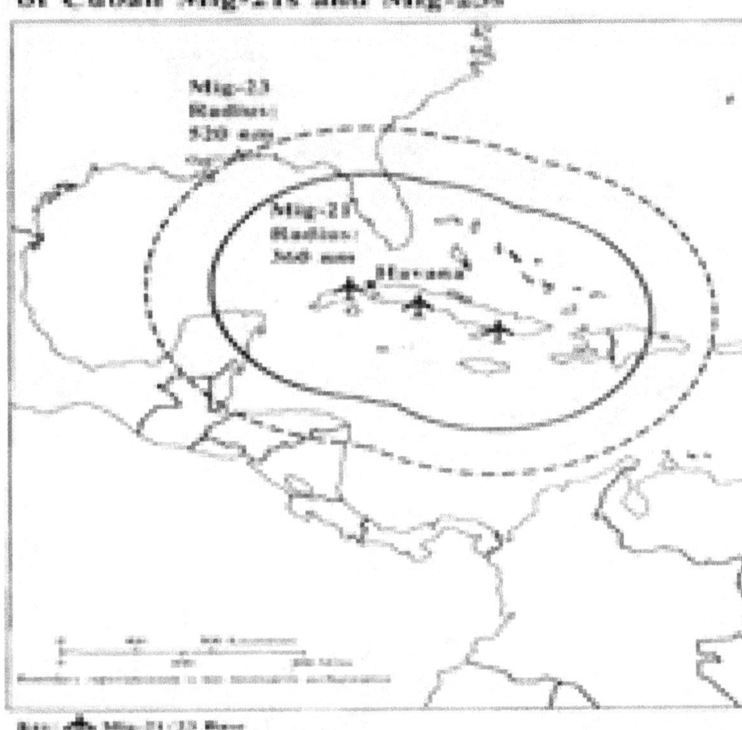

The Monroe Doctrine was an appropriate approach to the security of the entire continent, but the United States charitable paternalism has not worked, it has not bounced with gratitude, but rather .

The nearby Mexico, for many years, we are "smoke signals" with an introduction policy exaggerated of its citizens in American territory, which in fact become an "invasion", imitating the "model of behavior induced by a Plan of the KGB, known as "Brave" Operation. They applied against the United States from Cuba in May 1980. With the irregular immigration they create a political, economic and social imbalance with negative consequences in all spheres in United States.

The State Department seems to be clinging to allow everything that harms the United States, historically it has played this leading role with a lot of "pride".

The next country that is going to taste the "teeth" in a terrible way, I predict it is Canada, who has been subjected for many years to a strong campaign of political and cultural subversion from Cuba and as we all know his leadership is committed to the left for obvious reasons and does everything he can in "against who has depended on everything", for many years.

Chart 5
Operating Areas of OSA- and Komar-class Guided Missile Patrol Boats from Cuban Ports*

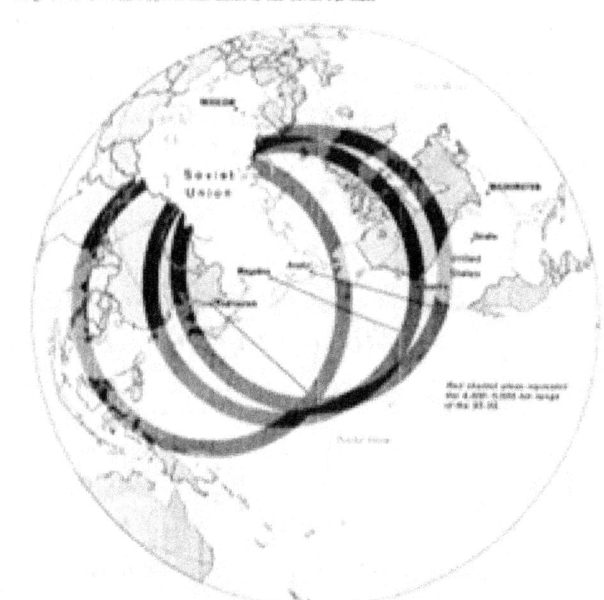

We come to the conclusion that Mexico, Canada, Cuba and Venezuela continue to push and abuse the benevolence of the United States, because they have proven that they have a lot of leeway to do so and have not had to pay the consequences of their unfriendly and continuous hostile gestures.

If we take into account that the defense of Canada is under the auspices of the United States. Its northern border is a stone's throw from Russia and its Siberia, always uncertain through the Arctic Circle. Of course, because of

100

their favorable disposition to the left, they do not feel very affected by what Russia can do to them, which they approach more and more politically every day.

The Department of State and its officials never apply the principles of reciprocity in diplomatic and legal relations with other countries and the consequences are grinding for the nation and the control of public opinion about this that is charged on the Congress, in a comprehensive manner He

seems not very aware of the problem.

Technical Data of the Russian Missiles

Russian container missile system is known as the 3M-54 Club-K. Artificially manufactured graphic. But it is a sample of how the rocket system masked inside a common container works.

Russian systems 3M-54 Kalibr and 3M-14 Biryuza, Turquoise (codename of NATO SS-N-27 Sizzler) can also be launched by surface ships and by submarines were developed by the Novator Design Bureau (OKB-8) Russian missiles hidden inside the container as nuclear carriers are illegal according to international treaties.
Tactical and technical data of:
Code: 3M-14 / Klub-A / Caliber-NK 3M14E (SS-N -30) 3M14E / P-900 Kalibr 3M14EE / TE / P-900Kalibr
Missile Range 2,500 km (1500 miles)

The 3M-14, part of the Russian contractor's Novato's Club-A series, is a ground-based cruise missile. The ground attack variant is designed to attack preprogrammed targets, such as seaports, aerodromes and command posts. The 3M-14AE missile has a range of 300 km.

In Syria, when launched from the Caspian Sea, these missiles hit 1,500 km. Working with photos of the launches of these missiles, the missiles have a launching size of approximately 8 meters, like the 3M10 "Granada" cruise missiles, which are already in the arsenal of the Russian Navy from 1980.

The latest missile version is designated as 3M14 and is part of the "CaliberNK" firearms complex. Klub missiles are narrow-range versions of Kalibr systems that can be exported without violating the MTCR. The 3M14E (E for export) Klub is a reduced range version (~ 300 km) of Kalibr 3M14

International Missile Control

There is a treaty known as the Missile Technology Control Regime (RCM) is a multilateral export control agreement. It is an informal and voluntary association between 35 countries to prevent the proliferation of missiles and unmanned aerial vehicle technology capable of transporting loads exceeding 500 kg for more than 300 km.
The missile technology control regime (RCTM) was established in April 1987

by the G7

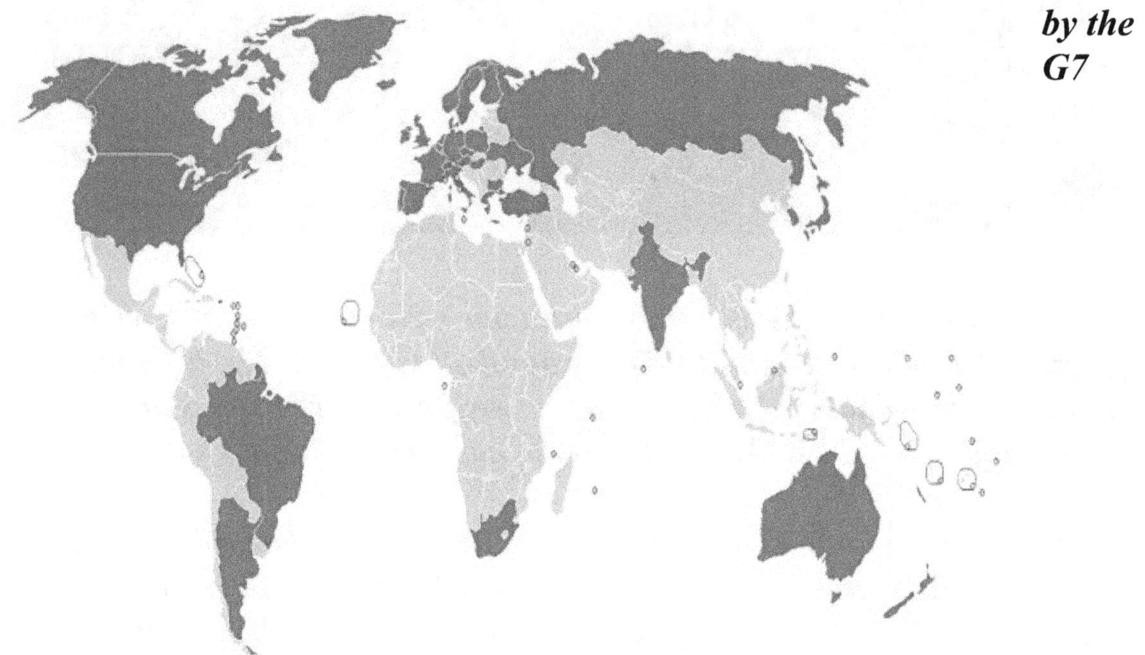

countries: Canada, France, Germany, Italy, Japan, the United Kingdom and the United States of America. The MTCR was created in order to stop the spread of unmanned delivery systems for nuclear weapons, specifically delivery systems that could carry a payload of 500 kg at 300 km. 35 countries are members of MTCR.
Legal or Illegal?

<u>Cuba is not a member, nor is this type of weapons allowed, especially if it is hidden and under the control of a third country, in this case is Russia.</u>

Maritime traffic of Mariel Port
Practically, there is no commercial movement in the port of Mariel.
Everything has been a "maskirovkas" or "a dirty play with a smile" for Russia to place medium-range missiles inside containers and transport

hidden anywhere in the country on ships, trains, or trucks. Let's clarify that these missiles were designed to be placed inside the containers.
If there is no maritime traffic in this port, why are these containers in the port? The information that arrives informs us that the containers are sometimes moved by foreigners to the underground warehouses of "food for luxury hotels" according to residents.

With the appearance of a container base, it is a complex military base with drones, radars, anti-aircraft missiles for the defense of the site with its control, command and orientation equipment that are inside the containers and can be transported secretly as freight containers. , in civil trucks, merchant ships, railroads or in conventional storage areas, but ready to be fired against the United States.

By monitoring the transit of merchant ships around the globe through the Internet, it is possible to know how many ships, which they contain, where

they come from and which are the next destinations. *This facilitates the knowledge that the port of Mariel has no cargo movement because it is not visited by merchant ships. There are testimonies of neighbors of the place of the manufacture of underground facilities, and the supposed use that they say to have as storage of food for the tourist industry. Cubans do not work in the area, nor do they observe merchandise movements. according to the sources consulted. Neighbors of Mariel.*

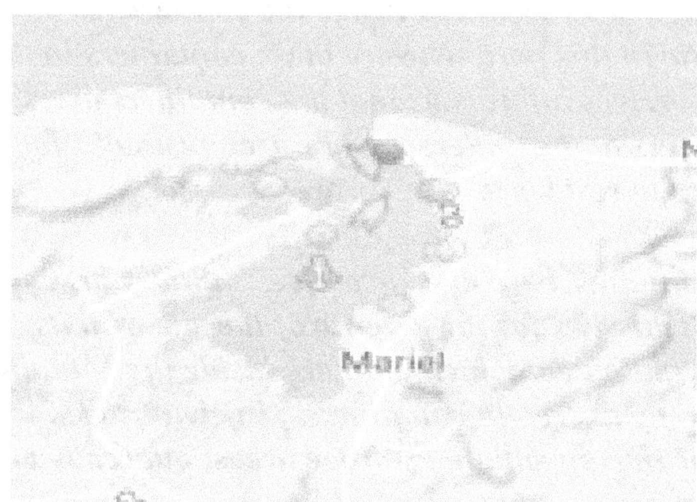

Any interested person can know daily how many ships arrive to Cuban ports or from any country, free of charge through some of the websites that I relate below.

The reported positions of merchant ships ready to arrive or leave Cuban ports is minimal, these are the Merchants report their positions in the last every 24 hours.

The Merchant ships are absent in Cuban ports. Mariel Today is June 25/2018. Satellite view taken thanks to www.marinetraffic.com
Puerto Mariel Cuba. Reported today Jun / 26/2018: An oil tanker and the port tug.
Other smaller vessels are national, Cuba Navy and Cuba Border Guard.

RE
F:

Marine Traffic: Global Ship Tracking Intelligence | AIS Marine Traffic
https://www.marinetraffic.com/

Marine Traffic Live Ships Map. Discover information and vessel positions for vessels around the world. Search the Marine Traffic ships database of more than ...

VesselFinder: Free AIS Ship Tracking of Marine Traffic
https://www.vesselfinder.com/

Vessel Finder is a FREE AIS vessel tracking web site. Vessel Finder displays real time ship positions and marine traffic detected by global AIS network. Top 3 Websites to Track Your Ship - Marine Insight https://www.marineinsight.com/know-more/top-3-websites-to-track-yourship/

Vessel Tracking & Monitoring | ORBCOMM
https://www.orbcomm.com/en/industries/maritime/vessel-tracking
The. fishing boats, merchant marine fleets as well as ocean buoys travelling global waters. ... Send real-time weather and safety alerts to crews at sea. Track vessel location to comply with Long Range Identification and Tracking (LRIT) and Ship ...

[PDF]Legal aspects of maritime monitoring & surveillance data - European

...
https://ec.europa.eu/.../sites/.../legal_aspects_maritime_monitoring_summary
_en.pdf

monitoring and surveillance takes place against the background of the sea, and the ... international voyages, cargo ships of 500 gross tonnage and above and ...

BigOceanData - Vessel tracking & management software, AIS reporting www.bigoceandata.com/ www.planet.com/markets/maritime/ Monitor Earth's oceans, open waters, and seas every day. Track moving vessels and ... Fishing boats; Cargo ships; Oil tankers; Naval vessels. Transshipments ...

Live AIS Vessel Tracker with Ship and Port
Database https://www.fleetmon.com/
http://www.cia.gov
Document CIA TOP SECRET. Declassification 2009/08/04 CIA-RDP78705449A0002001100001-0 Supplement 6 Joint Evaluation of Soviet Missile Threat in Cuba Prepared by: Guided Missiles and Astronautics Intelligence Committee, Joint Atomic Energy Intelligence Committee, National Photographic Interpretation Center

2
5

SUPPLEMENT 6

TO

JOINT EVALUATION OF
SOVIET MISSILE THREAT IN CUBA

PREPARED BY
Guided Missile and Astronautics Intelligence Committee
Joint Atomic Energy Intelligence Committee
National Photographic Interpretation Center

Documento CIA TOT SECRET Desclasificado 2009/08/04 CIA-RDP78705449A0002001100001-0 Suplement 6 Joint Evaluation of Soviet Missile Threat in Cuba Prepared by: Guided Missiles and Astronautics Intelligence Committee, Joint Atomic Energy Intelligence Committee, National Photographic Interpretation Center

James Jesus Anglenton

https://www.google.com/search?rlz=1C1CHBF_enUS799US799&ei=dfuc W_OO5Ly5gKO7LnYCw&q=angleton+cia&oq=anglenton+cia&gs_l=psya b.1.0.0i13.174187.189486..192625...0.0..0.104.2994.38j1......0....1..gswswiz... .....35i39j0i10j0i22i10i30.I51NUAKiVXk John Owen Breman

https://www.google.com/search?q=john+brennan+cia+wikipedia&rlz=1C1 C

HBF_enUS799US799&oq=john+breman+cia&aqs=chrome.1.69i57j0l5.19 7

29j1j8&sourceid=chrome&ie=UTF-8

James Comie

Comiehttps://www.google.com/search?q=james+comey+biography&rlz=1C 1

CHBF_enUS799US799&oq=James+Comie+biogra&aqs=chrome.1.69i57j 0.

18408j1j8&sourceid=chrome&ie=UTF-8

Aldrich Aimes

https://www.google.com/search?rlz=1C1CHBF_enUS799US799&ei=Mf6c W

83FLMGb5gLRjJrYAw&q=aldrich+ames&oq=ames+cia+robert&gs_l=psy =

ab.1.2.0i71l7.0.0..56185...0.0..0.0.0........0......gws-wiz.hk56IrC6AQ4

Bernard Barker "Macho"

*https://www.google.com/search?q=bernard+barker+CIA&rlz=1C1CHBF_*

en

US799US799&oq=bernard+barker+CIA&aqs=chrome..69i57.10513j1j7&s

o urceid=chrome&ie=UTF-8 Robert Mueller

https://www.google.com/search?rlz=1C1CHBF_enUS799US799&ei=kvcW

7D1CsyD5wLWv5zoBw&q=robert+mueller&oq=+rober+Mueller&gs_l=p

sy-

ab.1.0.0i10l10.97142.102788..115631...1.0..0.106.889.12j1......0....1..gwswiz.

....6..0j35i39j0i67j0i131j0i131i20i264j0i131i20i263i264j0i20i264j0i20i26

3.PtZyXMDb3l4

The Castro's regime has designed electronic equipment that calls and directs sharks to the beaches of the United States to create panic and damage to the tourism industry.
Better image could not be perceptually communicated this message: an aggressive shark, with the skin of the Russian bear and Putin's rider reins in hand to guide the jaws of the shark. This is not really humorous because hundreds of people die and others are severely injured by shark attacks on the beaches. The statistics of the attacks are eloquent by itself.

Background:

Because of the unusual behavior and without justification because it has no food purposes, no environmental changes are involved, there are no physical or chemical changes in the marine currents.

• The Cuban espionage network in Puerto Rico headed by Alfonso Silva Lee, marine biologist, had the mission of introducing a virus to create an epidemic in the population of Puerto Rico and to blame the United States

Navy for the use of chemicals in the explosives of the missiles launched by the planes in the practices on the coast and on the beach of Vieques. Work of previous preparation that the liberal organizations and the Democratic Party had carried out years before.

The laboratory and the deposit were in the ranch "Las Delicias" in the province of Ponce, Puerto Rico. The Cuban spy network escaped to Cuba before the FBI action. Dr. Alfonso Salva Lee son of the Captain Luis Alfonso Silva Tablada, who was shootdown in Playa Giron Beach on April 17, 1961 and his mother the Lady Edna Mae Lee(an American). Dr. Siva war received by Fidel Castro when he returned to Cuba from Puerto Rico, he is now

CARISUB CORP / Reyes Chirino Heyller A

florida.intercreditreport.com/company/carisub... ⌄

The current status of the **business** is Active. The **CARISUB** CORP principal adress is 12960 NW 9 TH LANE, MIAMI, 33182-5. Meanwhile you can send your letters to 12960 NW 9 TH LANE, MIAMI, FL, 33182-5. The company`s **registered** agent is REYES CHIRINO HEYLLER A 12960 NW 9 TH LANE, MIAMI, FL, 33182.

director of the Miramar Sea Aquarium in Havana.

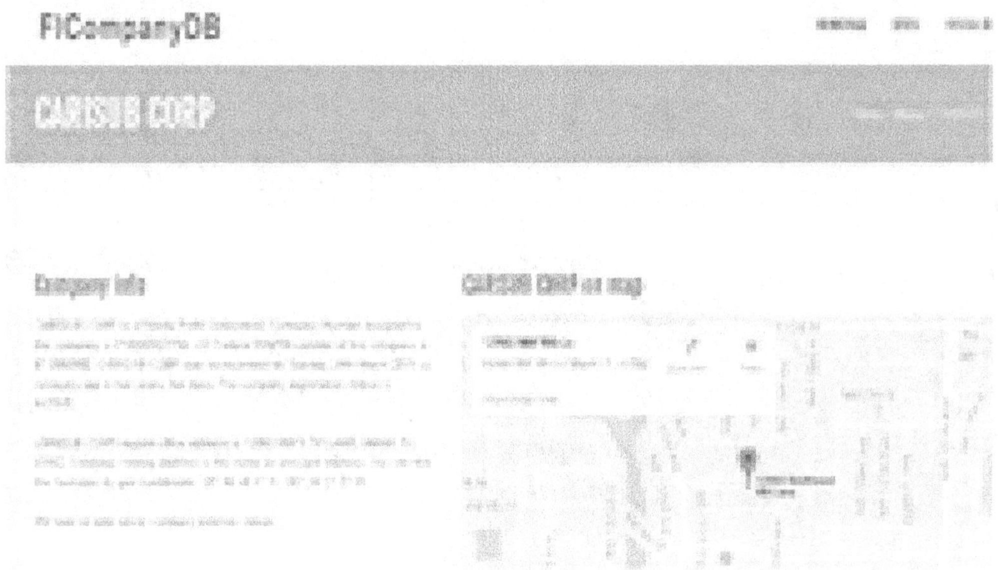

CariSub is here and there ... in Miami and Cuba. Carisub is a civil company attached to the Directorate of Special Troops, a group of military elites for the mission of support for Castro's Intelligence around the world. The CariSub is under the leadership of the Colonel Mike Montañez of Special

Troops, he is an American borne in Pompano Beach, Fl. also member of MC (Marihuana and Cocaine Section of Cuban Intelligence and very close of Cor. Antonio La Guardia Font).

Around the 1983, CariSub in coordination with the Institute of Oceanography under the direction of Dr. Darío Guitart, a renowned expert in sharks, was investigating on how to attract sharks and barracudas to a specific point, with the main idea to create "dangerous zones by the decade 80-90, it was initial objective was to defend from the submarine commando raids by the Beach of Viriato, close to Point Zero (Residential Complex of Castro).

The marine biologists of the Institute manage to get the frequency capable of attracting sharks, considered the call of "emergency" like that produced by other biological entities in the presence of sharks, identified this frequency, they needed to reproduce an autonomous instrument to be deposited on the seabed.

The result was equipment that emits electromagnetic signals like those emitted by smaller fish, when they are being attacked by sharks. Due to the physical characteristics of the saline water, the waves move at great distances, which is interpreted by the sharks as the existence of prey in abundance where this is the point or focus of emission of the signals.

The equipment has an energy source that provides the energy consumed by a device that takes advantage of the movement of the sea, are programmed to emit the signal intermittently and synchronized with other equipment in the area, simulating panicked fish that are being devoured by other sharks in the zone, this is interpreted as a sign of abundant feeding, as the sharks arrive at the emission point confused because they feel the signal but do not find other more specific signals of the supposed fish.

The United States and other centers of tourism in the Mediterranean and West Africa, which have been visited by the sons of Fidel Castro and with security personnel, which according to the press amount to 200 security agents, could also be an accessory and justified among them attract sharks and thus justify that the unusual phenomenon of sharks on Florida beaches, is also in other places, as well as make tourists flow to Cuba,

where the phenomenon does not exist.

The splendid yacht, by Antonio Castro at the level of bi millionaires like Bill Gate, property of Castro's son, should be a facade for some biological terrorism activity, such as the installation of equipment to attract sharks in some beaches. In some way, this yacht must be justified in the eyes of Uncle Raúl and the cousins who enjoy a certain executive power in the repressive area. His journeys through the Mediterranean are constant focus of attention of the press dedicated to the European Jet

This yacht could be "justified" for the use of propaganda of the Cohiba tobacco, or the cocaine of Moa, the Yumuri shirts, or epidemics created in Biotechnology, that could do more, it might be difficult to find on board the yacht, any product produced in Cuba .

The electronic device was developed and built in the Laboratory-Workshop of the Buro of Scientific Research and Center 3 (Air Force of Cuba) around

1983-84 where I worked as Scientific Investigator on Combat Aviation since 1981-92. The author of the book with my colleagues at the BIC, 1985.

An anonymous opinion on the Internet about the Cuban military company CariSub.

CARISUB - Castro's private treasure chest

"I'm reading a book called 'Silent Dead' by Randy Wayne White. It is part of a series of books by the author that I have enjoyed reading. The book is fiction, but, like all fiction, it is based on reality. In the story they mentioned Carisub, a lifesaving company run by Cubans that Fidel Castro created many years ago to rescue treasures from shipwrecks throughout Cuba. It must be nice to be a dictator.

Does anyone know of any material in the company or any of the remains they saved? I would be interested in reading a book on the subject if there is one out there. Do you know if any of the items found has entered the market?

There must be a very good hiding place somewhere in Cuba.

Thank you

N

J

World News Article published in THE SUNDAY TIMES on February 28. 1999

Divers seek 500 galleons with treasures

by Derek Baldwin. Havana

This underwater event described as one of the greatest discoveries of treasures in the world. A team of divers plunged into the crystalline waters of the Caribbean last week in search of the first of hundreds of Spanish galleons that sank off the coast of Cuba three centuries or more, loaded with gold and silver looted from Latin America .

In an unprecedented agreement with President Fidel Castro, a Canadian company, Visa Gold, has earned the right to excavate the remains of coral shipwrecks on the northwest coast of Cuba and around the small Isla de Juventud, which is located at south.

The adventure, which could be the most lucrative of maritime history, is expected to uncover the world's largest treasure of sunken Spanish gold and silver, but it also seems to provide new insights into the ancient civilizations of the Aztecs.
and the Incas, whose artifacts were captured and transported to Spain in armadas of up to 100 ships.

Where does CARISUB operate from within the United States?

The public document of the Miami Dade County website informs us:CARISUB CORP and 7 Non Profit organizations in subordination probably they also they are receiving money from Grant..for other 5 nonprofit organization...

The reason for this shark meeting is ... to thank the Environmentalists? The biologists did not answer ... Why are the sharks in Assembly on the beaches of Florida, North Carolina and California and how to stop the sharks. This propaganda for the CariSub Corporation has not been paid, it's free.
CARISUB CORP located: 12960 NW 9th, Lane Miami, Fl. 33192

CONCLUSION
• CARISUB is the façade, underneath they have several none's profit organizations and it really works as a biological terrorism network of Cuba

in Miami and represents the Castro regime. They are in charge of installing and maintaining this device near the coast. All officers of the Special Troops • First of all cowardly murder defenseless American citizens.

The goal is to create demoralization and terror in the United States. UU Create economic damage with the tourism industry due to the dangerous image of the beaches. Satirically speaking ... Emperor Alexander the Great liked to tame his horses, now Emperor Vladimir II Putin of Russia likes to tame sharks in South Florida ...

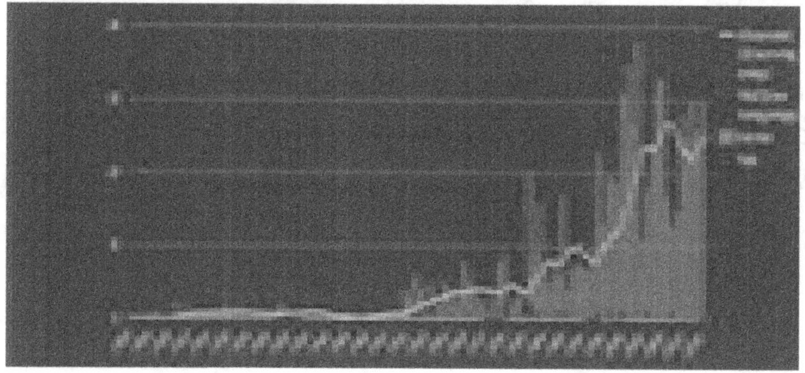

Non-Fatal Attacks and Evasions 782
Fatal 326
Fatal Missing 36

Total deaths 362

The 362 deaths could be enough for our institution of Counter Intelligence to wake up and detain them to the espionage and terrorism network that for years has committed all kinds of crimes with impunity in the United States, disguising their attacks with sharks. What we do expect from the FBI?

FLORIDA ATLANTIC UNIVERSITY ESTIMATED

Florida Atlantic University estimated;

WOMEN BETWEEN THE SHARKS

Thounsands of Sharks very close to the shores

SOURCES OF INFORMATION

- http://www.treasurenet.com/forums/general-discussion/262935-carisub-castros-private-treasure-chest.html (CariSub)
- https://www.youtube.com/watch?v=3KjZMqA7SyU&ab_channel=TheBrandNewWorld
- https://www.youtube.com/watch?v=WFJk-OUzqCE&ab_channel=Animalist
- https://www.youtube.com/watch?v=KuLwxpu7zFo&ab_channel=TheCosmosNews
- https://www.youtube.com/watch?v=kzr-NOxPhOM&ab_channel=MIKROFILMCHANNEL
- http://flcompanydb.com/company/P15000027794/carisub-corp.html
- Testimony:and Opinion:
- Dr. Ed Prida
- Further information upon request contact me.

Chapter 5

Cuba: Allied to extremist Muslims

Cuba has further strengthened its relations with the Muslim world to the level of allowing a mosque to be built in a central location in the capital. Contrary to Marxist ideology and atheist orientation. Rather, this is a symbolic fact to demonstrate its political unity with Muslim Arab terrorists. Iran and Arab Saudi Arabian extremists are in Cuba

Chapter 6

Cuba is the bridge of Political and Cultural Subversion of the Russians

Cuba exerts influence through the political and cultural subversion used in several countries such as Angola, Congo, South Africa, Mozambique, Ethiopia, Peru, Chile, Argentina, Brazil, Guyana, Haiti, Venezuela, Colombia, Jamaica, Mexico, Santo Domingo, Nicaragua , Honduras, El Salvador, Haiti, Puerto Rico, etc.

The long-term goal is first to obtain diplomatic support, and rewarded by credits and technical assistance that also generates economic dependence with a calculated debt, thus reaching political control and then the ultimate goal, a Russian military base against the United States.

Coup d'état in Portugal and later Angola

Cuba and the USSR coordinated Intelligence operations within the Armed Forces of Portugal, recruiting 5 Colonels, to give the coup d'etat, known as the "Carnation Revolution".
In April of 1974. The Carnation Revolution that makes its way through the wide door to Cuba in the political events of Portugal and its colonies, Angola and Mozambique and a little late to the socialist government of Mario Soares.

A whole Subversive Plan from the demoralization, to the seizure of power ... everything planned, Portugal from one day to the next dawns with Workers Committees in the work centers, neighborhood committees. Total persecution of former members of the government and the press.
The campaign for the decolonization of Angola and Mozambique did not wait, immediately the coup leaders, appear in Havana to be baptized by Fidel Castro and receive direct instructions from the Godfather.

The objective was to accelerate the decolonization to introduce Cuba in the name of the USSR in Angola as it had been doing without success in the Congo.

Everything obeyed a plan developed in almost 10 years, so that Moscow in 1974-75, Cuba would take a country in Africa and they would establish an Aero-Naval base for their operations in the South Atlantic.
All ready for the military invasion of Cuba in Angola with the "appearance that it was an initiative of Castro, flaunting his independence from Moscow and speaking of a supposed internationalist duty for our Latin-African blood." It has only been the sowing of death, misery and hatred, which can corrupt the human being more.
Troops from Cuba had been supporting the insurgent movements in Angola since years before and several high-ranking officers had died, others had been prisoners.

After the decolonization, Cuba instigates the struggle between the three forces fighting for power, instead of facilitating a process of democratic integration, Cuba selects only one of the three movements that developed the Independence of Angola, using the Doctor Agostino Neto, begins the war against the other Angolans, the supposed leader is an unknown and more domesticable doctor, but when he fulfilled his function, like Hugo Chávez, "an incurable disease" and they take him to Moscow to get him out of the game, later he is replaced by Eduardo Dos Santos, a young lawyer trained for more than 10 years in Cuba and everything under control, plunging him into the putrid band of Dutch prostitutes, drugs, and opening of Angola to the oil consortiums and the export of diamonds through only the President of Angola and her daughter with a total closure to agriculture, education and health.
However, Eduardo DosSantos became famous for being the best dressed man in the world, used the best European tailors, the most expensive fabrics and wore each suit only one day.

Isabel DosSantos. her daughter is a frequent visitor to Beverly Hill where she meets with her movie star friends. It is an exact example of the sacrifice of thousands of men and women, Cubans and Angolans who fought to create this caste of privileges and sow misery for both peoples. How to do justice? In those days the attacks of Cuba against the United States were on all possible fronts, but other secrets ... Diplomatic Forces of the Non-Aligned Countries against the United States in Panama, a blockade of South Africa for Apartheid, Independence for Angola,

Mozambique, Namibia, Guinea Bissau, the Greens in Western Europe, a worldwide movement against the United States based on falsehoods of subversive operations.
Through diplomatic channels Cuba manages to take the United States out of the Panama Canal, replacing it with Iran and China with the Woan Poa Division and political propaganda in the United Nations to block South Africa with the anti-apartheid argument.

The real reason for the war in Angola was the interest of the Soviet Union to take control of the Southern Cone of Africa and install a naval base in Lobito to control the South Atlantic region. This is also the case, Russia supports a dictatorial regime in Syria because, Russia built a Naval Base on the Mediterranean coasts of Syria to take control of the Mediterranean area.
As we see everything is a game of geopolitical

strategy.
<u>*Russian Military Posts around the World:*</u>
. Cuba (Mariel, Havana and Cienfuegos), Egypt (Alexandria and Marsa Matruh), Libya (Tripoli and Tobruk), Tunisia (Bizerte and Sfax), Syria (Latakia and Tartus),
Yemen (the island of Socotra and Aden), Yugoslavia (Split- today in Croatia and Tivat -now in Montenegro). In other countries it was enough for one, there was another fence in the neighboring country, such as Algeria (Cherchell), Ethiopia (in the Dahlak archipelago - now under the control of Eritrea), Guinea (Conakry), Angola (Luanda), Vietnam (Cam Ranh).

Moscow has military bases in 11 countries: In Ukraine, Moldova and Georgia it has them against the will of these countries.
The case of Ukraine is strange because now, after the annexation of Crimea to Russia, in theory, and by way of the facts, the base of Sevastopol

is already in Russian territory, it had previously leased it. It seems that Russia plans to even deploy nuclear weapons. Those deployed in the area are estimated at 13,000.

In Moldova, Russia is based in the region of Transnistria, where the influence of the Russian base is so great that, in fact, Transnistria is considered a Russian protectorate.

In South Ossetia and Abkhazia, territories broken off from Georgia after the lightning war against Russia in 2008, the respective Russian bases with infantry, armored personnel, helicopters and anti-aircraft artillery, make them function as Russian protectorates. At the base of Gudauta (Abkhazia) it has 3,500 personnel. At the base Tskhinvali (South Ossetia has 925 troops.

In Belarus, with the consent of the authorities, Russia created in 2007 a joint anti-aircraft defense device, with a powerful radar station. In addition, an airfield for Russian fighter jets 150 km from Minsk has been negotiated since 2015. It is estimated that 850 troops have been deployed. Kyrgyzstan rents to Russia an air base (Kant) on the periphery of its capital, Bishkek. It has about 700 troops.

More determined and more important seems the support of Armenia, in which the Russians have a base in Erebuni, next to the capital, Yerevan. In it there is an airport and a squadron of Mig-29. After the deterioration of relations with Turkey, the Erebuni base has been reinforced in men and helicopters. It has more than 5,000 personnel.

In Tajikistan, the Russian bases (in Dushanbe, Qurghonteppa and Kulab) are to help control its border with Afghanistan and have 5,500 troops. In Azerbaijan they have a radar base, Qabala, with 900 troops.

In 2013, an agreement was signed with Vietnam for the reopening of the former Russian base in Cam Ranh. It is intended to serve as a point of supply for Russian submarines.

In Kazakhstan, Russia has a small force deployed, with a number of unknown troops, in Baikonur, to protect its space installations.

In Syria, Russia has two military bases: the Tartus naval and the Jmeimim air base

Africa
An Angolan among the thousands killed by vesicant gases spread by the Cuban Armed Forces in Angola and reported to the UN Security Council

The political subversion of Cuba in South America is the tool to introduce Russia as a supply of weapons for the Armed Forces of South America, as they did in Cuba, Peru, Venezuela, Argentina, Brazil and Mexico, it is the last conquest in which Russia will build an aeronautical industry to supply combat aircraft for Mexico and other countries. We are very happy that Mexico and the rest of us will soon have the worst planes that are manufactured in the world ...

But the main interest is to take power in all countries. They have such low quality weapons and they know it, almost certainly no country in history has made such an offer, because a fighter aircraft factory carries a protection against intelligence to technological secrets, but the Russians have no secrets because they know that "their technology" has been stolen and in fact does not interest others, much less the United States.

The quality of its aircraft is terrible, the operating time of Russian aircraft is short, the capital repairs are very expensive, the fuel consumption is very high, the armament load is inefficient, the safety of the fighter pilots is considered As producers of wholesale widows, the Venezuelan pilots refused to fly the Mig-29 because it did not offer them the security that the American F-16s had.

The greatest difficulty of the Soviet aeronautical industry rests on three points, the metallurgy which, given the general level of the country, has never achieved what is necessary to produce light, resistant and anticorrosive metals and metalloids.

Castro's Covert Action in Mexico

New cover for Soviet spies

Reviving the terror networks

The basis of the

Russian aeronautical designs rests on the aerodynamic theory of Shuvkovski, who provided important ways of calculating cosmic speeds, but it seems not to be effective in vehicle speeds within the earth's atmosphere, and they have remained absolutely stuck to the classic calculations of the legendary 18th century Russian scientist. Soviet aircraft are characterized by instability during flights, high fuel consumption, very little lift in relation to their weight, so the minimum speed for landings is very high, which requires very heavy structures to withstand the impact of the landing. The Avionics is very backward and heavy. Low economic performance

In the aircraft manufactured by the Soviets and Russians an absolute disregard for human life has prevailed as an extension of their political system and they have treated Russian science in general in science and technology within the aeronautical industry, within the many concrete examples there is one that stands out, the contempt for the use of flight simulators, which have unquestionably contributed security and efficiency to aeronautical safety, it is not possible to evade Ronald Reagan who everyone does not know as the precursor of these teams when in the Second World War, he served as Captain of the Air Force and was the founder of the flight simulators for bombing missions in places where radio navigation did not exist and in meteorological conditions that provided cover for the aircrafts, so that deep bombings could be made in Germany and Japan. Biography of an American. Ronald Reagan.

Here in America, Cuba could make a cemetery only for fighter pilots who were shot down by Soviet technology. Peru has a museum arsenal of Russian airplanes and helicopters, so the two Illushin Il-96 of Cuba Airline did not reach 100 hours of flight and will be on land for life, because the factory canceled the production and there are no substitute engines.

The next step is "penetration into the military sphere" with the intention of obtaining information and recruiting high-ranking officials to support the leftist coup in the next stage and take power, or elegantly support a presidential candidate as was the case of Peru with President Ollanta Humala.

In fact, Cuba is the kind of "red bridge" to introduce Russian power in Asia, Africa and America.

Ref.:
Sunrise at the Higuera de Braulio
The Pinochet File CIA
The Mitrokin Archive
The removal of antipersonnel mines promotes the recovery of Angola ...
www.undp.org/content/.../ landmine-clearing-efforts-help-boost-ang ...
The United Nations Program for the Development (UNDP) has ... local, training more than a thousand specialists in de-mining in Eloy ... where more than 70% of the population lives on less than $ 2 per day.
BBC News
news.bbc.co.uk/hi/spanish/misc/newsid_7317000/7317594.stm
Mar 27, 2008 - In Angola, "Miss Mine" is celebrated, a beauty contest with survivors of antipersonnel mines. ... Survivors of antipersonnel mines will participate in a contest ... date chosen by the United Nations to celebrate the ... They're using rats to deactivate mines.

CHAPTER 7

Physical aggression against United States diplomats

Recently, in order to diminish the activity of diplomats in direct contact with the native population, Cuba has used sonic energy to create neurological disturbances to US diplomatic personnel on the island, with the aim of reducing the number of diplomats in Havana . This incident has created an imponderable precedent in Cuba-USA relations. But nevertheless, it has not had tangible consequences for the regime of the Island.

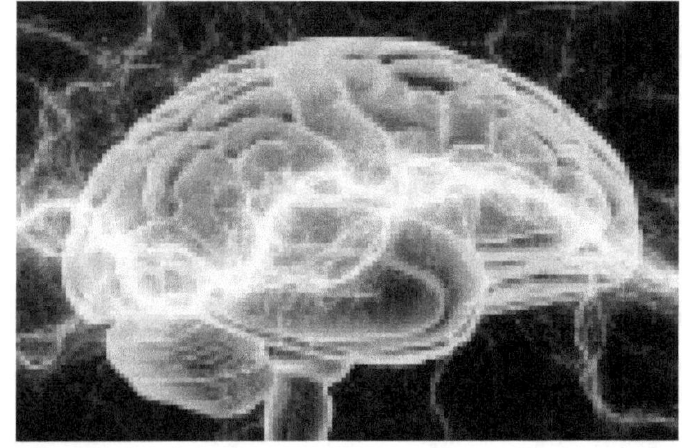

The Ministry of Foreign Affairs of Cuba offers absurd justifications and every more stupid comment to the previous one blaming even the insects that emit this same frequency is capable of causing brain damage.

"This is a slander of the United States," said Col. Ramiro Ramírez, a Cuban official responsible for the security of diplomats in the country, in response to Washington's accusations that sonic weapons were probably used to harm their diplomats.

Cuban investigators strongly denied that such weapons could have been used, even by third parties, without affecting the health of other people close to them at the time or attract much more attention.

"It's impossible, we're talking about science fiction," said Lt. Col. José Alazo, an expert in the criminal investigation unit of the Cuban Interior Ministry. "From a technical point of view, that argument is unsustainable." However, the recordings contain nothing that could harm human health, the researchers concluded. Noises included usual suburban sounds, such as traffic, steps and human voices.

They were also characterized by a deviation peak of 7 kilohertz (kHz) in the frequency band of 3 kHz, like the edge of a cricket. They said, however, that an audible sound would need to be very loud, over 80 decibels, or like the noise of an airplane engine, to have an impact on health. However, they said, only the victims heard the noise, but not their relatives who live in the same houses, nor their neighbors.

"We interviewed more than 300 people in the neighborhood, we also evaluated more than 30 medically, and nobody heard these things," said Alazo.

Finally, Cuban officials emphasized that only two or three of the alleged victims have presented hearing problems, according to the information provided by Washington, while any type of sound attack would have affected everyone in the area at that time.

Physiologically it is known that the human ear captures sound stimuli in this frequency range:
Frequency: 20 Hz - 20,000 Hz (corresponds to the tone)
Intensity: 10-12 - 10 watts / m2 (0 to 130 decibels)
Pressure: 2 x 10-5 - 60 Newton's / m2 2 x 10-10 - 0,0006 atmospheres

This means that the physical stimuli, called "sound waves" within these ranges, generate a conscious perception of them, but nevertheless, there are sound waves above and below these ranges, minimum and maximum that do not become conscious, but can produce "effects" for their energy, although it can not be perceived by the tympanic membrane and that some of these energies within different frequency ranges can be therapeutic like ultrasound, which is also mechanical waves, that is, non-ionizing, whose frequency is above the hearing capacity of the human ear (approximately 20 000 Hz).

There is also the infra sound, it is an acoustic wave or sound wave whose frequency is below the audible spectrum of the human ear (approximately 20 Hz). Infrasound is used by large animals such as elephants, whales and dolphins to communicate over long distances (sounds of 100 Decibels).

Another example, dogs have a different range of sounds as well as other types of animals, including fish. There are some instruments to call the packs that emit a sound not audible by humans, but for dogs. These whistles are widely used for training of sports or military dogs.

The effect of different forms of non-visible energies are ionic or active radio, sonic or magnetic, ultrasonic or subsonic if it is well known that it can affect the human body.

It is very famous the experiment of the English physicist, Maxwell who was the first to measure the acoustic waves, made an experiment with a whistle of the British police, but one meter in size and to blow the current of air into the whistle made to build giant blowers similar to those used in blacksmiths' forges to heat metals and make horseshoes ... the result of the giant whistle was the collapse of the four-story building where

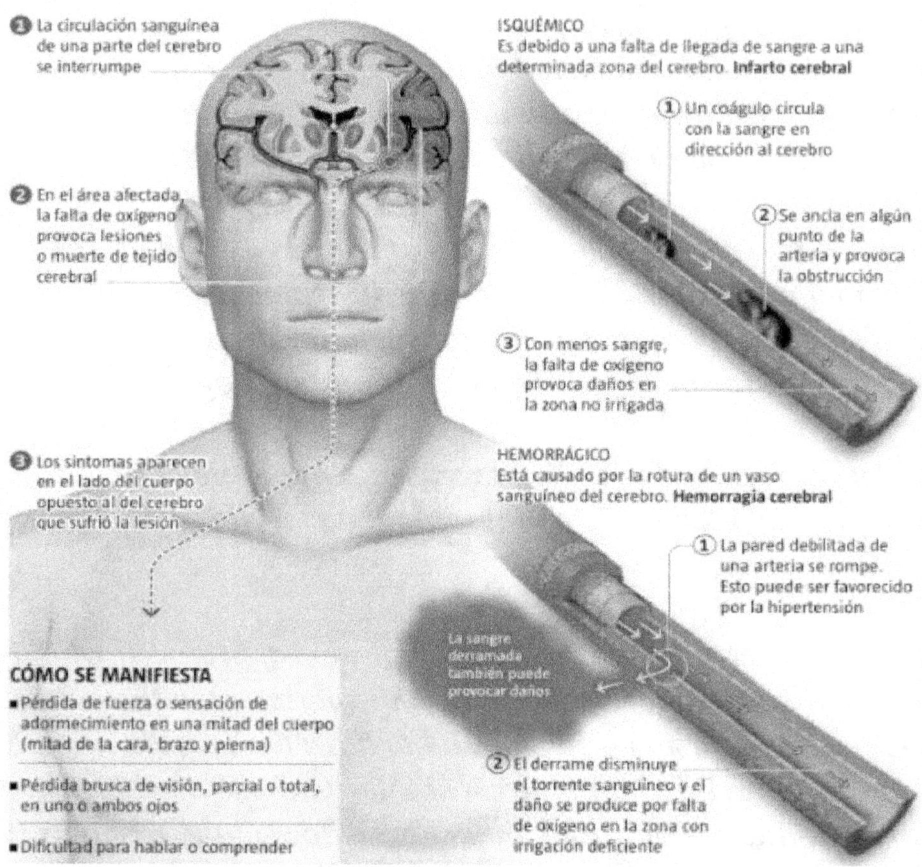

It is not very difficult to understand that any non-visible physical effect can cause injuries. They are experts in these homicidal articles with nuclear, electrical, chemical, etc. We already know this.

The physical effect on the brain or other tissue of the body produces, in broad strokes, two types of injuries: the rupture of blood vessels that produce spills in the brain or inhibition of the passage of blood, which produces the absence of blood where it should be and it does not arrive for any reason created by the physical effect.

We are not very familiar with the effect of sound as a physical phenomenon because it is not tangible like a blow with a mallet or a rifle shot.

It may be illustrative to know the effects of sound. For example, in 1839 a physicist Heinrich W. Dove discovered how certain sounds can alter the nervous system. There are certain ranges or spectra of frequencies that affect the normal activity of the brain.

Ultrasound of very short waves and rapid inaudible tone cause irritation and discomfort. Infrasound with wider frequencies between 4 and 8 Hertz produce dizziness, loss of sense of reality and spatial and temporal disorientation.

The consequences can lead to convulsions, conduction or electrical alterations of the cardiac muscle. It can also invalidate a person to calculate distances, sensations of movement, and estimated time, therefore, unable to operate machinery or drive vehicles.

The combination of tones and times for the left ear and another for the right creates problems in the processing of the acoustic signals that reach the 8th nerve pair or acoustic nerve, creating a sensation of waiting, which translates into an inhibition at the end.

All these acoustic phenomena achieved by the advancement of electronics and many others, have been manipulated to create the so-called "Sonic Drugs" capable of producing the same type of alteration and damage produced by drugs that unfortunately some people consume and reach the addiction. There are sounds that create the same psycho-physiological effect as drugs, only with the sound and it seems that the electronic drug displaced the drug produced in Colombia and Cuba.

With this minimal view on the matter, what Cuba does is not fiction, it is a reality. They can produce organic damage in the brain with sound, as they have done with nuclear energy.

REFERENCE:

Author's files
Press T V.com
PressTV.com
Press http://baneste.blogspot.com/2017/10/cuba-acusa-de-difamacionestados-unidos.html V.com

http://baneste.blogspot.com/2017/10/cuba-acusa-de-difamacion-estadosunidos.html V.com
https://es.slideshare.net/1Alejandra6/drogas-auditivas-52173097 **Chapter 8**

Note:- This chapter does not pretend to explain in detail the participation of

LOS HAVANA'S CUBAN BOYS EN DALLAS

Cuba and the USSR in the murder of JFK. Soon the book "Havana's Cuban Boys in Dallas" will be published where you will find all the details of the participation of Castro and Nikita in this sadistic event. We present by way of example another method without many precedents in history as two countries conspire to assassinate a President of the most powerful country on Earth and remain innocent. Many books, many dead, many falsehoods and a lot of money have run after the narrative about the events of November 22, 1963. Thank God we come to the Light.

Chapter
Nikita gave 'green light to Kill JFK

Col KGB Nicolai Leonov, Leonid President of Supreme Presidium, Captain Emilio Aragones, Nikita Khruschev, Nilolai Padgorni Vice Premier Minister and Castro. In the forest close to the Nikita's "dasha" April 6, 1963 Foto Tass Archive of the Author

The murder of JFK was part of a decision between the highest level of the Soviet Government and its order to his satrap in the Caribbean, Fidel Castro, was carried out without risk.

But not only the Soviet missiles threatened the United States, Cuba got introduce more of 600 agents in Canada and United States, they are a strong networks to do sabotages and subversion infested the United States in unimaginable ways as we will see: deep penetration of the KGB and DSE inside the CIA and White House presidential advisors, mafia, drugs, political subversion, administrative corruption to achieve blackmail, sabotage, etc.

Thanks to the FBI, many attempts to kill hundreds of thousands of people in

New York in December 1962 could be stopped

The objective of the Soviet Government was to stop the plans that JFK had to free Cuba from being a Soviet colony and turn it into a Soviet barracks to repress the people of Cuba as their nuclear hostages and to have an attack base against the United States.

They knew exactly the plans because they had penetrated the CIA and this agent infiltrated by his hierarchy imported from Cuba more than a dozen

agents who worked under the cover of the CIA to never kill Fidel Castro, as the case of the spy Antonio Veciana.

This compressed summary of a long investigation of dozens of years, brings us up to date on all the myths created by the USSR and Cuba, which are still promoting, but in the case of Fabián Escalante, he still pays in vain to be identified as Gilberto Lopez, still comes out in interviews made by an enchanted maiden where the "generalazo" creates an attenuated lighting scene, a super wide chest, a pillow in the abdomen and a false nose ... of Escalante escapes?

Taking Cuba reported to the USSR that its strategic balance multiplied to twice the combative nuclear efficiency in favor of the Soviets because of the geographical position, which they had conquered with a

"Trojan Horse" painted in red and black called July 26 for deceiving the Cuban people, the horse that came to free us from a supposed dictatorship, but the entire mantle was a trap for communist slavery and the service of a foreign power outside the American continent, the USSR.

CIA knew meeting in URSS

SUMMARY OF TRANSCRIPT OF JAMES ANGLETON

June 19, 1975

Record Number 157-10011-10034

CIA has a subject file on Oswald which contains all documentation that went to Warren Commission through Angleton's deputy, Raymond Rocca. (49)

Angleton has a very strong opinion on whether Oswald was a Soviet agent. He tried to prevail on Dulles that there should be a statement to the effect that the Commission's conclusions were based on available evidence. Given the fact that Department 13 was tasked with the assassination of Western leaders, Angleton felt the investigation should be continued. (49-50)

Angleton attempted to prevent the Warren Commission from concluding that Nosenko was a bona fide defector. Angleton thought Nosenko was a dispatch agent who was sent to mutilate the leads of very high grade Soviets which the CIA had acquired prior to the defection. (50) He was to mutilate leads relating to the JFK assassination, KGB agents, Vassily, the British agents, and many agents in France, and an alleged penetration in the U.S. (51)

Angleton doesn't feel the Oswald case is dead. There were too many leads that were never followed up. For example, in 1966, in a Soviet book on Cuba there is a photograph of Khrushchev, a photograph of Castro, a photograph of a man called Alexiev, real name Shettov, KGB, with the first Soviet Ambassador to Havana, and a man named Leontov, who was the Soviet KGB operational man in Mexico. When the Mexican police arrested Castro as a student, they found in his notebooks the name of Leontov, KGB, Mexico. (51-52)

CIA had a double agent after the assassination who made a number of allegations that he acquired from the Chief of KGB, Mexico, Yatskov

The JFK Plans

For many years I have had and analyzed the plans of JFK and his group to attack Cuba on December 1, 1963 at 9:00 p.m. by Casilda, Las Villas.

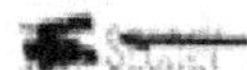

MEMORANDUM FOR THE PRESIDENT

SUBJECT: Future Policy Toward Cuba

Policy

    Our ultimate objective with respect to Cuba remains the otherthrow of the Castro/Communist regime and its replacement by one compatible with the objectives of the US and where possible sharing the aims of the Free World. To achieve this objective, the USG is prepared, if necessary, to apply increasing degrees of political, economic and military pressures until the Castro regime is overthrown. However, while applying these pressures, the USG will make it clear that there is another option available to the regime should it modify its position, with or without Castro. Initially, this modified position from which later broadening could be achieved, need be no more than one in which the Soviet presence is removed, trade relations with the U.S. are restored, and the U.S. has entree. Under either course, the U.S. would not seek to restore the status quo ante. Our immediate objectives are two-fold. On the one hand, optimum effort must be made to explore the possibility of rapprochement, through reorientation of the regime, by overt and covert communication of the reasonable nature of the shift in political orientation required and the economic benefits thereof. On the other hand, while exploring the above, we must seek to isolate the Castro/Communist regime from the Free World and from the Bloc; weaken it economically; promote internal dissension; erode its domestic

SECRET

JFK Memorandum

Because of the characteristics of the discretion of the AMWORLD Plan of JFK within the legal structure that moves the Executive of the United

States, the enemies knew that eliminating JFK, the Plan was without effect. For the relationship between the three branches, Executive, Legislative and Judicial, who were unaware of the Plan because by making it public, the effort would lose all effectiveness.

They knew in detail about these Plans for a chain of spies within the CIA and also within the anti-Castro organization created by them to cover all their actions and hold the anti-Castro movement in general accountable.

The Alfa-66 created by Antonio Veciana and Eloy G. Menoyo, agents of Castro and sponsored by the CIA by the person of Bernard Barker "El Macho", a Cuban American who since the 1930s fought with the ABC (Opposite terrorist organization against Gerardo Machado) along with other Communist militants against the Government of President Machado during years of work deceived many patriots and led them to certain death in all missions. He was in Castillo del Principe jail for two years joined to Fabio Grobart, Blas Roca and Victor Pina serving sentence for assassination of the opposition leaders.

On the other hand, the Soviet government and Castro was willing to turn Cuba into nuclear ashes because the Cubans were for them like cheap slaves, and Castro and his mafia had the way to take out of Cuba form the South shore of San Julian Air Force Base. The planning, coordination, organization and execution of the crime in US territory can be demonstrated with the photos and documents of the participants in the assassination of President JFK as well as the infiltration of KGB agents and Havana's Cuban Boys within the same preparations of President JFK ...

How do start this complex story?

If this event had been the product of a single person, and the executor of the crime took the decision 10 days before, could not have the complexity it has.
This was a decision of governments, planned almost two years before.
Perhaps this plot should start from the subjects involved since the more distant time and who participated as clandestine operatives

The two pigeons of Jews, Russians and communists one introduced the KGB in Cuba in the 30s and the other in the United States, in the 40s, both with the second name León, by the affinity of their parents with Leon Trotsky by Bernard León Barker and Jerome
León Rubinstein aka Jack Ruby, each with a history of "thugs" one against
President Gerardo Machado in Cuba and the other within the Mafia in the United States, "both with services rendered in the US Armed Forces to obtain a good credential and on the other hand, justified before the Party by the Forum of the Ye-Nan of Mao Tse Tung where he proclaimed that we had to fight with the tools of democracy and penetrate governments, "make the opposition from within." It is not surprising that Jerome León Rubinstein, later known as Jack Ruby, was the American weapon supplier for the 600 Spanish-Soviet soldiers who were inside the Soviet ship Zora, in the port of
Santiago de Cuba, on July 26, 1953. This officer, American
It is another case "sown" for years, which we give as an example. Taken from Wings and Shadows. Book on Víctor Pina.

The Pilot Commander of the United States Navy Mortimer Robson, also a

Jew who since the 1930s was in contact with the KGB through the Cuban Víctor Pina Cardoso, this is like a Jack Ruby, Davie Ferrie, Bernard Barker, Antonio Veciana, José Ricardo Rabel, Manuel Artime, Rolando Cubela and others who have served the cause of communism in an undetectable silence.

Both clandestine agents of the KGB infiltrated the CIA, one live and the other indirect, the Mafia used them for their domestic misdeeds and the CIA needed the information, because this group were the only Americans who had links with the island. through his former employees of the Casinos and Cabaret in Havana.

The Mafia members were cohesive, on the one hand against Castro for the frustration of the loss of property seized by the Castro and on the other hand with the CIA, since they were only seeking to establish a commitment that when a new government was restored in Cuba, they would have the privilege to restore their businesses. The main people in charge of doing business for this promise were the old politicians of Cuba with Tony Varona, Rolando Manferrer and others.
In one way or another, in the style of the Mafia, they played with the CIA with the story of killing Fidel. This explains the link that the Press presents us between the Mafia and the CIA.

The Macho Barker and other ex filtered some people of Cuba in coordination with the G-2 and with their legend and opened the door of the

Jack Ruby Biography

Joseph Rubinstein

Born Sokolov, in Russian territory. In 1871.
Artillery's men in Russian Army in 1883.
Serviced in China, Korea and Siberia. In 1898
went to England, Canada and USA in 1903. In
Chicago was founder and Leader of the
Carpenter Syndicate from 1906 to 1958
death.

Jack Ruby
March 11, 1911?
June 6, 1922
Jack referred to Institute
of Juvenile Research by
the Juvenile Service
Bureau for conduct
disorder and fight.
Temperamental and
disobedient behavior.
"He said, I can lick
anybody in any place".
Sexual deviation and
property damages.

Other members of the family were Red Army's officer
in Brest Fort in Aug 1941. They became **Soviet Union's
Heroes** and other part of this family emigrated to
Cuba in 1930-?
Jack Ruby cousin Maximo Bergman member of
Communists Party and Jewish was
Ministry of Internal Commerce between 1960-63.
Suspected political murder.

*CIA with the recruitment, as is classic in these cases, to clandestine
communists starting from the year 1959 from Cuba, USSR and
Washington.*

*Jack Ruby: A long family history from the Soviet Union itself and its
founding father of the Union of Carpenters of Chicago and communist
militant, on the other hand, in Cuba had a family, from the mother branch
to the Bergman, from the communist Jews who arrived in Cuba In the
1920s, one of his cousins was the Minister of Internal Trade of the Castro
government (1961-1964), Maxim Bergman, who dies months after the
attack on JFK inside his car, only 42 years old inside the car in the parking
lot of Ministry of Labor..*

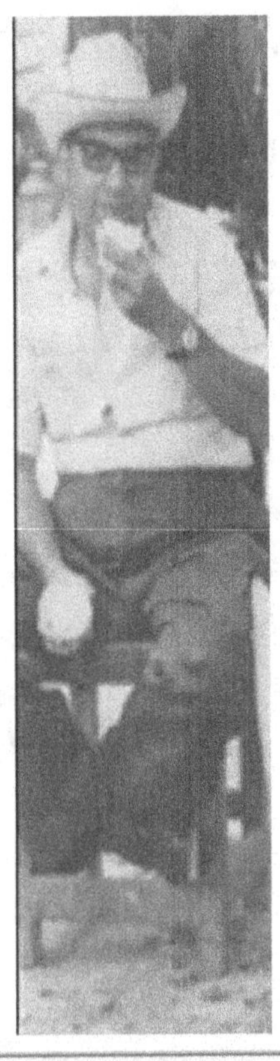

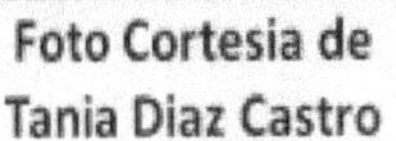

Foto Cortesia de
Tania Diaz Castro

Maximo Bergman Rubinstein, Interior Commerce Minister between 1960-1963. Cousin of Jerome Leon Rubinstein aka "Jack Ruby". The Bergman family was a Jews and communist family what arrived Cuba from Soviet Union as KGB's spy net code "Caribean's Fox" in 1924 with Fabio Grobart and Jose Cohen. This spy net had 200 members as Intelligence and Subversion and diamond cutter. They used as facade the little stores in Muralla Street in the center of Old Havana city specialist and diamond. They said, they came from Poland, no Russian.

Maximo Bergman false accused by Castro to buy in the Soviet Union 42 "Ice Sweeter" heavy equipment. He was found dead inside the auto in the Minister' of Labor's parking lot. He had just 42 years old in very good health.

Cuba cleaned with death the family bond of Maximo Bergman with Jerome León Rubinstein, it was necessary to silence him and that other family members assimilated the rules of the game. First, he was discredited by the false purchase of the "snow sweepers" and already without ministerial office he dies.

The snow sweepers were not purchased by the Cuban government in the USSR, they arrived in Cuba with the Mig'21 Jet Fighter Regiment of the 5th
Air Force of the Caucasian Army Corps that arrived in Cuba in 1962 in Operation "NADYR" which as part of a maskirovka supposedly went to Siberia for an exercise, but actually came to Cuba, this Aviation Regiment of Mig-21 arrived in Cuba with the snow sweepers for clean the air base airway, already in Cuba they were stationed in the back of hangar One of the San Antonio Base and it was not possible to adapt them to sweep the dust off the runway and Fidel Castro mentioned them in a speech as an error and ignorance of the Minister of Internal Trade who bought them to

143

remove the snow on the roads, this comment in a derisive and burlesque way to dismiss him and send him to plant eucalyptus in Guanahcavibes, where he was photographed by the journalist Tania Díaz.

 The commentary and the dismissal preceded the death. The 4 sweepers were for years on Ave. de Rancho Boyeros and Calle 100 in sight in a parking lot.

But Jack Ruby's starting the link with Cuba / Castro is that Jack had served the KGB to supply the 26 of July Movement and Rebel Army with weapons and for this service he obtained the License of Infantry Arms Exporter for Central America and the Caribbean, just in 1952 when the subversion begins in Cuba. He went to the Court in Louisiana for stolen the weapons from the Army Reserve depot.

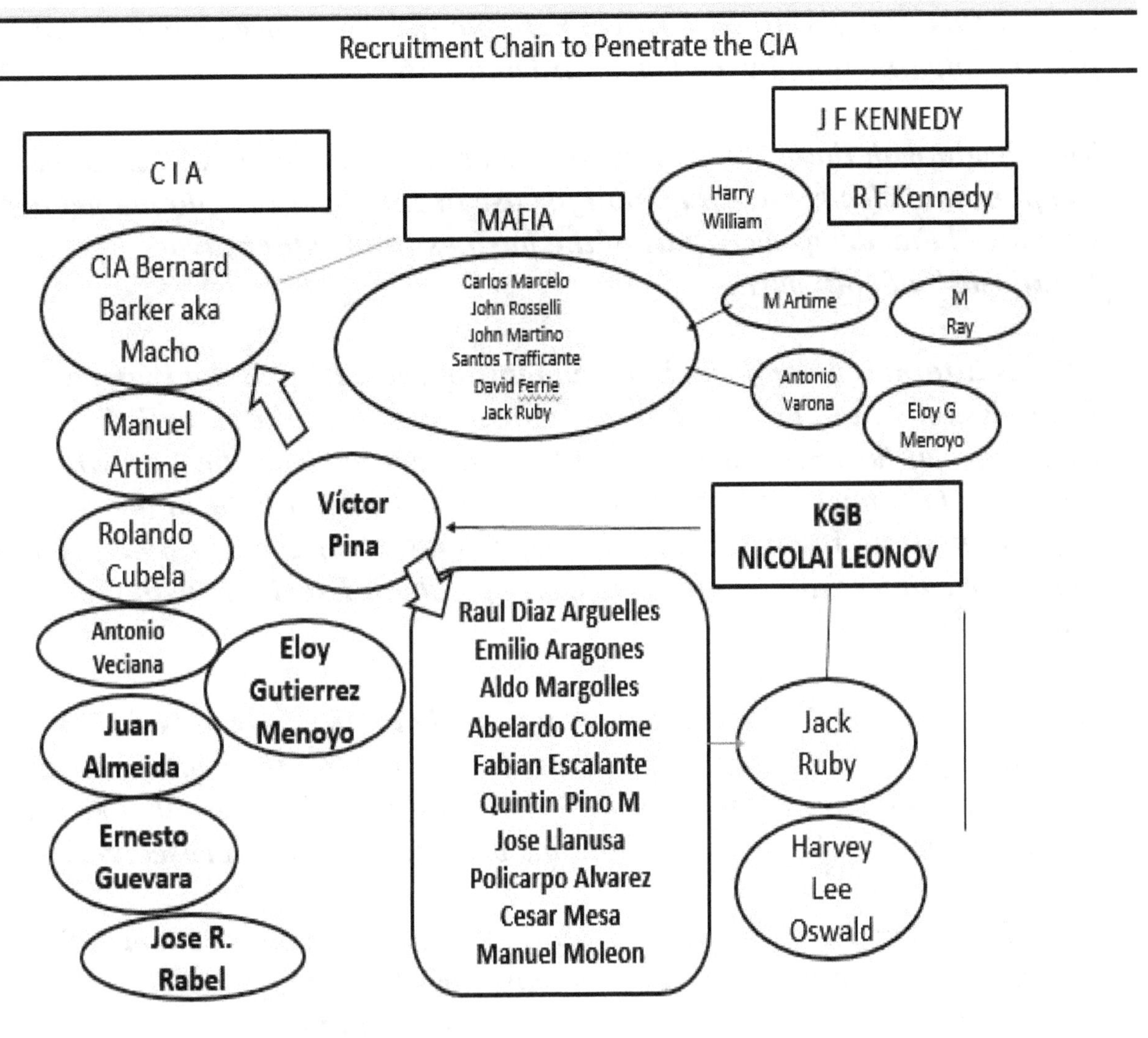

Ed Prida: Author

His contact with Cuba were the clandestine agents of the Popular Socialist Party like Víctor Pina, José LLanusa Gobel, but on April 27, 1959, in Houston they reached the level of Fidel Castro and Víctor Pina, in an interview that lasted 8 hours.

A few days later another chapter begins in Havana, Cuba when it is related to the Commanders Raúl Díaz Arguelles, Rolando Cubela, Aldo Margolles and Castro himself in negotiations for the freedom of the Mafia's American detainees in Cuba, including some mafia for the umpteenth chance this group of Cuban officers are the same as those shown in the photo, watching happily as they murdered JFK.

They begin with these conversations and certain businesses of exchange of weapons and electronic equipment for use in Intelligence, I do not get to be convinced that drugs were part of the business, but rather favors "mafiosos" of both parties.

All this information appears in documents of the CIA and the Warren Commission, but in my opinion these businesses were the so-called exchanges of favors, Castro offered him services to clean the way with murders to the enemies between mobsters and they would be in the disposition to fulfill missions of coverage that Cuban agents would need in the American territory. As was the case of Fabian Escalante with the Tampa Mafia.

Jack Ruby went to Cuba as the mediator to obtain the freedom of 128 American prisoners, some of them members of the fugitive mafia of the United States justice for the denunciations and investigations about their crimes of the then Senator JFK and his brother Robert as Prosecutor.

This element underscores that the Mafia was in fact a direct enemy of JFK, as Castro was also an enemy of Kennedy, for which he effectively converted the American Mafia, a strategic ally of the G-2.

Therefore, an action plan will be established focusing on Bernard Barker, Jack Ruby and secondarily, Lee Harvey Oswald.

If we analyze the dynamics of the factors involved, we can obtain a clearer idea of how these factors were used to achieve the JFK assassination and at the same time create an erasure of traces and an impenetrable cloud of plots where the researcher loses his way through infertile paths.

During his efforts in Cuba, Jack Ruby, at that time Jerome León Rubinstein was in official contact with the commanders Raúl Díaz Arguelles, Emilio Aragonés, Rolando Cubela and Aldo Margolles who were in charge of the detainees by the Technical Department of Investigations (DTI) , the hostage gangsters in Havana for Castro.

However, a rare coincidence, "beyond any rational doubt" as Fabián Escalante says, they are also meeting at JFK's death scene, seconds before the shot in Dallas.

This photo of the Revolutionary Studio shot by Naon perhaps fulfilled the mission to keep alive the facade of Fidel Castro's trips to Varadero by the year 1963, the trips were true but it was not Fidel Castro, it was his double to keep the "doubt" reasonable "that Antonio Veciana was the killer eager to kill" handsome as Cheo Malanga. "

The behavior of Veciana with Alpha 66, call the attention. This is part of the Congress of Assassination Committee Report.

1960, Alpha 66

Veciana settled in Miami with his family, and after Bishop contacted him there, under the direction of Bishop, he founded Alpha 66 in mid-1962, [4] [5] [1] becoming his chief civilian and chief tax collector. funds, and recruiting his military chief of another Cuban organization in exile. [1] Alpha 66 became one of the most active Cuban exile groups, acquiring weapons and ships and launching attacks against Cuba. [one]

From August 1968 to June 1972, Veciana was active in Bolivia. Formally banking advisor of the Central Bank of Bolivia in contracts financed by the United States Agency for International Development, his office was located in the passport division of the Embassy of the United States, and his main activity was to organize anticommunist and anti-Castro activities. This included another assassination attempt on Castro in Chile in 1971 [1] that involved a plan to put a gun inside a television camera. Veciana's recruitment of Cuban associates who prepared a plan to blame the Russian agents for the murder led to a confrontation with Bishop and the eventual cessation of their relationship. When Bishop broke the relationship in 1973, he paid Veciana $ 253,000 in recognition of his services; Veciana had previously rejected the payment. [one]

1970, and HSCA interview

In 1974, Veciana was found guilty of conspiracy to supply narcotics; [6] he served 27 months, and still professes his innocence after his release.

[one] In 1976, Veciana told the Select Committee on Assassinations of the US House of Representatives (HSCA) that at a meeting with Bishop in Dallas in late August or September 1963 he had arrived to see Bishop speak with Lee Harvey Oswald. [1] Veciana said that several months after the murder, Bishop had offered to pay a family member of Veciana who worked at the Cuban Intelligence Directorate in Mexico City to publicly say that he had found Oswald there. [1] On September 21, 1979 in Miami, Veciana was shot in the head during a drive-by shooting as she traveled in her car. [5] Initially she was admitted to the Pan American Hospital with a small caliber bullet embedded in her left ear, then transferred to Jackson Memorial Hospital. [5] Veciana's family and friends said that Cuban government agents had tried to kill him. [5] Veciana was not active on Alpha 66 at the time of the shooting. [5] His wife said he had received death threats eight months earlier, and Nazario Sargen, the then current leader of Alpha 66, said Veciana said a few months ago at a press conference that the Cuban government planned to kill him after he met. the plot of the Federal Bureau of Investigation

Veciana was briefly employed as treasurer by Maurice Ferré's 2004 campaign for mayor of Miami-Dade. He resigned after a few days, as he did not meet the state requirement of being a registered voter.[7]

In 2013 Veciana gave interviews saying that he believed that the assassination of John F. Kennedy was carried out by senior military and intelligence officials.[8][9] On January 16, 2016, the Assassination Archives and Research Center published a video on Youtube of a conference in which Veciana unequivocally stated that Maurice Bishop was in fact David Atlee Phillips[10][11]

Veciana is the husband of Sira Muino[5] and father of journalist Ana Veciana-Suarez.[12]

References[edit]

1. ^ Jump up to:a b c d e f g h i j k Appendix to Hearings before the Select Committee on Assassinations of the U.S. House of Representatives, Volume X 1979, pp. 37-56.

2. Jump up^ Giraud, Gabriel (May 28, 2017). "Un ex-espion de la CIA se décrit en "terroriste"". Le Figaro.

Retrieved May 29, 2017. Il a été recruté en 1959 par l'agent David Atlee Philipps - connu sous l'alias Bishop - dans le but de tuer Fidel Castro.

3.   **Jump up^** Jay Mallin, *The Miami News*, 23 November 1961, <u>A BAZOOKA DIDN'T FIRE IN HAVANA AND CASTRO TALKED ON</u>

4.   **Jump up^** *<u>"III. Antonio Veciana Blanch"</u>. <u>Appendix to Hearings before the Select Committee on Assassinations of the U.S. House of Representatives</u>. X. Washington, D.C.: United States Government Printing Office. March 1979. p. 37.*

5.   ^ **<u>Jump up to:</u>**[a] [b] [c] [d] [e] [f] [g] *Williams, Dan (September 22, 1979). <u>"Anti-Castro Leader Shot In the Head"</u>. Miami Herald. p. 2-B. Retrieved April 30, 2017.*

6.   **Jump up^** <u>United States vs. Ariel Pomares and Antonio Veciana (Docket 74-1219, Decided July 5, 1974)</u>

7.   **Jump up^** Noaki Schwartz, *Miami Herald*, 2 June 2005, <u>Audit: Ferré camp broke the law</u>

8.   **Jump up^** Alfonso Chardy, *El Nuevo Heraldo*, 17 November 2013, <u>La conexión cubana en el asesinato de JFK</u>

9.   **Jump up^** Iliana Lavastida, *Diario Las Américas*, <u>"A Kennedy lo mató la CIA", asegura un exagente de la CIA</u>, November 2013

10.   **Jump up^** *Antonio Veciana,) (September 26, 2014). Antonio Veciana - Admissions and Revelations HD (Conference). Bethesda Hyatt Regency, Bethesda, Maryland: Assassination Archives and Research Center..*

11.   **Jump up^** <u>JFK files: As Donald Trump looks to release classified documents, last living link to assassination drops bombshell</u>, The Independent, 23 October 2017.

12.   **Jump up^** Jay Weaver, *Miami Herald*, 19 January 2006, <u>Herald writer pleads guilty to 2003 contempt charg</u>

This photo of the "double" or doll of Fidel Castro in Varadero was taken

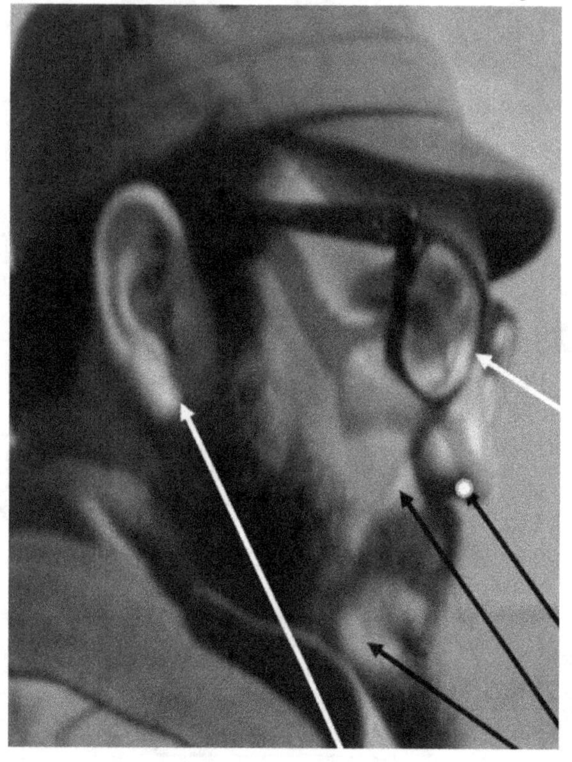

to excite the minds of his supposed enemies who prepared with double agents Bernard Baker and Antonio Veciana the famous attack on Castro on his Saturday trips to Varadero.

There are many reasons to show that far beyond the doubt this photo is not Fidel Castro, from a distance without going into detail the shoulders and arms do not have the proportion of Fidel Castro. His back was smooth, the trapezoids and the deltoids were never marked as we see the double, who is carrier of athletic structure by the muscles of arms and back, the back and the arms of Fidel Castro was totally

smooth, his muscles had no definition and with almost zero glutes. The 3-4 inch heels he used inside and outside the boots, created deviations from his structural pond balance and his spine was bent over and covered with his bulletproof and isothermal safety vests.

The weight of the 40-shot Stiche pistol on his right hip unbalanced his body and created injuries to his spine, and he also wanted to be taller than any of the bodyguards and ordered to put on his boots a heel of almost three inches outside and many others inside the boot. As we see in the photo, the eyeglasses support a supposed Hellenic nose, but undoubtedly it was a good double and an excellent job. In the lower part of the pavilion of the ear is one of the points of grip of the whole mask, which presumably was made with human skin

We can detect two different types of tones in the skin and it follows all over the upper lip on the mustache and around the mouth.

Beyond reasonable doubt, this plastic on the nose could have been justified, because the imperialist blockade did not allow Cubans to have a cream to block the effects of the sun's rays on the skin. Then the commander decided to cover his nose and not use a Mexican hat to cover the sun of Varadero. Clarifying the reader this it is an explanation in the style of Fabián Escalante.

The man who played this double role, must have suffered some terrible headaches with these glasses for extreme myopia so that his eyes would not be identified, due to physical characteristics, it seems to be General José Castro, Magaly's husband.

Why devote so much space to a double, Castro had the right to defend himself as he could, of course.

The importance of this photo in Varadero in 1963 is related because the agents infiltrated in the CIA entertained the Americans with plans to assassinate Fidel Castro in his trips to Varadero, the Vía Blanca has places near the so-called Fundora point, the Cayuelo, the Narigón, Arroyo Bermejo and many others where explosions or shots of frank shooters or a commando attack against the caravan could perfectly be implemented. The person in charge of these attacks was Eloy Gutiérrez Menoyo and Antonio Veciana, who made one first in the west of Miramar, but forgot to take the bazooka. Then for years, these plans of attacks that according to his book gave him years of training and then accuses the CIA of his training, if he wanted to kill Castro because he curses the training that the CIA provided him ... and that the CIA was the godmother by Lee Harvery Oswald. Attributed to an officer that he does not know, as it was called and baptizes him with two different names. There are documents linking Harvey Oswald with Raúl Díaz Arguelles, Ramiro Valdés, Rolando Cubela, Víctor Pina or Eusebio López Azcue at the consulate and at the party, Emilio Aragonés, Oswald travels to Cuba from October 2 to 9, 1963, they say that they deny him the Visa and nevertheless he had permanent Visa to travel to the USSR he and Marina with the girl ... these evidences do not have importance for Veciana. But, nevertheless, they exist and if they link Lee Harvey Oswald with the Cuban government, his G-2.

However, the head of the CIA Office in Miami, according to the text, appears in a memo about Veciana that had to be dismissed as an agent of "disinformation" because what Miami knew, Havana already knew thanks to Veciana's contacts with other Cubans, who trusted in their loyalty.

Agent of misinformation means that they always knew that it was from the other side and used it to misinform the enemy.

This photo in part shows that the Cuban side was connected to infiltrators in the CIA and they were "giving the dam cord" during all weekends to Varadero and staying near the house of Rolando Cubela, another supposed plot to assassinate to Fidel Castro, it was a siren song for the CIA and to continue charging money to the CIA,

There are throughout this operation to kill JFK, as in others, something that will surprise readers, the continuous use of makeup, false beards. eyeglasses with ears, glasses with nose, many makeups we are going to show you, but there are some that even more than 50 years of the fact, they continue using make-ups and deformations of the body as the case of Fabián Escalante trying not to look like a Gilberto Policarpo López, identity abandoned by Escalante in Mexico on November 27, 1963.

In the dim light it appears, "beyond reasonable doubt", a sexy lighting for girls because it looks 20 years younger, but for others, not badly thought, is that it is accustomed to his work in the shadows, in the falsehood and never present your true face. The habit makes the monk, the milkman's horse always follows the path, accustomed to his plastic nose can not leave without a plastic nose, soon, he says having an accident, and then in the CIMEQ, they make another face

Rolando Cubela and Aldo Margolles, who arrived in the United States through El Paso, Texas, on August 23, 1963, along with his brother-in-law Emilio Aragonés, is our neighbor in Miami and has more courage than Fabián, who even in Nuevo Vedado, with chosen neighbors and watched by panic.

This "reasonable and doubtful" interview with the General "in the dim light", a pillow on the abdomen, shoulders with an oversized dimension, two additional inches of shoulder on each side and a false nose.

The carnival costumes for the communists. They are nothing new. Dr. Fisin and Víctor Pina oversaw these makeups to the KGB agents who arrived in Cuba and the clandestine of the PSP for more than 60 years.

In the A times, Blas Roca used a face for each place. in Guanabacoa he was a babalawe, almost black mulatto, he had a different face and a wife Justina and in Marianao another face, another wife and children. When he left the country, they put on another mask. Everything about them has always been very legal, and after 1975, to top it all, Blas Roca conformed the new "socialist legality"

In the 60s, masks or adjustments with beards were made with dissected human skin. In the Institute of Legal Medicine were extracted skin segments dissected with formalin aldehyde, even many years later, therefore I assume that in previous years they did the same.

This chapter is just an introduction to the reader about participation and why the USSR and Cuba prepare in 1963 the death of President JFK, who committed his life to freeing the United States from the subversive and nuclear threat of the USSR through Cuba, kidnapped by the Russians, as the same JFK called it.

I present below a small sample of the collection of photographs, documents, logical arguments and identification of the main officers of Castro involved in this sad action.

You will have a reading friend, the opportunity to know in detail the full story in next publication of 'The Havana's Cuban Boy in Dallas' in English and Spanish, "God through".

It refers to Castro's assassination team, like "Cuban boys from Havana in Dallas," to make a difference between the "Cuban boys of Miami" because the exiles had been "designated" as enemies of JFK and the United States by Castro's propaganda machine.

I invite you to enjoy those photos ... what the fact brings down the lies created by the enemy of the CIA conspiracy against JFK

.

Nikita Khrushchev threatens to give a strong and devastating blow to the United States, on May Day, 1963. If Cuba receives a military invasion. This shows that they knew the JFK Plan and the coup d'état of commander Juan Almeida and Ernesto Guevara against Castro. Photo Agency Tass. Author file. May 1,1963.

With the white arrow, Captain Emilio Aragonés and Eloy official Nicolai Serguei Vich Leonov, individuals who will look like a front row operation in Chicago, Tampa, Miami, New Orleans and finally in Dallas and the Soviet from Mexico.

Secret meeting outside the house of Nikita ... First to the left Colonel Nicolai
Leonov, second Leonid Brezhnev President of the Presidium of the Soviet Supreme: Captain Emilio Aragonés: Nikita S. Khrushchev, Prime Minister and First Secretary of the Central Committee: Nicolai Podgorny Secretary of the Council of Ministers and Commander Fidel Castro. Photo by Tass, March 5, 1963. Author's archive. Those marked with the arrow Colonel Nicolai Sergueivich Leonov and Captain Emilio Aragonés Navarro, "coincidentally" will be involved until the end of the operation to eliminate JFK.

Castro and Khrushchev knew from different intelligence sources that JFK had the decision and the Plan of attack, Coup d'État, the Contingency Plan for the State Department because five Cuban leaders from Miami were working and involved with Robert Kennedy with the Plan, 3 of them passed the information to Castro. Also, the CIA Political Advisor for Cuban Affairs went to Cuba and gave the

information to Fidel and Raúl Castro

```
                          AGENCY INFORMATION

              AGENCY :  CIA
       RECORD NUMBER :  104-10308-10146
       RECORD SERIES :  JFK
 AGENCY FILE NUMBER :  80T01357A
- - - - - - - - - - - - - - - - - - - - - - - - - - - - - - - - - - - - - - -
                         DOCUMENT INFORMATION

          ORIGINATOR :  CIA
                FROM :
                  TO :  UNOFFICIAL TO MR. ALFRED COX
               TITLE :  ALDO PEDRO MARGOLLES Y DUENAS AND EMILIO ARAGONES Y NAVARRO PLOT TO
                        ASSASSINATE THE PRESIDENT OF THE UNITED STATES.
                DATE :  00/00/
               PAGES :  1
            SUBJECTS :  MARGOLLES Y DUE
                        ARAGONES, EMILI
                        PLOT
                        ASSASSINATE
                        PRESIDENT
                        UNITED STATES

       DOCUMENT TYPE :  PAPER, TEXTUAL DOCUMENT
      CLASSIFICATION :  UNCLASSIFIED
        RESTRICTIONS :  OPEN IN FULL
      CURRENT STATUS :  OPEN
 DATE OF LAST REVIEW :  09/19/98
    OPENING CRITERIA :
            COMMENTS :  JFK-WF02:F7 1998.09.19.11:55:02:513031:
```

This superior meeting in Moscow on March 5, 1963, Moscow and Havana made the decision to kill JFK and assigned Captain Emilio Aragonés for this mission.

What kind of humor would be running in this select group from left to right, Emilio Aragonés Navarro, who will appear in the photo next to the caravan of JFK, to dismiss him in the name of Castro.

The first Soviet Ambassador in Cuba, who was several times in the Sierra Maestra in 1958 and was the head of the KGB in Buenos Aires and the father of someone known in this environment, Ernesto Guevara, Fidel Castro, with the beard, then follows him who will always be present as the intimate representative of the Russian Empire in Cuba, Nicolai Leonov and the late Nikita K, Soviet Prime Minister. The group of women behind are the wives of the nomeklatura in Nikita's resting hut (dacha) near Moscow.

Ready for the mission against the United States. Ambassador Extraordinary and Plenipotentiary of the USSR Alexei Alexiev, the commander Ernesto Guevara and the "happy" Captain Emilio. Aragones.

Commander Aldo Margolles Dueñas. He came to repented exile, but not enough to make public his knowledge and participation in the missions assigned by the Soviets to the Cubans. Your information would be welcome.

Commander Aldo Margolles Dueñas. He came to repented exile, but not enough to make public his knowledge and participation in the missions assigned by the Soviets to the Cubans. Your information would be welcome.
There is a large declassified documentation of the CIA to locate and identify
José "Pepe" LLanusa during the preparation of the fateful attack against JFK. He was a professional basketball athlete very popular at that time and a disguised communist before 1959. He went into exile in Miami in 1957 and worked as a weapons

MEMORANDUM FOR THE RECORD   1998

SUBJECT: AMBLOUCH Project

                    Job #   69-827/91   (Box 20)
                                       71-739/68   (Box 13)

                    File #   [ ]4-93

                    Volumes: 15 and 4

    1. Description:

        Formerly AMRANGE and [ ]BLOUCH, Material couriers
around AMBLOUCH-1, honorary [08   ] in Havana, trained
in ORTG and SW; and AMBLOUCH-2, contract type employee,
[10   ] Havana.

    2. Findings:

        RBOO 2944 (IN 83333) 18 Dec 63:

        [05   ]
        [10   ] reported to Rio Station contact in
Rio: a. Wide rumor of assassination attempt against
Fidel CASTRO after his TV appearance 6 Dec resulting in killing
of man next to him. CASTRO uninjured. Would be killer at large.

        b. Wide rumor Cuban Juan "Pepe" LLANOSA met Lee OSWALD
in Mexico before Kennedy assassination.

Attachment: LAD/JTF Task Force

Researcher: DG

*supplier for the so-called Rebel Army in the Sierra Maestra in coordination
with Jack Ruby (KGB), with gun license exporter Infantry, which he stole
in an arsenal of the United States Army. Jack Ruby went to Court accused
of stealing a shipment weaof weapons.*

Aldo Margolles, Emilio Aragones and Harvey Oswald

The commanders Aldo Margolles, Raúl Díaz Argüelles and José LLanusa worked to coordinate the action with Jack Ruby and Lee Harvey Oswald between August / 63 to November 26/1963 in the United States.

In Cuba, he held the position of director of sporting activity and later became Minister of Education. In the 70s, he was replaced as Minister and disappeared from the public scene. According to unconfirmed information, Castro assigned him to work on a pig farm near Menocal, in Cienfuegos.

Instead, his daughter was a prominent member of the Commander's Coordination and Support Group for scientific affairs in the military area. I study Mathematical Sciences.

José LLanusa, Director of the Institute of Sports, Physical Education and Recreation known by INDER with the rank of Minister, was in contact with Jack Ruby in Dallas, New Orleans and Tampa in October and November of 1963.

The photo was taken in front of the Book Depository, very close to where Pina bet Policarpo Álvarez Pileta, the pilot who would take Oswald, Oswald's supposed double, who would be able to show that Oswald was at the door at the time of the shooting, but the checkered shirt with no pocket showed that it was not Oswald and a character who gave him an alleged epileptic seizure at the time of the passage of the caravan, that everyone would turn their attention and the cameras towards the door and that for several photographers the image of the double of Oswald.

It seems that the epileptic disease was the favorite of Víctor Pina, because also Fabian Escalante, they put within his legend the Epilepsy "Great Evil" so that a doctor "conspired" with the same root as Fabio Grobart, José Cohen, Bernard Barker , Moray, David Ferrie, Rosselli and others more infiltrated by the KGB, he entered for several days at the Jackson Hospital in Miami and there he enjoyed a safe place for contacts or other maneuvers, such as leaving a double in the hospital and moving towards Cuba or another place

Número de registro de NARA: 104-10308-10143
RAUL JAIMO DIAZ ARGUELLES Y GARCIA

The identification of General Raúl Díaz, I was able to establish by the two photos on the far right, is the same, one with the normal negative and the other opposite. The mouth is tilted in both photos for different place, one on the right and one leaning to the left. The same applies to the photo with a beard, where you can see the mouth indicating to the left.

Exposure of the mouth to the opposite side in the photo of the far right is because it is transposed the negative as we can show in the bottom photo, with the letters in the opposite direction and its inclined to the left ...
The border of the hair was taken exaggeratedly backwards, which called attention to Sylvia Odio when Arguelles Days was late in the night accompanied by Lee Harvey Oswald; Sylvia declared it that way in the Police and in the Warren Commission. Diaz Arguelles showed up with Harvey Lee Oswald in Sylvia's apartment to introduce the American who can hit a candle 100 meters away and who was willing to kill JFK.

There is no room for "reasonable doubt", this was Raúl Díaz Arguelles. There is still some doubt if I know who you are with and I will tell you who you are ... then if they were with Lee Harvey Oswald in Dallas ... that could happen to General Escalante, who was a G-2 Commander in Dallas with the President JFK's killer. Tested with the documents of his entry into the United States with Commander Aldo Margolles, identified by Silvia Odio, identified in the photo, greeting President JFK for the last time ... in addition to his stay in Chicago and Tampa.

The Cubans in Havana learned of the location and attitude of Mrs. Odio because she wrote to her father, who was imprisoned in Cuba for an attack on Fidel Castro. The letter must have been intercepted by the State Security.

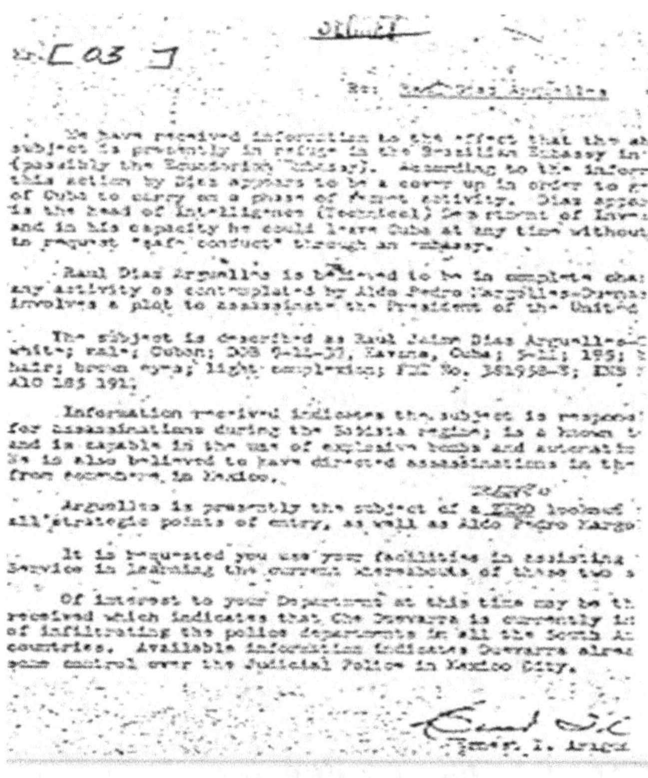

Then they assigned Raúl Díaz Arguelles to include her in this operation to erase the prints. Arguelles posed as two characters, Loran Eugene Helt and Leonardo. Their telephone calls are recorded by both and it could be detected that English was not consistent with their identity.

The visit was intended to leave false fingerprints to involve the Miami Cuban Boys in the death of JFK, playing the anti-Castro role of the Alfa-66 movement, also the declassified documents indicate that the rented houses in Oklahoma and Texas for the operation against JFK, were rented under the name of said organization. The residents of the residences were able to identify the Cubans who occupied these residences and who left the same day of the death of JFK.

Declassified document of the CIA that indicates on the entry of the subject Raúl Díaz Arguelles with Aldo Margolles, penetrated to the United States through some diplomatic documentation in August of 1963.

The Cuban Boy of Havana managed the infiltration of Captain Emilio Aragonés and the commander Raúl Díaz Argüelles visiting the military training facilities in Louisiana, a military unit of the United States Army where Cubans were trained for the invasion of December 1, 1963. Captain José A. Brigade, Pedro members of the 2506 fighters who have not

trained for the invasion of December Pérez San Román, Chief of the Encinosa and Erneido Oliva, Brigade, and other Cuban exile yet been identified.

The

presence
of at least three

*infiltrators of Havana's Cuban Boys inside the camp in apparent role of
visitors along with a high level group leads us to investigate who could
introduce them, under what justification and what purpose they attended*

*this meeting, as well as what type of information the "infiltrators"
eventually obtained in the camp.*

*Fabian Escalante Font aka Gilberto Policarpo Lopez, played epileptic roles
and husband of a "grandmother" in Tampa.*
*Fabián Escalante was born in Tampa, his grandfather with his same name
was Secretary of General Calixto García during the War of Independence.*

*The Escalante family members of the Communist Party lived in Tampa for
more than 130 years. Fabian met Lee Harvey Oswald when the KGB
favored the meeting, when a very select group of Cubans passed a school
of Counter Intelligence in the same city that the Cubans studied.*

*Sergio "Sergito" Escalante is identified as the younger brother of Fabián,
as well as that it was never known that he had suffered from great epilepsy
by Jorge Rodríguez, owner of the Radio Station "La Poderosa y Cadena
Azul", as Antonio Castell also a classmate who was a fellow student of
both brothers in the American school before 1959, Candle College of
Vedado, Cuba and by a doctor who attended him professionally in the
Carlos J.Finlay Military Hospital in Havana and in the CIMEQ, Captain
of SM Noel Gumersindo Villa.*

*The supposed epilepsy was a cloak to cover the days that disappeared from
Tampa and also have a safe place to contact other agents.*

*Dr. Irving Perlmutter was a communist Jewish neurosurgeon who met the
same biographical parameters as Jack Leon Ruby, Bernard Leon Barker,
Davie Ferrie, Mortimer Robson "Morthy", etc. they all served in the
United States Armed Forces to create trustworthy facades, but they were
Marxists.*

*Fabián Escalante Font has never suffered from Grand Mal Epilepsy,
therefore, the doctor facilitated coverage with the disease. Dr. Perlmutter
was a contributor to the Havana's Cuban Boys.*

*General Escalante during the interview of the documentary "Cita con la
Muerte", ironically evades the question whether or not he was in Dallas ...
he replied "There have been so many lies, that you no longer know that it*

is a lie and that it is true ... the American government says who was on the moon and I do not know, because they have said so many lies ... just what he said is true and is very applicable to it, still uses a removable nose as we see in the photo, a wig, glasses, gloves to avoid leave footprints and also pretends to be an epileptic patient, etc ... perhaps the one who gave the epileptic attack when the caravan passed could be Fabian Escalante ... it is perfectly understood the disorders of the self, which can suffer living among so many falsehoods, there are so many lies written in the books to defend his boss that he himself does not know what is true and what is a lie

CIA's Report for Gilberto Lopez

1. Attached are copies of a photograph of Gilberto LOPEZ, U.S. citizen, Subject of reference. This photograph was taken the night of 27 November 1963 at the Mexico City airport by Mexican authorities.

2. As previously reported, Subject secured a fifteen day Mexican tourist card (FM-8-#24,553) at Tampa, Florida, on 20 November 1963. Subject entered Mexico on this document at Nuevo Laredo on 23 November 1963 - the day after President Kennedy's assassination in Dallas, Texas.

3. Subject checked into the Hotel Roosevelt, Avenida Insurgentes 287, Mexico, D.F., at 1600 hours (Mexico City time) on 25 November 1963. He stayed in room 203 at this hotel. At 1900 hours (Mexico City time) on 27 November 1963, Subject checked out of the Hotel Roosevelt and at 2100 hours on 27 November 1963 Subject departed Mexico for Habana.

4. Subject was listed on Cubana Flight #465 of 27 November 1963 as the only passenger. A crew of nine (9) Cubans was listed. On departure from Mexico, Subject used U.S. passport #310,162 which contained a Cuban "Courtesy" visa.

(continued)

Attachment:
Photograph (3)

Distribution:
3 - WH, w/att

Gilberto Lope[

Nariz plástica supuesta utilizada por el General Fabian Escalante Font, el hombre que dice que se han dicho tantas mentiras que no se sabe ahora que es verdad y que es mentira, este es un ejemplo también que primero se coge a un mentiroso que a un cojo. En fotos públicas en los últimos anos….trata de alejarse de su personaje Gilberto Policarpo López.

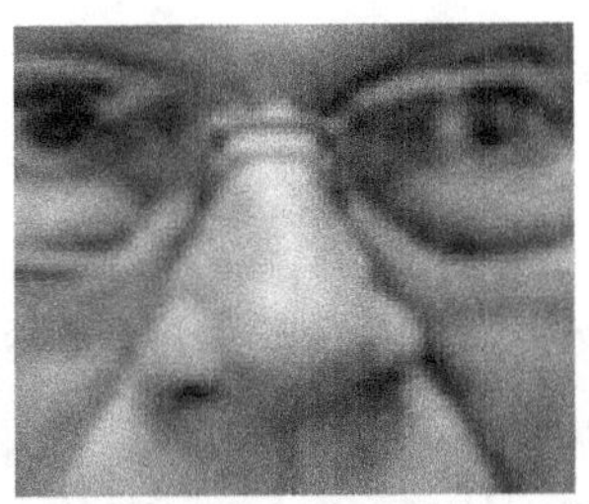

La nariz, pabellón de la oreja esta adherido al espejuelo, y su barbilla o mentón tiene el mismo corte en el centro. La foto de pasaporte del pasajero misterioso del Britannia de Cubana. Llego de Dallas y tomo el avión que lo esperaba. El Capitan Fabian Escalante junto a Policarpo Alvarez quien aparece en la foto al lado de la puerte del Deposito de Libros en el momento que la caravana de JFK gira frente al edificio estaba supuesto a evacuar a Lee Harvey Oswald de Dallas junto a Quintín Pino Machado, algo sucedió que no pudo ser como estaba planificado con auto con letreros del Partido Republicano apoyando a

Many officers have told Fabian not to use false noses anymore, including Colonel Fisin, who adjusts it to the CIMEQ ... but he does not hear advice.

Captain Fabian Escalante (1963) was supposed to evacuate Lee Harvey Oswald from Dallas with Quentin Pino Machado, Grossi Knoll was evacuated from visitors by double agent Bernard Barker.

Bernard Barker, Cuban infiltrator in the CIA who used a Secret Service ID and was officially identified by the Dallas Sheriff, something happened that could not be as planned with the car with signs of the Republican Party supporting Goldwater who was parked behind Deadly Plaza, near the

train line. Then they went to Plan B, shut up Harvey Oswald, already arrested.

Some authors have elaborated hypotheses that Oswald did not use the shirt to identify him, but this identification could be appropriate for the police officer Tippit, who drove a patrol car, if there was any link between them and the JFK murder.

Which after reading a lot of the information available about Tippit, there does not seem to be any kind of plot, nor Tippit's death, it makes sense, because if Tippit had the mission to kill Oswald, he never took out the weapon and walked around his car, without any gesture indicating his willingness to take out his weapon, only to identify a suspect with whom he did not want to use the weapon. Many witnesses from the apartment building and the bus stop clearly saw the scene.

The residence from which Oswald left was rented by the organization "anti castro Alfa-66" led at that time by Antonio Veciana, the great matador with the "impossible mission" and neighbors saw Oswald enter with a curtain where he wrapped his rifle to transport it by bus days before.

Oswald's shirt appeared in the parking lot of a car dealer. For the Cubans, especially for Fabián Escalante, such a shirt would not be necessary, since Oswald and Fabián had known each other for years before in the city of Minsk, USSR.

On the validity of this information there is documentary evidence that, in addition, they were in contact in Tampa since January 1963

The Soviet flag in years 1959 – 1961 in the room is unmistakable sign that this office was a very special place only for those who were in those years, former members of the clandestine of the PSP, these Soviet flags were only in the premises without access for civilians inside the offices of the Department of State Security, this is one of the office in 5th, Ave and 14th. Street in Miramar, Headquarter of Department of State Security, which Antonio Veciana has never declared ... he has said he worked for Julio Lobo and the Ministry of Internal Trade. However, his retroactive behavior shows that always, Veciana and his family in Spain were communists.

Close to Veciana the Commander Raul Diaz Arguelles, Captain Jose Abrantes, some time after, he was a Minister of Interior and the Chief of Pinar del Rio Department of State Security G-2. IN the corner of the office, the Soviet Union's flag.

There are many makeups throughout this operation that we are going to discover but there are some that even more than 50 years after the fact, they continue to use makeup and deformations of the body such as Eloy, Fabián Escalante's case ...

In the next photo we find the Consul of
Cuba in Mexico, Eusebio López (Víctor Pina) inside the Dallas Police Office, just as the shots fired against Oswald. Also made-up and balding ...

also discovered beyond the unacceptable lie ... of General Escalante.

Captain Víctor Pina Cardoso, the Colonel and Master of the KGB,

architect of this difficult plot of events. His false name as the Consul in Mexico Eusebio López Azcue. Supervising how Jack Ruby closes the mouth of Harvey Lee Oswald inside the Police Office in Dallas, Texas.

Captain Víctor Pina Cardoso, was also a Kommandeur der Division der deutschen Armee, also Colonel (KGB) Dahud, in addition Captain Alberto, his mantle as Consul was reinforced by José Ricardo Rabel, whom he had prepared for his desertion in the Aviation Section of Peasant Housing and is recruited by the CIA, at the proposal of the CIA Bernard Barker.

Captain Rabel (debrifing) in making his debut in the United States, ratifies "the identity of López Azcue as an architect devoted to rebuilding the homes destroyed by the Batista dictatorship", which reaffirms his loyalty to Castro, as a double agent . Rabel worked in Cuba with the rank of Captain and pilot of the executive airplanes at the service of "Viviendas Campesinas" he was obliged to know the high rank of Víctor Pina in the Intelligence and in general on all the Aviation, both civil and military after 1959

In March of 1963, Víctor Pina began to perform as the Consul of Cuba in Mexico, and his constant trips to Cuba because he remained in his other functions of Government. Captain José Ricardo Rabel returns clandestinely to Cuba once JFK was assassinated.

The Rural Housing Aviation Section of INRA was a "screen institution" of the Department of State Security to move its "operatives" of Intelligence to third countries in the Caribbean and Central America or within Cuba, in practice the chief was the Captain Pina, who during those years was the Chief of the entire apparatus of State Security and Civil and Military Aviation.
Behind the Constellation Super G of Cubana de Aviación, there were three small buildings, Meteorology that on its roof is the sleeve that indicates the prevailing wind, a small office of CAISA Fuel and then a hangar of corrugated aluminum sheets with space for two or three light airplanes where Peasant Housing worked.

Víctor Pina, who supposedly had left for Cuba from Mexico on November 21, found him in Dallas in a photo taken by NBC, as a person similar to Jack Ruby in the role of "interpreter of Hebrew" without credentials but in reality he was the Supervisor or emergency hit of Jack Ruby, on his mission to close Oswald's mouth inside the Police Office in Dallas, Texas.

The behavior of Jack Ruby, highlights a conscience and a discipline as required by the Communist Party, commissioned by a prominent figure of the regime as Commander Ernesto Guevara, this happened in a clandestine contact in Panama, a few weeks before. This meeting served as a positive reinforcement stimulus and this interview is recorded in the book titled "Che Compañero" by Jorge Castañeda, a Mexican communist who was the
Minister of Foreign Affairs of Mexico, since he took it from official sources and files in Cuba, according to the fountain.

Víctor Pina (Eugenio López Azcue) Cuba / KGB Head of Technical

Operations of the Department of State Security (G-2) inside the Dallas Police Office when Jack Ruby shot Lee Harvey Oswald. NBC Picture. This photo is conclusive evidence of Cuba's participation in Eloy last step of the operation of the assassination of President JFK.

In the photo. The "amplitude of the back" of Víctor Pina stands out, contributed by the shoulders of the sack, similar reinforcement of the width of his body, equal to the one used with a guayabera, at the time of his arrest by Lt. Colonel Esteban Ventura Novo during the strike of April 9, 1958 in Havana.

The magazine "Life", who makes the report identifies him as an operative of international communism, but incredibly, he is not identified with his true identity being an official of the Civil Aeronautics Commission of Cuba, and head of the Department of Aeronautical Licenses and not was identified by the authorities, he presented credentials and the personality of a French journalist and also very effeminate in their gestures and voice inflections. Very different from his real personality.

Pina had confessed this specific event and many years later Commander Jaime Costa reaffirms it with a spontaneous testimony when he saw the photo of Pina with Ventura when he was arrested, but this contact resulted

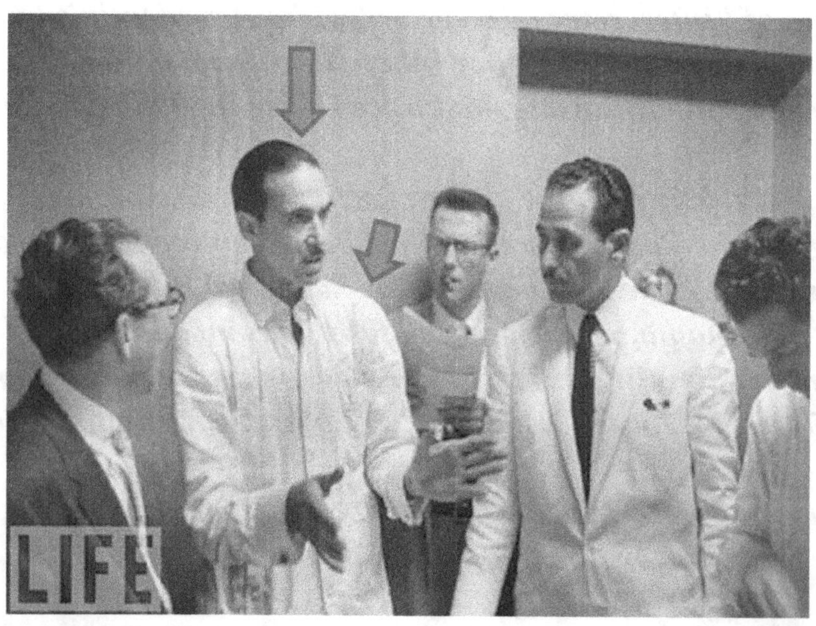

in convincing the "alleged torturer" Tte. Colonel Esteban Ventura Novo, cousin of the Commandant and member of the Political Bureau José Ramon Machado Ventura, also proposed as a guarantee for his physical integrity

*the presence of José Pardo LLada, later turned into Castro's influence
agent, planted in Colombia,*
*this is confirmed his encounter with Castro at the end of his days, like Eloy
Gutiérrez Menoyo, as there are others in exile with the same mission. With
the difference that appears in the list of spies of the DIA, in this same book*

*. In the interview, Castro proposes to kill Fulgencio Batista and then
appoint him provisional president, until, the restoration of democracy
through elections.*

*The meeting was held in La Plata at 3 am after a day and a half of waiting
hidden in a mountain valley where Comandante Costa kept them to protect
them, the meeting ended at 7 in the morning in April 1958. Castro sent
Ramiro Valdés away because he wanted to kill Esteban Ventura Novo.
Commander Costa is detailed in the interview recorded for that purpose.
The blue arrows in the photo indicate the parts of the body that were
altered to avoid their identification, width of shoulders over dimensioned
with the shoulder pads of the guayabera, and the entrance of the hair as
well as the straight hair that in fact Víctor Pina had him frizzy.*

*The National Identity Directorate of the Judicial Police seems to have had
Víctor Pina with fingerprints or false fingerprints. He could never be
identified. Something really significant, as well as his long absences from
work in the Civil Aeronautics Commission of Cuba.*

*In addition to speaking 6 languages, Pina was able to adopt different
personalities, such as dyslexic, sick, "crazy", invalido, deaf and dumb, etc.*

*From the complete event that began with his capture described in details in
an interview recorded to former Commander Jaime Costa, a direct
participant of these events will appear in the book The Sovietization of
Cuba and its consequences of the author.*

An NBC journalist took a picture of an unidentified person in the Dallas Police Office room and wrote that someone was trying to be confused with Jack Ruby and said he was a Hebrew interpreter who had not found anyone who had it. hired. It was as we see Victor Pina Cardoso, who left Mexico four days earlier and supposedly replaced

in his position by Miraval, his departure from Mexico officially justified because his son Victor Pina Tabio was ill in Havana. The whole scene was to justify his presence in Dallas, Texas. How can we compare the profile of Victor Pina with Jack Ruby and there are very few coincidences.

The photo of the bottom line of the extreme left was taken on January 10, 1959 during Ed Sullivan's interview for US TV, the photo of the center on November 24, 1963. It is difficult for a natural baldness to advance, other photos 10 years later in the official photo of the Warren Commission when he gave his testimony it seems again with all its lush hair that always kept.

NBC took on November 24, 1963 at 10:34 p.m. The image and they wrote that some Jewish journalist was posing as Jack Ruby. He is not a Jewish journalist; He is really a Cuban boy from Havana, Captain Victor Pina Cardoso, the Master and boss of this Operation.

The photo on the right is Jack Ruby and the photo on the left is Victor Pina with hair. Identified by Ed Prida.

Víctor Pina Cardoso Official of the KGB, Nicolai Leonov Official of the KGB appointed by Nikita Khrushchev in Moscow to supervise Operation Jovenzuelo and Raúl Castro.

Photo taken on board the Italian ship during the return to Havana, two weeks before the assault on the Moncada barracks. Raül Castro was arrested for bringing documents and propaganda from the USSR. Nicolai Leonov and Víctor Pina threw themselves into the water and were rescued by José Abantes' father and taken to a port warehouse.

Nicolai Leonov remained in Cuba hidden in a cave discovered by Ing. Antonio Núñez Jiménez, clandestine militant of the Communist Party of Cuba and president of INRA after 1959. The cave is located in Menocal, Matanzas. Years later, this point became the alternative and secret Central Command Post of the Armed Forces of Cuba, when Diocles Torralba was Chief of General Staff of the FAR. According to Comandante Jaime Costa, very close to where Fidel and a group of his gang executed Camilo Cienfuegos.

The assault plan for the Moncada barracks with Eloy uniform of the National Army had an aggregate force of 600 armed Hispanic Soviets camped on the Soria ship in Santiago de Cuba. The objective was to simulate that the massacre of the population had been the work of the Army to demoralize the Batista government, the false soldiers had identification and spoke Spanish, if they were taken prisoners they would have identification of the Army so that the press could create confusion.

The death toll demanded by Nikita was more than 10,000 people. The late arrival of Fidel Castro made abort the original Plan of the Soviets. This within the Subversion Plan is the stage for Demoralization

As of July 1953, the Soviets were directing through Nicolai Leonov how and when any movement should be made. Everything was guided by Víctor Pina and Nicolai Leonov.

We identify and highlight the story of these characters because they will appear on the scene of JFK's death. We will see these two characters in all the important events and in others that there is no photographic record.

Until the time of writing these notes, Nicolai Leonov is the adviser and direct contact of Raúl Castro with the government of Vladimir Putin. Leonov reached the rank of Second Chief of the KGB with the rank of General and is also a member of the Russian Parliament and Advisor to Vladimir Putin for the affairs of Cuba. He wrote a biography of Raul Castro recently and distributed only to party militants, as in his previous accounts everything is masking the scam and the betrayal of the USSR to the Cubans.

Victor Pina from the year 1967 was abruptly removed from power and returned to his apartment where he always lived and with his V W yellow that we will see in Mexico. He died in 2005, being the man most watched by Section KJ, special section of the Military Counter Intelligence, according to testimony of Lt. Colonel Orlando Mayeta, former Chief of the KJ of the Military Counter Intelligence, of Germany, went to Canada where he requested exile and then moved to Miami. Mayeta abandoned communist ideology and was assassinated in Miami by the CIM. His wife

*and children suffered cruel treatment from Colonels Gil and Socorro, of
the Counter Intelligence of the Air Force*

The KGB colonel Nikolai Leonov was inside Cuba

*clandestinely from a week before July 26, 1953, later in the cave, other
times in Cayo Coco and in this picture with Raul Castro in Sierra Cristal in
1958, on January First, 1959 he was in the Hotel Sevilla,Havana, before
he visited the Sierra Maestra with Alexei Alexeiev many times. Sometimes
it was infiltrated by Soviet submarines the same for Manzanillo as for the
Bay of Nipe.*

*Leonov will be involved in the two subversive operations applied in Cuba
by the USSR. The commander Raul Castro and the KGB Nicolai Leonov in
Sierra Cristal, Cuba, 1958. The Soviet intelligence had total control of the
actions of the alleged Rebel Army. The operations of the guerrilla and its
logistics planned by the KGB years before.*

Commander Pedro Luis Díaz Lanz, former Chief of the Rebel Air Force witnessed what was "3 Soviet officers infiltrated the Nipe Bay from the Soviet submarine and returned by the same route 3 days later". His testimony along with that of Edward Whitehouse is in the archives of the United States Congress.

As you can see, Nicolai Leonov started as KGB supervisor appointed by Nikita Khrushchev on July 14, 1953 for the assault on the Moncada Barracks, then in Mexico preparing the expedition of Granma, in the Sierra Maestra, Missile Crisis in 1962, the March 5, 1963 in Moscow in the decision to assassinate JFK. As part of the Soviet Embassy in Mexico, leading the operation with Captain Víctor Pina Cardoso (Eugenio López Azcue) with other KGB Colonels stationed in Washington and Havana.

Nicolai Leonov is still the main "political adviser" of Raúl Castro and Alejandro Castro Espín. For the Soviets or the Russians, a "political adviser" is the chain of command between Moscow and Havana.

AP Photo

For a long time these images had been seen by thousands or millions of people ... Only Havana's Cuban Boys in Dallas knew what would happen after this moment ... in the background, first of all Captain Emilio Aragonés, on his back Commander Aldo Margolles and on the right Commander Abelardo "Furry" Colomé Ibarra. Why are you watching the caravan of cars with a smile for the camera?

Commander Abelardo Colomé in the upper left, Captain Emilio Aragonés with the red arrow and Aldo Margolles in the back. Do you need more evidence to consider that Khrushchev and Castro prepared the operation to kill JFK?

There are thousands of documents, photos and logical arguments that demonstrate the direct participation in four attempts of attack, the first in Washington with the commander Juan Moleón Cabrera and the first lieutenant Quintín Pino Machado, the second in the Chicago stadium by Aldo Margolles, Raúl Díaz Argüelles, Emilio Aragonés and Abelardo Colomé Ibarra. The third was in Tampa, FL, by Captain Fabián Escalante Font, Aldo Margolles and Raúl Díaz Argüelles.
Desinformación exclusiva, derroche de picardía cubana, hay que reconocerlo.

In this historical photo, it is striking that some people, including Secret Service officers, turn their gaze to a special stimulus, and it is a person with an epileptic seizure, but this fact was prepared by Víctor Pina, to draw attention to the door where a man with physical resemblance to Harvey Oswald and the photographer hired has the justification to focus his camera to the event and it seems as if Oswald was accidentally taken at the door and therefore, Oswald was not the executor of the shots, if it is at the door, it was later discovered that although they had similar shirts, that of the man at the door, he had no pocket.

The recovery of the details of this photo, thanks to Professor Larry Rivera, years later by digital means, gave me the possibility that Eloy ex Cor.

Alfredo Lima, pilot of the Air Force of Cuba and former political prisoner for 15 years, my classmate, without a doubt we identified Captain Policarpo Álvarez Pileta, a Cuban pilot who would pick up Oswald to take him to the Dallas airport in a "possible" direction. Mexico or the base of San Julián, west of Cuba.

Finally, in Dallas, Texas, by Quintín Pino Machado, Abelardo Colomé Ibarra, Aldo Margolles, Fabián Escalante and Captain Víctor Pina. If you want to know more details, read "Cuban boys of Havana in Dallas", I offer you to know the details of the Master Plan, who, how and why Castro and Nikita killed JFK. This is not fiction, photos, documents and history that are known about Castro's forces in the United States of America.

The man in the doorway identified
By Larry Rivera © 11/06/15

In the photo you can easily identify Policarpo Álvarez Piletas. The Cuban pilot and member of the Cuban Air Force. He died in Angola War.

\

For some researchers, the man with the hat and scarf on his back is Jack Ruby. "I was with Jack Ruby and he was standing at the corner of the post office building in front of the Texas school bookstore building at the time of the shooting. Immediately after the shooting, Ruby left and went to the Dallas Morning News Building area, "the document continues.

Others have placed Ruby in the nearby Dallas Morning News building that day, but Vanderslice may be the first to place him among the crowd that actually testifies to the murder.

Ruby, they have links with the members of Havanan's Cuban Boys as we saw 20 years ago, but in Dallas at the time of the murder he had invited this FBI member to see "fireworks", beyond his undisputed role as the murderer of Oswald. You can easily identify Jack Ruby with shade and Policarpo Alvarez Pileta.

The newly published records do not speculate on whether Ruby used the "fireworks" reference as an innocent metaphor for "hoopla," or something more sinister.

Ruby did not say anything immediately after the shooting, Vanderslice told the agents. This was Eloy exchange of words between Ruby and informant Bob Vanderslice of Dallas on Nov. 22, 1963. This was not known until April, 1977 after an interview with NBC.

The Cuba's Delegation to the Murder of JFK

It seems that Castro sent a delegation to dismiss JFK and Nikita another delegation for a football game in honor of JFK, perhaps if we only have these photos anyone could present this elementary hypothesis. But hundreds of documents from the CIA, FBI, rent of houses, hotel accommodations, makeup, infiltrated Cuba in the CIA and four attacks on President JFK, it would not be easy to justify hi mong this group there are Viceministers of MinInt, officers with the rank of Commanders and a hierarchy of the Party like Emilio Aragonés, does not have many reasons to be of good will in the place of the fact. With these photos it seems that many conspiracy theories involving the CIA against President JFK, will not have much to explain ... This is Commander Raúl Díaz Arguelles, behind Commander Abelardo
Colomé Ibarra, Commander Aldo Margolles Dueñas and Captain Emilio Aragonés, National Coordinator of the ORI. In the group, an unidentified Soviet with a nose and glasses, his hair masked in black.

General Escalante insists on demonstrating that Antonio Veciana, Bernard Barker, José Ricardo Rabel, others were at the crime scene or in Dallas at this time, and it is true, they were in Dallas because they were agents of Cuba, not because the CIA had intention to kill JFK.

There were agents of the FBI, Police, Fire, CIA were fulfilling their functions within the territory of the United States. What is not causal and beyond the reasonable doubt is that the Cuban officers who entered American territory without legal documentation, were in link with Jack Ruby and Lee Harvey Oswald for months and then we found Victor Pina supervising the death of Lee Harvey Oswald inside the Dallas Police office.

Thanks for this strong affirmation. They even had rented houses in the name of the organization that founded Veciana, Alfa-66.

Nor does Eloy General Escalante remember that exactly at the time of Oswald's shot, his "Tavarich" from Minsk and Tampa, are the commanders
Abelardo Colomé Ibarra, Raul Diaz Arguelles, Aldo Margolles and Captain Emilito Aragonés, accompanied by Lady Babuska, the Russian make-up artist, who put hair on Emilio Aragonés. You do not remember, neither from your false nose when leaving through the airport in Mexico.

The "Moscow-Havana's Boys in Mexico and Dallas"

Coronel KGB
Nicolai
Leonov
•Coronel Nikolai
Leonov
•Coronel Oleg
Nachiporenko
•Coronel Georgi
Bolshakov
•Coronel Valery
Kostikov
•Coronel Pavel
Yatzov
•Coronel Yuri
Montinsky

I could not miss Nicolai Leonov in all the fateful history related to the USSR and Cuba against the United States in the Soviet Embassy in Mexico on November 22, 1963 at the The Soviet assassin team played football in the backyard of the Soviet Embassy in the City from Mexico at 12:30 pm on November 22, 1963. Why were the KGB / GRU colonels of service in Washington and Havana playing soccer in Mexico City? They take the picture just at the time of the murder, check it with the position of the shadow of the midday sunlight. All happy, the Russians usually ake the serious photos 12:30 pm. presence as a simple tourist visit to see the President up close JFK.

Many Cubans know that this yellow V VV car was owned by Captain Víctor Pina for many years, it was transported by an Antonov AN-12 from Cubana de Aviación to Mexico City. Captain Pina drove this car until General Raúl Castro presented him with a 600 cc FIAT Polsky as a replacement in 1985. I drove this V W many times when Captain Pina visited my house in Rancho Boyeros.

Colonel Valery Kostikov of Section Z of the KGB, known as "kill 7". I was waiting for the "news" on the Radio of the car on November 22, 1963 at 12:30 p.m. in Mexico City.
Notice the shadow exactly at 12:00
Proof of them all knew what would happen in Dallas with JFK.
Two Lady "Babuskas", only one known
The Cuban government will have some answer beyond the "unreasonable lies" with signs of admiration, with this photo. Fabián, American, he born in Tampa, who refused to comply with the Mandatory Military Service in the United States, where he was born, who passed himself off as an epileptic and entered Miami's Jackson Hospital, thanks to another Communist who served him as a doctor, that he wrote to his brother Sergito, that he married a Puerto Rican lady in Tampa, who could be his grandmother, he will have to write the seventh book to invent an argument, well you are completely naked, calm that everything is known ... surrender. All roads lead to Rome, despite the amount of obstacles and false signals that were put on the road, there are always errors, there are no perfect crimes that seems above all to be a Law of Divine Order, more than a Law of Men .

Two Babauskas Ladies in Dallas

Newly arrived girls from Moscow, did not want to be contaminated ideologically with American fashion and they did not give them money to buy American clothes and dressed in the typical Russian dress and not even Moscow, rather it is a Ukrainian-type clothes, in this form of mantle on the head.

But we can say that there are two Ladies Babuskas, the main hitherto unknown and cannot be the same because the photo of the first Lady Babuska to pass the car of JFK, is not accompanied by four tall men and dressed in suits.

All Cubans are with hair dyed black, Emilio Aragonés has fake hair and dyed black and the other three men were light brown hair, they also have black hair, we can think as we have said, that the lady who accompanies them was the technique of disfiguring faces. In the years following the event, many people who were present were identified, perhaps trying to divert the attention of real

"individuals", leaving false and confusing traces.

The first identified Lady Babuska is dressed in the Russian style standing on the grass between Elm and Main Streets, photographing the moment they shot JFK, with a male body position. Because it had rained earlier that morning, some women in Dealey Plaza wore headscarves; but the rain had stopped at 10 a.m., as we know the shots were at 12:30 p.m.

I have found, several events of disinformation in the area of projectile impacts, there is the epileptic attack in front of the door of the Book Store, just in Eloy moment that a Secret Service car passes, which in the form of exploration makes the trajectory 5 minutes before where JFK was actually transported:
First: A man physically similar to Oswald at the door, wearing a shirt similar to the one Oswald wore, so that the photographer hired take a "casual incident" a man with an epileptic seizure in the grown and on the scene. Second: In the main door, Lee Harvey Oswald appeared and with this make the defense that Oswald could not be in two places at once, shooting and in the main door, but one detail saves the Truth, the shirt was the same but the double of the door had no pocket in the shirt.
Third: The Havana's Cuban Boy José LLanusa Gobel is in the area.
Fourth: Policarpo Álvarez Pileta, waving militarily at the passage of the caravan and very cheerful.
Fifth: Jack Ruby is next to Policarpo Alvarez.

Coincidentally s these events are in the stretch where even JFK was alive, from this point to the hospital they had nothing prepared. In addition, the photographer hired appeared dead in his room a few days later. All this incident will be more detailed in the next book.

It has never been seen that images took the alleged camera, which could well have been a pointing device of reinforcement for Oswald was more accurate in his shots or a camera capable of at least two shots.

The Cubans and the other Soviet, did not have optical or photographic instruments in their hands, although their glasses and artificial nose are evident. It seems strange, that the Babuska of the Cuban group, with typical Russian clothes and sunglasses, would not have been taken into account by so many amateur researchers, even with an atypical group, four men and one woman.

A visitor from Dallas, former star of Jack Ruby's Cabaret Carousel, Marie Muchmore (which has become one of the main chronicles of that day), at Eloy Zapruba Film the Babuska is at 0:41 seconds, behind a man , Charles Brehm, and his 5 year old son, Joe.

We can only see his back, a long tan coat, his hands are on his face and his legs are open as if waiting for a force of a shot.
At that time there was no synchronization of clocks by satellite or other form, for this reason the times of the photographic shots are slightly altered. Another visitor was Mark Bell, Babuska appears at 0:47 after the shooting and the cars accelerate. With his back to the camera, he walks towards the center of the street to the grass mound. She is untouched standing and the others are running or are stuck to the ground.
Zapruder, the front shot at 0:37, but his camera is hidden and his face is blurred.
The Soviets have a tactic to close the stories, but still nothing is perfect. Seven years later, a friend of Jack Ruby and who knew Oswald, as a member of the CIA, a cloak that were using the group of Bernard Barker, Manuel Artime, David Ferrie, Eloy Gutiérrez Menoyo, Antonio Veciana and José Ricardo Rabel as members of an Anti Castro Plan.
The beautiful Beverly Oliver claims to have taken a view of the crime with a Yashica Super 8 camera, and argues that two FBI agents took her camera. that Oswald was a member of the CIA.
A liar is detected faster than a lame man, Beverly at age 17 did not have the sturdy body of Lady Babuska, the Yashica Super 8 camera was on sale after 1966. It is clear to me that Beverly received an order for blackmail or money to get involved in these statements, somewhat absurd and that the press has given so much importance for so many years, is significant.
It is obvious to reinforce Lady Babuska or to discredit her, it is really to end the "concept" of the participation of the Soviets in the JFK case and in fact, not to draw more attention in the future on the other Babuska, that if she was in that group by a tactical error or they were to reinforce Oswald's mission to kill JFK, and the accurate shots did not need such support, which could have been with explosives, nerve gases, tear gas, suffocating, etc. Nor is the Havana's Cuban Boys group justified in the place of the act as mere spectators.
The hypothesis about the participation of Cubans and Soviets, with the appearance of a ridiculous affirmation of Beverly, has the purpose of

causing the attention to drop on the event, since she did not have to volunteer to appear involved when she met Jack and Oswald, and even always the dark CIA is involved by the enemies, to discredit as they always have.

Ref.:
Analysis of the author of declassified documents
Author's files
Conversations and the Testimony of Captain Víctor Pina (Eusebio López Azcue, Consul of Cuba in Mexico in 1963) Colonel of the KGB.
Conversations with Rolando Barros
Conversations with commander Jaime Costa
Photos and Documents donated by Víctor Pina since 1982, copied in the Photography Section of the IACC authorized by Commander José Álvarez Bravo.
Photos and declassified documents of the CIA had exhibited in Eloy chapter.

Chapter 9

Cuba is factor of the destabilization

 The Brheznev's Doctrine

**The Warsaw Pact aimed at invading Europe, during
the 70s and deploy a gigantic force of Armored
Troops
with the support of medium-range missiles (less than 3417.5 miles) of
mobile location than NATO baptized with the code SS-20.**

**The propaganda of the left parties was aimed at making
 NATO members will refuse to defend their defenses. Clearly,
If this happened, the Soviet Union would have an easy victory in its
endeavor to take himself, all to Eurasian continent.**

**The subversive Soviet measures ran through the
organizations unions, students and academics putting**

*millions of young people in demonstrations of protests so that
there was no Parity of Nuclear Forces in the European
continent.*

*Cuba's participation after the Festival of Youth
and the Students (1978) increased the activity of the
"pacifists" in Holland, Italy, Belgium and Germany, who had
the thesis of accept Soviet superiority on the Continent
because the Socialism represented World Peace.*

*These confusing messages created conflicts in domestic politics in
Germany. Then the German Chancellor Helmut Schmidt proposes in 1977
that The United States will negotiate with the USSR an agreement on the
"Euromisiles" or, in case of not reaching a commitment, that the United
States deployed missiles in Western Europe compensate for the imbalance
caused by the location of SS-20 in the countries of socialist Europe.*

*NATO in 1979, takes the "double decision" if the USSR does not
withdrew its SS-20 missiles the NATO would deploy 572 missiles
Pershing type and Cruises in the territories From Great Britain,
Belgium, Holland, Italy and RFA.*

*Then, the wise President Reagan proposed the "Option Zero" is The
withdrawal of the SS-20 in exchange for not deploying the Pershing
missiles and Cruise ships. After many negotiations, the USSR abandons
the negotiating table in October 1983.*

*The following four years were typical of the protests they increased by days
and It take the government of Germany towards
Internal crisis. The struggle between the pro-Soviet and the realist, the
center-right German under the leadership Helmut Kohl ended with the
signing of a Treaty between the USSR and the United States, eliminating
missiles from Mid Range SS-20 and the Pershing and Cruises.*

*The crisis ended in 1987 with the signing of the Soviet-North Treaty
American that eliminated the nuclear missiles of Intermediate Range in
Europe.*

The energy crisis resulting from the amount of expenditure on forces armored vehicles, submarines, aircraft, etc. and induced errors such as search of the energy solution in Siberia, a spectacular plan of pipelines and gas pipelines, without even finding the fuel sources and giant gas with the Baikal-Amur Train took the economy to ruin internal, and the readjustment, dismantled in fact and right, its system economic and political had only one possibility with his Economy and Politics Forces centralized, the structure of the government would come down when two lines of reforms: restructuring (perestroika) and transparency (glasnost).

The Soviet Union faced dangerous reforms for the stability of The totalitarian regimes and the rest of the countries of the Warsaw Pact, who in full rejected the changes because they lost their power.

Castro maintained his Minister of Foreign Affairs Isidoro Malmierca, for months visiting the countries of the socialist camp trying to make some patch or a conspiracy that was able to stop the reform movement in the USSR, "Coup d'État or an attack on Mikhail Gorbachev" both events were executed but did not give the expected result.

The coup d'etat and the ninth man of the coup d'état arrived It was Fidel Castro, who prepared a toast in the lounge in advance protocol with the Minister of Justice of the USSR, who had been the coordinator of the event, for Monday night, just on the date of the so-called "Hand Strike" to stop the collapse of the USSR with the diplomatic support of the rest of the countries Socialists

The tanks took Moscow. Mikhail Gorbachev, under Domiciliary Arrest in the Crimean Peninsula. With this event, the Union Soviet suffered a change. But Hundreds of thousands of citizens went to streets of Moscow and Leningrad to defend their expected freedoms.

The newly elected Russian president, Boris Yeltsin, gave an incendiary speech on the war tank before the parliamentary seat.

On the third day of the coup collapsed, and the conspirators fled. Gorbachev returned. The clumsiness of the coup leaders helped, especially the victory of his rival Gorbachev.

And the conspirators did nothing but advance the fall of the empire Soviet, what they really wanted to prevent.

Castro Armed with Nuclear and Chemical Weapons
This left Castro, with weapons of mass destruction, with his a new Scam campain, "The War of the Whole People", which guaranteed even in absentia of the USSR a solid nuclear shield and internally a system Repressive and Incalculable Ofensive Power. Castro now, he is not thinking in defense, he was thinking in offensive. When he said…"I'm a poisoned lamb"….

Castro assassinated his subordinates to clean the international argument of the Cuba's Drug trafficking.

The only conceivable explanation seems to be linked to a minor condition in the INF treaty that allows what is called "exhibition of museum pieces" of the SS 20, configured for viewing in a disarmed deployment. But the treaty requires a full consultation of the Soviet government with the United States before putting any weapon on public display. A US official stated, "He told us that there is absolutely nothing that justifies the explanation of the "museum article".

This same little-known condition was used by the Soviets and Cubans when a medium-range missile SS 4 banned by the treaty was anchored on Cuban soil near the coastal land in front of the Naval Hospital in Alamar, as a "reminder" of the October Crisis or the Missiles, there was a strong objection from the United States, the location of the rocket as a monument angered the Bush administration. The real reason for the "monument" was the arrival in Cuba of another 25 missiles that were located in La Campana, Escambray and others in the area of Florence in Ciego de Avila.

When the Soviet Ministry of Foreign Affairs told the United States that

Moscow wanted to send an SS 4 to Cuba for that purpose, the State Department protested. Despite the INF treaty, he said, even a tourist missile, capable of firing warheads against the United States, would damage relations with the Soviets and generate a strong political reaction on the part of US politicians, particularly conservative Republicans. The episode has never been widely publicized.

The then Soviet Foreign Minister, Eduard Shevardnadze assured the United States in July that no SS-20 would be sent to Cuba. The missiles were already located in Cuba, when they were asking permission to put the clause of the INF Treaty to leave some for museum or study as a teaching material base.

Six months later, in December, the Soviet General Staff surreptitiously sent the missile to Cuba and established itself as a "museum piece". It is believed that Shevardnadze's position on this issue, and his swift dismissal by the military, was one of the factors that contributed to his resignation, when he warned about the upcoming Soviet dictatorship. Eduard Shavardnaze on his visit to Cuba was put aboard the plane a few servings of lobster Termidor and charged by order of Fidel Castro $ 100,000 by the food. Shevarnadze ordened to send this lobster to the waste: I ate part of this lobster. The Il62M flew without foods to Moscow.

The discovery of the SS-20 is a much more dangerous issue for SovietAmerican relations. It comes at a time of apprehension about the growing power of the military within a Soviet system that seems destined to stop. However, the latest CIA studies suggest that the great country, divided by the divisive issue of nationality, a bankrupt economy and the collapse of Gorbachev's reform programs, continues to produce strategic weapons, including mobile missiles, that eclipse everything that is produced in the United States. In fact, it is likely that Congress will not fund a mobile missile in the next year for a US strategic force that does not yet have one of them.

Unreported elements of this surprising attention to military power have been observed in Cuba, along with the discovery of one or more SS 20. A new unit of signal intelligence (SIGINT) has been located both by observation in the field and by spy photography -satélite near Havana. The military garrison surrounding the naval base at Guantánamo Bay of the US Navy. UU It has been reinforced with the incorporation of several thousand new Cuban troops.

More ominous are the intelligence findings that suggest that Cuba, with Soviet backing, could be developing a nuclear reactor capable of producing armament fuel in a new facility near Cienfuegos, the same area in which one or more SS 20 have been placed. Illegal The Soviets have long had a suspicious installation of manipulating nuclear warheads to arm their strategic nuclear submarines

Declassified document of the CIA on the SS-20 as a forecast of the location of the missiles in Cuba:

This issue was discussed in 1988. This telephone conversation was very strong and must be recorded in the White House. I was able to read it in the Chicago Tribune archive and comments on this serious crisis, wrote journalist Robert Novak in the Washington Post.

MEMORANDUM FOR: Chairman, NIC

FROM   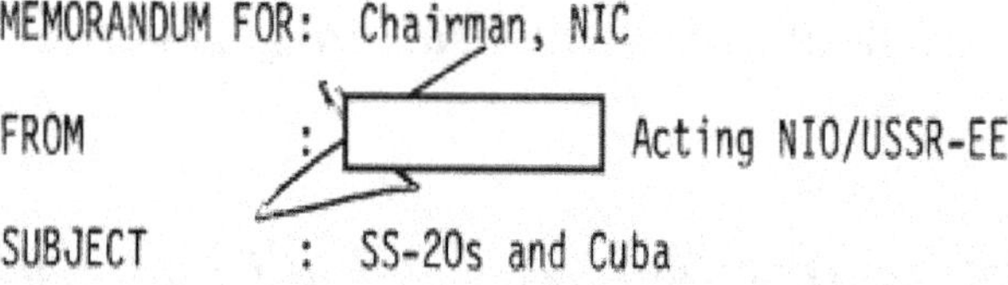   Acting NIO/USSR-EE

SUBJECT   : SS-20s and Cuba

1. <u>Thesis</u>.

    I believe that the Soviets are positioning themselves to be able to
deploy SS-20s to Cuba on short notice. The primary purposes of such a move,
should they decide upon it, would be to prevent US INF deployment in Western
Europe and to weaken the Atlantic alliance.

2. <u>Supporting Evidence</u>:

    A. <u>SS-20s</u>. They have been or are being modified for tropical
        climates, i.e., for deployment outside the USSR.

    B. <u>Political Preparation</u>: In discussions (most recently on ABC TV,
        Sunday, 14 February) Soviet representatives have been arguing
        that the 1962 Cuban missile crisis was resolved by having the
        USSR withdraw its missiles in exchange for a withdrawal of US
        IRBMs from Europe (Thors from Turkey).

    C. <u>Military Developments in Cuba</u>: Over the last year the Soviets
        have upgraded their military representative to a 3-star general
        [   ]
        [   ] They have also increased their
        military deliveries to the Cuban forces, and given particular
        emphasis to Cuban air defense capabilities (<u>inter alia</u> by the
        delivery of SA-6 and additional MIG-23s, which improve the Cuban
        air defense capability no matter what their primary mission is.

considered in 1962) all the more costly and less certain of success --
particularly against mobile missiles; (3) Have Castro satisfied with Soviet
military support so that he does not have to be mollified post facto (as was
the case in 1962) if a Soviet-US deal were to result in non-deployment or
withdrawal.

4. Soviet Purpose.

In contrast with 1962, the Soviets do not have to search for a quick
expedient in order to close their missile gap. While the deployment of
missiles to Cuba would improve their current capability somewhat, I believe
its primary purpose would be to support Soviet political and military ends in
Europe. Deployment would create a political outcry in the States and face the
administration with unpalatable choices: (1) Take military action in much
less favorable circumstances than in 1962, risking both escalation and
increased European fear of US adventurism; (2) accept a new deal which would
make explicit the linkage between non-deployment of Soviet missiles to Cuba in
exchange for non-deployment of US missiles to Europe; such a deal would
preserve the current Soviet military advantage in Europe. More important, it
would be used to demonstrate to the West Europeans that US INF modernization
plans were really intended to serve US (not European) strategic purposes and
could be jettisoned unilaterally and at the expense of the allies in the US
search for its own security -- i.e., widen the wedge between the US and
Europe; or (3) Acquiesce, demonstrating both the US loss of power since 1962
and inability to match rhetoric with action, thereby doing incalculable damage
to the US global geostrategic position.

5. Conclusion.

To repeat, I do not see SS-20 deployments as imminent but do believe
that the Soviets are creating the military capability and the political
justification for it. Such a move -- while associated with substantial risk
-- would become more attractive to the Soviets if they were unable to stop INF
modernization in some other way and if they saw NATO coming closer to a final
decision point. The
implications of such a Soviet action would be so grave that I strongly
recommend that: (1) my analysis be examined for its logic and (2) if that
initial examination warrants, it be brought to the attention of policymakers
for further consideration and development of a US counterstrategy.

*Now, there is no doubt with the finding among sugar bags of SS-20
missiles inside the Nor Koreano freighter.*

*Journalists as always described these obsolete weapons to reduce the
danger and the value of the finding. The same action is repeated and
again, reducing the level of danger of the enemy. The dangerous thing is
that so many stupid people believe them in a relaxed, calm and serene way.
According CIA's reported in 1960' s years Cuba keeps 44 missiles with
nuclear weapons ready to be launched against United States.*

Weapons technically cannot be obsolete for Russians in Cuba, they still can kill thousands or millions of people, even without being precise and modernized. Your main enemies are inside and the deadly charges could be used without launching the missile.

This nexus of Cuba and North Korea highlights the close coordination and common objectives ... the United States. Everything said, is manifested when in moments

SOVIET MILITARY STRENGTH IN CUBA — AN UNDERGROUND INTELLIGENCE REPORT

The following figures on Soviet armed strength in Cuba come from intelligence reports of anti-Castro underground organizations working inside Cuba:

Troops: At least 18,700 Russians, perhaps as many as 35,000, including five Soviet generals.

Missiles: Soviets removed 42, but 44 medium and intermediate-range missiles are reported still in Cuba, hidden in caves, manned by Russians. In addition, 140 or more ground-to-air or ground-to-sea missiles are in Cuba. All missiles are capable of carrying nuclear warheads.

Planes: 184 MIG fighters have been counted, capable of carrying nuclear bombs into U. S. Also in Cuba are 37 Soviet transport planes, 83 Soviet helicopters. No jet bombers are known to remain in Cuba.

Submarines: 12 to 15 Soviet submarines are manned by Russians, operate from at least four new Russian-built bases.

Tanks: 260 Soviet-made T-34s and T-54s.

Patrol boats: 32, including nine with launchers for nuclear rockets.

Guns: 1,900 artillery pieces, 2,200 antiaircraft guns, 2,720 mortars, 425,000 rifles and small arms.

of tension is sent from North Korea to the
Minister of Foreign
Affairs (to reaffirm the order of attack (Foreign Minister of North Korea Ri
Yong Ho) jointly between the two countries)
In the decade of 60s, after October Crisis, Cuba keep nuclear offensive capacity with 44 missiles of medium range ready to launch against United States, according CIA's report:

The 100% false statement:
The statement of the Ministry of Foreign Affairs said that "Cuba reaffirmed its commitment to peace, disarmament, including nuclear

disarmament and respect for international law." Nothing more absurd and grotesque insult to the intelligence of others, they detect missiles hidden between sacks of sugar and they say they are defending La Paz.
He said the ship was transporting 240 tons of obsolete defensive weapons: two anti-aircraft missile complexes, nine missiles in parts and spare parts, two MiG-21bis fighters and 15 MiG engines.
The Cuban declaration said that all were made in the mid-twentieth century and should be repaired and returned to Cuba.

"The agreements signed by Cuba in this field are based on the need to maintain our defensive capacity to preserve national sovereignty," Lies Cuba because the important thing of the cargo not of anti-air missiles but the SS-20 ballistic missiles. If those missiles are obsolete, why did they send to repair in North Korea? They have 21 more in Cuba. Why do the missiles have to be hidden among the bags of sugar, if this type of weapons is legal?

Cuba is the Open Door and the Bridge for

Communism in
America

and perhaps most significantly, the Lebanese terrorist organization Hezbollah has been allowed to establish a base in Cuba to add to its facilities on the island of Margarita in Venezuela and the "tripartite" region between Paraguay, Brazil and Argentina.

"Technical assistant" for Terrorism, Drugs and Subversion

In return, Iran has provided key technical assistance to Caracas in the areas of defense, intelligence, security, energy and industry. Among other initiatives, it agreed to build an explosives plant in the state of Carabobo and it is known that it produces weapons in the "tractors" factory in Bolívar. In addition, the Revolutionary Guard of Iran has been involved in the training of the secret services and the police of Venezuela.
Iran, in addition, is prepared to help Venezuela in the area of nuclear energy.

This represents a particularly curious development, given that Iran has limited experience in the peaceful use of nuclear energy, and that in any case nuclear energy is a known and mature technology applied in numerous countries and by numerous companies throughout the world. world.

Therefore, it is reasonable to conclude that the "technical assistance" provided by Iran (and Russia) to Venezuela will be for the purpose of finding and exploiting uranium deposits.

Recent reports that Iran has established missile bases in Venezuela, This photo confirms that there are missiles in Venezuela, this does not seem to be two tubes of toothpaste.

Drug traffic
The Iranian involvement in drug trafficking through Venezuela to Central America, Mexico, EE. UU., The Caribbean and Europe through West Africa is extensive and is well Interested in Iran in the region, as well as at least partially finance the terrorist organizations mentioned above.
Detailed reports from the Anti-Drug Agency and the United Nations have reported on the extensive drug trade from eastern Venezuela to West Africa, and then to Europe.

It is believed that the supply for this pipeline comes from the Iranian facilities in the Orinoco River delta, where "tuna" boats and other ships load cocaine from Iranian facilities and then ship it upstream.

Other narcotics routes through Venezuela also channel cocaine through Santo Domingo (Haiti and the Dominican Republic) to the Gulf Coast of the United States and the west coast of Florida. Cocaine is also transported through Central America, particularly Honduras and Guatemala, to Mexico and the US. UU
The protection of drug trafficking by the Venezuelan National Guard is so frequent and notorious that the Guard is sometimes referred to as an additional drug cartel (Cartel de los Soles, after the rank insignia of the National Guard).

Cuba maintains an installation to produce cocaine in paste, and other narcotics in Sierra Cristal, south of Nipe Bay. Rare square clouds are to hide the installation. Like a fachade close to the Laboratory the "Gaviota" Hotel (Gaviota is a military interprise)

Thanks to the Cuban plan of subversion with Iran and Russia are in Venezuela.

The second objective is to facilitate the financing of radical organizations and terrorist movements in the Hemisphere. This includes, first and foremost, Hezbollah, the radical Lebanese militia that serves as the main terrorist detachment in Iran.

In the last three decades, the Iranian regime has facilitated the establishment by Hezbollah of a large regional presence throughout the American continent, and has aided and abetted the organization's participation in a series of illicit activities, from drug trafficking to drug trafficking. money laundering.4 (In 2008, for example, the Bush administration accused the Venezuelan diplomat Ghazi Nasr al Din and the Arab-Venezuelan businessman Fawzi Kanan of laundering money and facilitating the travel of Hezbollah members from Iran to Venezuela.5) In recent years, academic analysis has also revealed the use of radical mosques in Caracas and elsewhere in Venezuela as a center for Hezbollah fundraising activities, and most notably the existence of Hezbollah "support cells" in the Isla Margarita.

The Iranians are in frank expansion of their intelligence resources throughout South America to better understand and introduce the regional presence of the Iranian regime.

This report was prepared by the American Foreing Relation by Norman A. Bailey, translated verbatim

Cuba Spy's Network

Cuba maintains an active network of military and political, subversive, technological, scientific, academic, cultural and political intelligence of thousands of men and women, Cubans and other nationalities.

Cuban intelligence agents known and suspected in Eurasia, North America and South America. (Confidential Cuba, Colonel Simmons DIA) Updated on June 24, 2012

Ana Belén Montes (DIA)
Giraldo Abreu Morales
Ramon Aja Castro
Alina Alayo Amaro
Carlos Alfaras Varela
Roberto Alvarez Barrera
Miguel Amantegui Perez
Jose Antonio Arbesu Fraga (Master)
Ricardo Azcuy Rodriguez
Enrique Benavides Santos
Alberto Betancourt Roa
Orlando Boullon Castellon

Orlando Cabrera Garcia
Ricardo Belen Cabrisas Ruiz
Pedro Brugues Ortega
Juan Carretero Ibanez
Benigno Castellar Sánchez
Moises Cheni Plaza
Dr. Carlos Diaz Larranaga
Jose Diaz Puga
Alberto Diaz Vigo
Ricardo Espino Martinez
Manuel Estevez Perez
Ulises Estrada
Oscar Fajardo Garcia
Cristobal Fajardo Rabasa
Tomas Fernandez Cisneros
José Fernandez Perez
Ramon Fernández Rodríguez
Manuel Figueral Prado
Raúl Fornell Delgado
Armando Galán Arias
Mauro García Triana
Mario García Vázquez
Saul González
Wilfredo González Ramírez
Manuel Guillot Pérez
Aleida Gutiérrez Acequiera
Francisco Iglesias Iglesias
Pedro Miguel Lobaina-Jimenez de Castro
Armando López Orta
Virgilio Lázaro Lora Quesada
Menocal Luis Martinez
Pedro Machado Fernandez
Gustavo Machín Gomez
Roberto Mulet del Valle
Martin Navarro Báez
José Luis Ojalvo
Gregorio M. Ortega Suarez
Luis Palacios Rodríguez

Rene Pérez Acosta
Antonio Pérez Caneiro
José Luis Pérez Hernández
Adalberto Quintana Suarez
Pedro Luis Pineiro Eirin
Jose Antonio Rabaza Vazquez
Francisco Ramos Alvarez
Luis Reyes Mas
Aldo Rodríguez Camps
Rene Rodríguez Cruz
Eduardo Rodríguez Diaz
Fermín Rodríguez Paz
Alfonso Rodríguez Pérez
Mario Roque Tariche
Raúl Samper
Carlos Sánchez Bosquet
Armando Arle Sánchez Castro
Eduardo Sánchez Pena
Guido Sánchez Robert
Pablo de Jesús Sarduy Darías
Jorge Solís
Darío Urra
Jacinto Vásquez de la Garza
Raúl Valdés Vivo
Agustín Vargas Vargas
Fernando Vecino Alegret
Pedro Fumero
Ernesto Wong
Raúl Ceferino Zayas Linares
Reynaldo Zepeda Hernández

Known and suspected of being agents of Intelligence of Cuba in the areas of
South America and the Caribbean. Updated February 20, 2016

Bienvenido Abierno
Juan Emilio Aboy
Ortelio Abrahantes Bacallao

José Abrantes Fernández
Ramiro Abreu Quintana
Manuel Abstengo Carmenate
José Raúl Acosta Campuzano
Juan Acosta
Teófilo A. Acosta Rodríguez
Philip Agee
Manuel Agramonte Sánchez
Uver Ángel Aguilar Sánchez
Ramon Aja Castro
Alina Alayo Amaro
Carlos Alfonso González
Alejandro Alonso
Guillermo Alonso Pujol
Percy Francisco Alvarado Godoy
Carlos Conrado de Jesús Alvarado Marín
Roberto Regalado Álvarez
Lázaro Amaya La Puente
Armando Tomas Amieva Dalboys
Carlos Eugenio Antelo Pérez
Raúl Aparicio Nogales
Guillermo Arastaguia Fundora
José Antonio Arbesu Fraga (Master Spy)
Andrés Armona Ramos
Damian Arteaga Hernández
Noel Ascanio Montero
Juan Rafael Astorga Frometa
Francisco Ávila Azcuy
Roberto Asanza Páez
Eusebio Azcue López (Victor Pina Cardoso)
German Barreiro Carames
Gonzalo Bassols Suarez
*Jesus Bermudez Cutino (General Ex Jefe de la Inteligencia Militar y
MININT)*
Frank Bestard
Alberto Betancourt Roa
Jorge Bolanos Suarez
Alberto Boza-Hidalgo Gato

Emilio Brito
Orlando Brito Pestana
Miguel Brugueras del Valle
Ángel Brugues Pérez
Javier Martínez Buduen
Ricardo Cabrera Amoedo
Alberto Silvio Cabrera Barrio
Ricardo Belén Cabri sas Ruiz
Martin Tomas Cala
Maria del Carmen y Ruiz
Luisa Calderón Carralero
Armando Campos Ginesta
Raúl Antonio Capote
Osvaldo Cárdenas Junquera
Sergio Cardona Illizastigui
Julio Carranza Valdés
Juan Carretero Ibáñez
Jorge Castaneda
José Nivaldo Causse Perez
Joaquín Penton Cejas
Julio Sergio Cervantes Padilla
Carlos Sixto Chain Soler
Enrique Miguel Cicard Labrada
Carlos Coello
José Manuel Collera Vento
Carlos Manuel Collazo Usallan
Abelardo Colomé Ibarra (General /JFK)
Fernando Pascual Comas Pérez
Julio Concepción González
Luis Conte Agüero
Omar Ramon Córdoba Rivas
Vladimir Cruz
Luis Ismael Cruz Arce
José de Jesús Cruz González
Ramon Cesar Cuenca Montoto
Mario Dagoberto Diaz Orgaz
Roque Dalton García
Rafael Dausa Céspedes

Manuel de Beunza Rivero
Rene de los Santos
Ramiro del Rio
Adrián Francisco Delgado González
Eduardo Delgado Rodríguez Izquierdo
María Cristina Delgado Suarez
Luis Felipe Denis Diaz
Gastón Diaz Evaristo
Carlos Andrés Diaz Larrañaga
Santiago Eduardo Diaz Páez
Alberto Diaz Vigo
Antonio Diegues
José Dirceu de Oliveira de Silva
Helmut Doménech González
Fabian Escalante Font (General /JFK)
Ricardo Escartín Fernández
Héctor Esplugas Valdés
Mario Estebes Gonzales
Armando Ulises Estrada Fernández
Heriberto Falcon Medina
Pedro Fariñas Diaz
Osmin Fernández Concepción
Luis Fernández de Oña
Gonzalo Fernández Garay
Luis Fernández Ojeda
Antonio Bruno Fernández Pajón Roberto Fernández Vásquez
José Fernández Vilela
Jorge Antonio Ferrera Diaz
Carlos Freites
Raúl Fornel Delgado
Humberto Omar Francis Pardo
Juan Francisco Fernández
Olga Francisco
Rubén Rafael Franco González
Arsenio Franco Villanueva
Osmel Fuentes Lavín
Guillermo "Bill" Gaede
Rico Galán

Héctor Pascual Gallo Portielles
Julio Cesar Gandarilla Bermejo
Alfredo García Almeida
Gilberto García Alonso
Fernando García Bielsa
Enrique García Diaz
José Antonio García Lara
Oscar Garcia Manzano
Jorge E. García-Bango Dirube
Justo Cesar Gelabert Martínez
José Gómez Abad
José Fernández Gondi
Fernando González
Marta A. González
Raúl González
René González Sehwerert
Saul González
Caridad Pérez González
Francisco González García
José González Marrero
Carlos Alberto Gonzalez Mendez
Elicio Gonzalez Moreno
Flavio Delfín González Nunes
Pedro Silvio González Pérez
Pedro González Pineiro
Wilfredo Gonzalez Ramírez
Victor M. Gonzalez Valdés
Gines Silvio Gorriz
Alfredo Victor Guerra Fernandez
Francisco Guerrero Veliz
Arturo Guzman Nolasco
Abel Haidar Elias
Geraldo Hernandez
Juan Hernandez Acen
Linda Hernandez
Nilo Hernandez
Rafael Hernández
Roberto Hernandez Caballero

Tomás Hernández Cruz
Norberto Hernandez Curbelo
Eduardo Hernandez Gispert
Luis Hernandez Ojeda
Daniel Enrique Herrera Perez
Manuel Hevia Cosculluela
José Miguel Hidalgo Rodriguez
Ramon Hurtado
Rogelio Iglesias Patino
Robert Infante Pupu
Jose Imperatori
Elpidio Interian Comezanes
Néstor García Iturbe
Jesus Jimenez Escobar
Florentino Jimenez Padron
Herberto Jorrin Munoz
Thelma King
Roberto Koro
Guillermo Jimenez Soler
Jorge Luis Joa Campos
Ramon Labanino
Jose R. Labrada Torres
Ida Paz Lago
Jose Lain Martin Gonzalez
Roberto Lasalle
Jose Francisco Llagostera Garcia (JFK)
Pedro Miguel Lobaina-Jimenez de Castro
Antonio Lopez
Adis Lopez Cervino
Julian Lopez Diaz
Armando Lopez Orta
Alfredo Luis del Valle
Jose Luis Ponce
Jorge Luis Rodríguez
Virgilio Lora
Ivan Luis
Remijio Luna
Felix Luna Mederos

Pedro Machado Fernandez

Gustavo Machin Gomez

Oscar Madruga

Rodrigo Malmierca Díaz

Manuel Celestino Marcano Carrasquel

Eduardo Martinez Borbonet

Roberto Marquez Orozco

Adelfo Martin

Sergio Martin Vidal

Manuel Martinez Galan

Sergio Manuel Martínez González

Fernando Martinez Heredia

Jose Maria Martinez Tamayo

Rene Martinez Tamayo

Jorge Ricardo (Jorge) Masetti

Jorge Ricardo (Ricardo) Masetti

Jorge Luis Mayo Fernandez

Jose Mendez Cominches

Tomas Isaac Mendez Parra

Enrique Miguel Mesa Levis

Felix Martin Milanes Fajardo

Jennifer Miles

Rafael Mirabel Fernandez

Alfredo Mirabell Diaz

Luis Molina

Luis Raul Molina Montes de Oca

Luis Mones Lafita

Michael Montanez

Renan Montero Corrales

Ana Belen Montes

Arqueles Morales Mendoza

Omar Morales Bazo

Miguel More Santana

Pepe Nova

Julian Novas Fernandez

Rafael Nunez

Alwin Artilano Odio Tamayo

Jose Ojeda Santana

Julio Cesar Oliva Perdueles
Manolo Orgalles
Ramon Oroza Naberan
Isaac Orrantia Orrantia
Dario Ortega
Rodolfo Paez Perez
Orlando Pantoja Tamayo
Ida Borja Paz Escalante de Gomez
Jose Paz Novas
Victor Pena
Leda Elvira Peña Hernández
Joaquin Rodobaldo Penton Cejas
Orlando F. Pereira Gonzalez
Santiago Perez
Jose Ramon Perez Ayala
Ernesto Perez De Cardenas
Earle Perez Friman
Luis Jesus Perez Martinez
Alfredo Jose Perez Rivero
Ramón Pérez Soria
Gerardo Perez Tejera
Alejandro Pila Alonso
Ricardo Porfirio Pimentel Roger
Pedro Luis Pineiro Eirin
Manuel Pineiro Losada
Berta Louisa Pla y Badia
Jose Luis Posada Torres
Orlando Prendes Gutierrez
Eugenio Prieto Valido
Carlos Puig Espinosa
Raul Pujol
Adalberto Quintana Suarez
Daniel Rafuls
Vivian Rafuls
Julio A. Ramirez Otero
Fernando Ravelo Renedo
Oscar Red ondo Toledo
Osvaldo Relova Penichet

Juan Manuel Reyes Alonso
Raul Reyes Goicochea
Jorge E. Reyes Vega
Pedro Anibal Riera Escalante (in prison)
Jose Miguel Roa
Raul Rodriguez Averhoff
Juan Manuel Rodriguez Camejo
Rene Rodríguez-Cruz
Ramiro Rodriguez Gomez
Ramiro Rodriguez Gonzalez
Rogelio Rodriguez Lopez
Juan Carlos Rodriguez Lueje
Jose Rodriguez Rodriguez
Charles Romeo
Mauricio Rosencoff
Juan Pablo Roque
Jose Francisco Ross Paz
Tania Rouco de Zayas
Alberto Manuel Ruiz
Alfredo Ruiz
Angel Ruiz
Orestes Guillermo Ruiz Perez
Homero Saker Rivero
Jaime Salas
Lino Fernando Salazar Chia
Ovidio Sama Viamonte
Ernesto Samper
Guilermo Samper
George Sanchez
Ramon Sanchez-Parodi Montoto
German Sanchez Otero
Gerardo Sanchez Robert
Carlos Manuel Lazaro Felix Sanchez y Basquet
Roberto Santiago Humet
Roberto Santiesteban Casanova
Joseph Santos
Ismael Sene Alegret
Pedro Serrat

Orlando Silva Fors
Amarylis Silverio Santos
Ramon Sinobas Casado
Juan Enrique Sosa Mompie
Mario Sosa Navarro
Amado Nicolas Soto Ga rcia
Carlos Augusto Suanes Flexas
Felix Suarez More
Edmundo Suarez Hernandez
Luis Suarez Salazar
Johana Tablada
Romilio Tambutti
Jorge Timossi Corbani
Armando Torres Mesones
Julian Torres Rizo
Neuris Trutie
Teudys Trutie Matilla
Dario Urra Torriente
Ramiro Valdes Menendez
Juan Valdés Paz
Edgardo Obdulio Valdes Suarez
Oreste Varela
Michael Vazquez Montes de Oca
Manuel Eugenio Vega Perez
Gustavo Veliz Olivares
Ernesto Vera
Ilya Felicia Villar Martinez
Ricardo Villareal
Felix Wilson Hernandez
Carlos Rafael Zamora Rodriguez
Tania Rouco de Zayas
Raul Ceferino Zayas Linares

Bienvenido Abierno
Maria Caridad Abierno Gobin
Juan Emilio Aboy
Jose Abrante Fernandez
Ramiro Abreu Quintana

Jose Raul Acosta Campuzano
Juan Acosta
Teofilo A. Acosta Rodriguez
Philip Agee
Manuel Agramonte Sanchez
Uver Angel Aguilar Sanchez
Ramon Aja Castro
Alina Alayo Amaro
Carlos Alfonso Gonzalez
Alejandro Alonso
Guillermo Alonso Pujol
Percy Francisco Alvarado Godoy
Carlos Conrado de Jesus Alvarado Marin
Lazaro Amaya La Puente
Armando Tomas Amieva Dalboys
Carlos Eugenio Antelo Perez
Raul Aparicio Nogales
Guillermo Arastaguia Fundora
Jose Antonio Arbesu Fraga (Master Spy)
Jesus Arboleya Cervera
Andres Armona Ramos
Damian Arteaga Hernandez
Noel Ascanio Montero
Juan Rafael Astorga Frometa
Francisco Avila Azcuy
Roberto Azanza Paez
Eusebio Azcue Lopez (Victor Pina Cardoso / JFK)
German Barreiro Carames
Gonzalo Bassols Suarez
Jesus Bermudez Cutino
Frank Bestard
Alberto Betancourt Roa
Jorge Bolanos Suarez
Emilio Brito
Orlando Brito Pestana
Alberto Boza-Hidalgo Gato
Miguel Brugueras del Valle
Angel Brugues Perez

Rolando Salup Canto
Ricardo Cabrera Amoedo
Alberto Silvio Cabrera Barrio
Ricardo Belen Cabrisas Ruiz
Martin Tomas Cala
Armando Campos Ginesta
Osvaldo Cardenas Junquera
Sergio Cardona Illizastigui
Julio Carranza Valdés
Luis Carrera Martorell
Jose Nivaldo Causse Perez
Joaquin Penton Cejas
Sergio Cervantes
Carlos Sixto Chain Soler
Enrique Miguel Cicard Labrada
Carlos Coello
Alberto Coll
Carlos Manuel Collazo Usallan
Odilia Collazo Valdes
Abelardo Colome Ibarra
Fernando Pascual Comas Perez
Luis Conte Aguero
Omar Ramon Cordoba Rivas
Angelica Cruz
Vladimir Cruz
Luis Ismael Cruz Arce
Jose de Jesus Cruz Gonzalez
Ramon Cesar Cuenca Montoto
Roque Dalton Garcia
Rafael Dausa Cespedes
Manuel de Beunza Rivero
Rene de los Santos
Ramiro del Rio
Adrian Francisco Delgado Gonzalez
Eduardo Delgado Rodriguez Izquierdo
Luis Felipe Denis Diaz
Gaston Diaz Evarista
Carlos Andres Diaz Larranaga

Alberto Diaz Vigo
Antonio Diegues
Jose Dirceu de Oliveira de Silva Helmut Domenech Gonzalez
Fabian Escalante Font
Ricardo Escartin Fernandez
Hector Esplugas Valdes
Mario Estebes Gonzales
Armando Ulises Estrada Fernandez
Pedro Farinas Diaz
Osmin Fernandez Concepcion
Luis Fernandez de Ona
Gonzalo Fernandez Garay
Luis Fernandez Ojeda
Antonio Brunol Fernandez Pajon
Roberto Fernandez Vasquez
Jose Fernandez Vilela
Carlos Fle ites
Raul Fornell Delgado
Humberto Omar Francis Pardo
Juan Francisco Fernandez
Olga Francisco
Ruben Rafael Franco Gonzalez
Arsenio Franco Villanueva
Osmel Fuentes Lavin
Guillermo "Bill" Gaede
Hector Pascual Gallo Portielles
Julio Cesar Gandarilla Bermejo
Alfredo Garcia Almeida
Fernando Garcia Bielsa
Enrique Garcia Diaz
Nestor Garcia Iturbe
Jose Antonio Garcia Lara
Oscar Garcia Manzano
Jorge E. Garcia-Bango Dirube
George Gari
Marisol Gari
Justo Cesar Gelabert Martinez
Jose Gomez Abad

Manuel Fernandez Gondin

Fernando Gonzalez Llort

Marta A. Gonzalez

Raul Gonzalez

Rene Gonzalez Sehwerert

Saul Gonzalez

Francisco Gonzalez Garcia

Jose Gonzalez Marrero

Carlos Alberto Gonzalez Mendez

Elicio Gonzalez Moreno

Flavio Delfin Gonzalez Nunez

Pedro Silvio Gonzalez Perez

Pedro Gonzalez Pineiro

Wilfredo Gonzalez Ramirez

Victor M. Gonzalez Valdes

Gines Silvio Gorriz

Alfredo Victor Guerra Fernandez

Antonio Guerrero Rodriguez

Arturo Guzman Nolasco

Abel Haidar Elias

Gerardo Hernandez Nordelo

Juan Hernan dez Acen

Linda Hernandez

Nilo Hernandez

Rafael Hernández

Norberto Hernandez Curbelo

Eduardo Hernandez Gispert

Luis Hernandez Ojeda

Manuel Hevia Cosculluela

Jose Miguel Hidalgo Rodriguez

Ramon Hurtado

Rogelio Iglesias Patino

Robert Infante Pupu

Jose Imperatori

Elpidio Interian Comezanes

Jesus Jimenez Escobar

Florentino Jimenez Padron

Herberto Jorrin Munoz

Roberto Koro
Guillermo Jimenez Soler
Jorge Luis Joa Campos
Ramon Labanino Salazar
Jose R. Labrada Torres
Jose Lain Martin Gonzalez Roberto Lasalle
Jose Francisco Llagostera Garcia (Mexico-JFK)
Pedro Miguel Lobaina-Jimenez de Castro
Antonio Lopez
Adis Lopez Cervino
Julian Lopez Diaz
Arturo López-Levy
Armando Lopez Orta
Jorge Luis Rodriguez
Virgilio Lazaro Lora Quesada
Ivan Luis
Remijio Luna
Felix Luna Mederos
Pedro Machado Fernandez
Gustavo Machin Gomez
Oscar Madruga
Manuel Celestino Marcano Carrasquel
Roberto Marquez Orozco
Adelfo Martin
Eduardo Martinez Borbonet
Manuel Martinez Galan
Fernando Martinez Heredia
Jose Maria Martinez Tam ayo
Rene Martinez Tamayo
Jorge Ricardo Masetti ("Jorge")
Jorge Ricardo Masetti ("Ricardo")
Jose Mendez Cominches
Enrique Miguel Mesa Levis
Felix Martin Milanes Fajardo
Jennifer Miles
Rafael Mirabel Fernandez
Alfredo Mirabell Diaz
Luis Molina

Luis Mones Lafita
Michael Montanez
Renan Montero Corrales
Ana Belen Montes
Mario Monzon Barata
Arqueles Morales Mendoza
Miguel More Santana
Pepe Nova
Julian Novas Fernandez
Alwin Artilano Odio Tamayo
Jose Ojeda Santana
Julio Cesar Oliva Perdueles
Manolo Orgalles
Ramon Oroza Naberan
Isaac Orrantia Orrantia
Dario Ortega
Rodolfo Paez Perez
Orlando Pantoja Tamayo
Ida Borja Paz Escalante de Gomez
Jose Paz Novas
Victor Pena
Joaquin Rodobaldo Penton Cejas
Orlando F. Pereira Gonzalez
Santiago Perez
Jose Ramon Perez Ayala
Ernesto Perez DeCardenas
Earle Perez Friman
Luis Jesus Perez Martinez
Alfredo Jose Perez Rivero
Gerardo Perez Tejera
Alejandro Pila Alonso
Ricardo Porfirio Pimentel Roger
Pedro Luis Pineiro Eirin
Manuel Pineiro Losada
Berta Louisa Pla y Badia
Jose Luis Posada Torres
Orlando Prendes Gutierrez
Eugenio Prieto Valido

Carlos Puig Espinosa
Raul Pujol
Adalberto Quintana Suarez
Daniel Rafuls
Vivian Rafuls
Julio A. Ramirez Otero
Fernando Ravelo Renedo
Oscar Redondo Toledo
Osvaldo Relova Penichet
Juan Manuel Reyes Alonso
Raul Reyes Goicochea
Jorge E. Reyes Vega
Pedro Anibal Riera Escalante
Raul Rodriguez Averhoff
Juan Manuel Rodriguez Camejo
Rene Rodriguez-Cruz
Ramiro Rodriguez Gomez
Ramiro Rodriguez Gonzalez
Rogelio Rodriguez Lopez
Juan Carlos Rodriguez Lueje
José Rodríguez Rodríguez
Charles Romeo
Juan Pablo Roque
José Francisco Ross Paz
Tania Rouco de Zayas
Alberto Manuel Ruiz
Alfredo Ruiz
Angel Ruiz
Orestes Guillermo Ruiz Perez
Albor Ruiz Salazar
Homero Saker Rivero
Jaime Salas
Lino Fernando Salazar Chia
Ovidio Sama Viamonte
Gilermo Samper
George Sanchez
Ramon Sanchez-Parodi
German Sanchez Otero

Gerardo Sánchez Robert
Carlos Manuel Lázaro Félix Sánchez y Básquet
Roberto Santiago Humet
Roberto Santiesteban Casanova
Joseph Santos
Pedro Serrat
Orlando Silva Fors
Amaryllis Silverio Santos
Ramon Sinobas Casado
Nicolas Alberto Sirgado Ross
Juan Enrique Sosa Mompie
Mario Sosa Navarro
Amado Nicolas Soto Garcia
Carlos Augusto Suanes Flexas
Felix Suarez More
Edmundo Suarez Hernandez
Luis Suarez Salazar
Johana Tablada
Romilio Tambutti
Frank E. Terpil
Jorge Timossi Corbani
Cosme Torres Espinosa
Armando Torres Mesones
Julian Torres Rizo
Neuris Trutie
Teudys Trutie Matilla
Dario Urra Torriente
Juan Gabriel Valdes
Ramiro Valdes Menendez
Juan Valdés Paz
Edgardo Obdulio Valdes Suarez
Oreste Valera
Michael Vazquez Montes de Oca
Manuel Eugenio Vega Perez
Juan Velasco Alvarado
Pedro Luis Veliz Martinez
Pedro Jesus Vidaurreta Font
Napoleón Vilaboa

Ilya Felicia Villar Martínez
Ricardo Villareal
Félix Wilson Hernandez
Hugo Ernesto Yedra Díaz
 List of Col. Simmons DIA CubaCnfidential.com

It is important that this long list and other infinitely more agents that we do not know, come here with the evident purpose of promoting these points that we see below. Detecting those who promote these points is a good sign ...

Points to create social conflict. Written in 1919 in Germany.

1. Corrupt young people, away from religion. Make them interested in sex. Make them superficial. It destroys his intellectual and moral robustness.
2. Obtain control of all advertising media.
3. Keep the minds of the people in your government away by focusing on sports or absurd shows, bodybuilding, pornography, sexy books and other trivia.
4. Divide people into hostile groups by constantly insisting on unimportant controversial issues.
5. Destroy people's faith in their natural leaders by leading the latter to contempt, ridicule and gift.
6. Always preach true democracy but take power as quickly and as ruthlessly as possible.
7. By encouraging the extravagance of the government, destroy their credit and generate fear of inflation with rising prices and general discontent.
8. Encourage unnecessary strikes in vital industries, foment civil unrest and encourage an indulgent and soft attitude on the part of the government toward such disorders.
9. By a deceptive argument causes collapse of the old moral virtues, honesty, sobriety, continence, faith in the promised word, harshness.
10. Cause registration of all firearms under some pretext, in order to confiscate them and leave the population defenseless.

<u>Conclusion on the relations of the USSR / Russia and Cuba since they sent Fabio Grobart to Cuba in 1925. It has an strategic purpose of Russia's relations with Cuba has not been, nor will it be to defend Cuba from the</u>

"enemy" that they themselves have created for us. Cuba is destined to attack the United States. From 1962 to date they have maintained different types of weapons and offensive techniques against the United States

Re
f:
American Foreign Relation Norman A. Bailey February 2012 No. 5 Dr. Norman A. Bailey is President of the Institute for Global Economic Growth and Adjunct Professor o f Economic Statecraft at the Institute of World

Politics in Washington, DC. He previously served at the National Security Council and in the Office of the Director of National Intelligence. T
"Iran Using Venezuela Ties To Duck Sanctions: Report," Associated Press, December 21, 2008,
http://www.google.com/hostednews/afp/article/ALeqM5h1fferlbgjsi06XFgT k lru3hbatA. 21. Sarah Diehl, "Venezuela's Search for Nuclear Power – Or
Nuclear Prestige," The Nuclear Threat Initiative, May 7, 2009, http://www. nti.org/analysis/articles/venezuelas-search-nuclear-power/. 22. Simon Romero, "Venezuela Says Iran Is Helping It Look for Uranium," New York Times, September 25, 2009, http://www.nytimes. com/2009/09/26/world/americas/ 26venez.html. 23. See, for example, Michael Braun, "Counternarcotic Strategies in Latin America," testimony before the House Committee on International Relations Subcommittee on Western Hemisphere, March 30, 2006, http://www.justice.gov/dea/ pubs/cngrtest/ct033006.html. 24. Author's personal correspondence and contacts with regional experts, ongoing. 25. "Drug Control: US Narcotics Cooperation with Venezuela Has Declined," United States Government Accountability Office Report to the Ranking Member, Committee on Foreign Relations, US Senate, July, 2009, http://www.gao.gov/ new.items/d09806.pdf. https://cubaconfidential.wordpress.com/cuban-intelligence-personnel/known-suspected-cuban-officers-and-agents-in-the-us-or-canada/ http://www.prensalibre.com/internacional/golpe-contra-gorbachov-de-1991sello-fin-de-la-urss https://www.cia.gov/library/readingroom/document/ciadp65b00383r000200 230060-1

Chapter # 10

Cuba bridge of the Soviet subversion "Operation Bravo" of the DSE/KGB of May of 1980.

The execution of this subversive operation was scheduled years in advance ordered by Yuri Andropov, minister of the State Committee for State Security of the USSR.

The design of this operation was based on academic studies of the Social Sciences, taking references from the historical analysis of different social factors such as Economics, Demography and Psychology, a detailed Analysis of all the open or public information that they could obtain over the years. the United States and Cuba, seeking the vulnerability of American and Cuban society, as well as looking for ways to destroy the

ethical foundations of society with the modification of attitudes (brain cleansing).

The social upheaval and the resulting vector when introducing the "active measures" that can be used very easily in a totalitarian system, without considering the individual rights, it was easy to create a true "invading" army to destabilize the order within States. United and create changes that could undermine patriotism, family, school and contribute to the modeling of the "New Man" that they need to create in other countries to encourage the phase of demoralization and weaken the United States.

The actions taken by the Government are the so-called "active measures" and are linked consecutively to create partial and staggered conditions to eventually provoke an event that produces an appearance of "spontaneous and surprising phenomenon".

A cloak is also used, which are the subjective conditions created by rumors and opinions created by the press and the leaders in their speeches, which become a law and guide for immediate action.

For the average individual it is almost impossible to concatenate or relate an event with another to demonstrate or prove to oneself, that the result had been planned and calculated down to the smallest details.

This lesson teaches us with enough eloquence, our enemies prepare the terrain, take us to where they best suit us and at the moment, we cannot choose any option. Everything is under control.

It is not idle to remember a speech by Nikita Khrushchev at the United Nations when he already felt he was the master of the Island of Cuba and knew that from there he could weaken first and then attack the United States. It is still incredible, that the United States does not take into account this plan that has been fulfilled on their behalf and the results hit us day by day to each of the citizens of this

Operation "Bravo" was a reinforcement to the subversive operation that started in the 40s with the Frankfort school that we have put at your disposal in the book, previously entitled "Subversion against the United States and Cuba".

If we remember and defend ourselves daily from Nikita Khrushchev's message when we respond to the Philippine Delegate at the United Nations who asked her to respect the rights of the men and women of the countries invaded by the Soviet Union in Asia and Europe, taking off disrespectfully his shoe and hit the atrium strongly and said:

"Your children's children will live under communism. You Americans are guilty. No, you will not accept the advantage of Communism: but we will continue to feed you with small doses of socialism until you finally wake up and discover that you already have communism. We will not have to bother you: we will weaken your economy so much, until you fail like too ripe fruit in our hands "

These words have been prophetic, every day local governments impose on us the "gothic of socialism" in our lives, with multiculturalism, immigration, so we fall asleep, because we do not give them importance, we let them pass and we rest on our laurels: everything they do with drugs, corruption, terrorism, low productivity, defense spending, sharks, environmental pollution, weather disturbances, epidemics one way or another degrade our economy, make us weaker and vulnerable, this is the plan.

Operation "Bravo" was carried out between 1975 and 1980.

To introduce 128,000 Cubans in Florida in order to destabilize the deepest roots of the United States. The Plan had different stages, each with a certain cover or mantle. Could any observer be possible just by canceling the police post of the Embassy of Peru, in Miramar on April 4, in minutes have thousands of people willing to enter an Embassy of a country that did not sympathize with an anti-communist stance and that neither had reasons, nor conditions to be hospitable with the "Cuban worms".

Could somebody imagine that this was the beginning of a crisis to force the United States to accept.

Liberty City became a victim of Plan de Castro, a small town predominantly populated by African-Americans, unemployed incited a black murder by a white policeman and this led to the removal of Cuban refugees to take jobs from blacks. Tourists moved away from Miami, which caused the economy to decline and increased rejection of newcomers.

While the Federal government sent 700 million dollars to the local government to create conditions for the new arrivals and every day the behavior of some newcomers identified themselves as violent criminals, drug addicts, deviant and sexual transgressors, which Castro had introduced among the true refugees.

Even worse hundreds of Intelligence operatives. According to a former officer of Castro's intelligence, Gerardo Pérez Pérez, Castro had as alternative plan to send another contingent of 200,000 Cubans, if not they would pay the damages for the 20 years of embargo, and then open talks on the normalization of relations between Cuba. and the United States.

At almost 40 years from the event, as everything was planned, the statements of the DGI official seem to be also within Operation Bravo, creating an image of only economic blackmail and never talk about Moscow and the introduction of HIV . But the same facts show that this did not have the nature that Gerardo Pérez Pérez said.

Let's see:

Between 1975 there were political events in Cuba, gathering political, diplomatic and military forces against the United States based on the interests of the USSR.

The Conference of the Communist and Workers Parties, the Summit of the Movement of Non-Aligned Countries, the Assembly of the Solidarity Organization of the Countries of Asia, Africa and Latin America, the Festival of Youth and Students, the World Confederation of Women La Paz,
World Congress of Communist and Workers Parties, World Peace Council, Forum on the Industrial Military Complex, World Congress of Forensic and Social Medicine and every two months a Head of States or Government of the Third World countries was officially received World.

These popular mobilizations created a very favorable political movement to justify a "good impression for visitors" with a propaganda of "My cheerful and beautiful house" that psychologically supported the application of Law 59 of Social Hazard making massive "raids" and operations against street vendors, such as the Pitirre in El Alambre operation, Operation Petunia and Operation Trash, more than 60,000 men were captured and subjected to collective trials of 50 in 50 to receive automatic sentences of 4 years of deprivation of liberty. The women were accused of Prostitution in several about 13,000 (absolutely false accusation).

Both men and women were detained when they got off a bus, into a movie theater or on the beach arbitrarily, anyone could be arrested, only military and party militants were excluded.

The Judges themselves did everything possible to stop that wave of injustice and cruelty, many people, both men and women committed suicide. The

judges and lawyers formed a small beachhead with their opinions adverse to the measures of the government and immediately, an operation called the "Toga Cagada" began against the officials of the justice that did not agree with the repressive wave, among them Dr. Nicasio Hernandez de Armas, President of the Criminal Chamber of the Supreme Court (who died in prison) who had led the rejection of that massive injustice, was imprisoned among the defendants was the distinguished lawyer and patriot Dr. Aramis Taguada (died in prison) and many others almost 200 lawyers, prosecutors and judges went to fulfill the 4 years, also appears suicidal the former President of the Republic, then Minister of Justice, Osvaldo Dorticos Torrado, according to the press release, the reason for the suicide was a
"Pain in the back"

His death happened at dawn on a Friday after the meeting of the Political Bureau, where he had exposed the conduct of Ramiro Valdés, newly appointed Minister of the Interior and Fidel Castro agreed with Ramiro and strongly offended Osvaldo Dorticos. His body was not necropsy, Dr. Francisco Ponce Zerquera, Director of the Institute of Legal Medicine was called at 3 o'clock in the morning to extend the certificate of natural death in his residence.

All this repressive wave was to create a high internal pressure that demanded escape at any price of the manifest injustice of thousands of incarcerated people, their relatives and friends were the "guinea pigs who left terrified before the opportunity to leave the hell created against them"

During these five years, Cuba gave a coup in Peru, Argentina, Iraq, Yemen, Ethiopia, Portugal and began the War that lasted 15 years in Angola and Ethiopia.

Very active subversion work in Panama, Spain, Argentina, Uruguay, Chile, Colombia, Venezuela, Iraq, Yemen and Ethiopia.

All this responded to the mandates of the USSR for their hegemonic interests. A naval base in Lobito, Angola for control of the South Atlantic, another naval base in the Mediterranean in the territory of Syria.

Overthrow the government of South Africa and impose Robert Mandela to destroy and form the war of blacks against blacks, as Africa is today.

The Bravo Plan, and its alternate Alpha, actually reinforced and deepened the "Eleven Points of the Frankfort School", now introducing a lethal sexually transmitted disease with chronic psychiatric patients and prisoners.

This disease brought bi-million-dollar expenses in medical care and social tension with mourning and insecurity to contract the lethal and disastrous disease that we now know as HIV.

The demoralization of American society on a superlative scale. In addition to introducing in the prison population in addition to the epidemic of sexual transmission, which at first was baptized "only for homosexuals" the prison system and its population of 70% of black race, takes a new direction with a new culture, which would begin within of the prisons and then the street would gradually come out of where the so-called "anti-culture" comes, pushing to exclude African Americans from cultural and social advances, inducing them to rebellion, extravagance in fashions and ways of life, rejection to work and study, drugs, gambling, alcohol, prostitution, robbery and love for the easy life and get away from the defense of the country.

Everything the enemy needs to take the country easily, as Nikita and Stalin said. I wonder, why our politicians do not bravely face these serious problems that get bigger every day.

This step was executed in Mariel in bell-houses that they armed as of eleven at night and disarmed them at 5 o'clock in the morning by a Medical Services team composed only of Soviets.

The Crisis of Mariel, culminates with the sending of 128,000 Cubans as refugees to the United States, Spain and Peru.

This event coincides with two previous elements that join in May 1980 to manipulate the masses and create the so-called May Crisis. Let's see the three steps:

Number 1; The Ministry of Defense of the USSR in 1978 gives the Virus of the disease that we know today as HIV to the KGB, because it did not meet the military requirements to be put on board the intercontinental missiles, the selected epidemics had to be lethal in less than 15 days.

For this reason the KGB had by that date, 1978 with the virus for its subversive operations and decided to introduce it in the United States as witnessed by the Head of BIOPREPARAD, the Directorate of Biological Warfare of the Ministry of Defense of the USSR, the medical Colonel Ken Alibek in his book (Alibek, K. and S. Handelman, Biohazard: The Chilling True Story of the Largest Covert Biological Weapons Program in the World -
Told from Inside by the Man Who Ran it, 1999. Delta (2000) ISBN 0- 385-33496-6 [1] page 223)

I insert this narrative for and I invite you to watch Dr. Eduardo Palmer's documentary "Red Alert" on YouTube where you can see Dr. Ken Alibek and the author of this book, explaining the programs of the KGB in Cuba with relation to Chemical and Biological Weapons.

ttp://www.abc.es/sociedad/20140811/abci-virus-marburgo-arma-biologica-201408101715.html

2nd. The celebration in Cuba of the Festival of Youth and Students in July and August of 1978, this event facilitated in the first place the recruitment of thousands of young visitors to collaborate with the intelligence organs

of the countries of the Warsaw Pact and especially to Cuba for the Psychological Warfare campaign to deactivate the NATO Pershing type missiles and they maintain the superiority with the 9 Armored Troops Armies to devastate the Western European countries in surprise attack.

The Festival in Cuba fulfilled another fundamental objective for the Operation that they would later carry out, increase the repression against a layer of population that had remained neutral to rebel against the regime.

It was necessary to create a population stratum of "unacceptable for the system" called lumpen, antisocial, habitual vagrants, scum "these qualifiers awarded to a person were sufficient to be in prison for 4 years according to the Law of Social Hazard, the number of affected would be greater when family and friends felt the injustice by identifying with the victims.
Only in the City of Havana were more than 50,000 male prisoners and 13,000 women for the Crime of Predelictive State, by Law 59 that justified the "clean the image of Cuba before the Festival visitors." They were tried

collectively in groups of 50, the same accusation, the same Fiscal conclusion, the same sentences of the Judges, all unanimous, without exception.

3rd: This repressed mass, their relatives and people who considered this massive judicial procedure unjust, prepared the conditions for the social stampede towards the Embassy of Peru and then to the United States in May 1980 as the only escape route for the repressed.

On the other hand, Castro had received in Havana with much publicity the famous "representatives of the Cuban community in the United States" which he had prepared, to use if President James Carter rejected the

Cubans who requested refuge, Castro I had prepared the detonator in part of the exile to advocate family reunification, etc. The show was coldly calculated as my friend says, Frank Alonso.

This stampede was designed in detail, because it was part of a Subversive Operation orchestrated by Yuri Andropov.

The Academy of Sciences of the USSR did a study for years to reinforce the Subversive Plan of the Frankfort School that had advanced much more than expected, but still promised much more to reinforce it. As explained by the KGB defector specializing in Subversion Yuri Bezmenov, former Colonel of the KGB in his lectures on the subject. Thank you Yuri for your information and your abnegation. Yuri Bezmenov was murdered in Montreal. The conferences are subtitled in Spanish. https://trinityatierra.wordpress.com/2009/10/14/ex-agente-desertor-de-lakgb-yuri-bezmenov

The details of this Operation can be read in the book "Subversion against the United States and Cuba" by the author.

Acts of Repudiation, Current Fascism

One can speak of a civil war in Cuba in May 1980. Fidel Castro said in his May Day speech in 1980, "It is good for enemies to stumble over the fist of the Revolution." This was enough for the CDRs, the Communist Party pushing behind, began acts of repudiation with beatings, offenses, stones, eggs, paint, where many people were blind or mutilated, others died.

A case among thousands
The case of the Cubana Airline Flight Engineer José Barreiro's son, with 37 years of impeccable service, and Pepito when he went to ask for the cancellation from his job, they stripped and tied him in a fork lift in the supine position and they walked through the airport and the residential areas near it, where they threw food waste, garbage, and with sticks they injured his anus, Pepito Barreiro was blinded by lime paint and could reach Spain, the herd of henchmen was directed by Hipólito Villamil Forte, militant of the PCC and neighbor of the Residential Calixto Sánchez.

To the Institute of Legal Medicine 87 corpses arrived for the acts of repudiation and siege, these incidents were ordered by Fidel Castro. Of the thousands of cases that occurred only in the City of La Habano, one was published with a version completely different from the real one. There were four dead, two by projectiles fired by the Captain of Special Troops Ricardo Lopez, alias Chomoncito, brother of General Manuel López "Chomon", the wife and brother of the dead man by projectile were killed with kicks and blows by medical students that they took to the place in omnibus for acts of repudiation.

The woman was blond, and her body was completely blue from the blows she received. Two days later I showed up at the scene on Velarde Street in the Cerro and found on the edge of the street.

Operation Bravo among other costs to the people of Cuba were more than 50,000 men and 12,000 young women imprisoned for 4 years accused of prostitution (false) always applying Law 59 of Social Hazard.

HIV this Soviet / Cuban aggression had resulted in millions of deaths of people all over the planet, billions of dollars in medical services, lost family members, broken families and national demoralization.

Ref.
Author's personal file
Testimonies of the author in the Provincial Court of Havana as Expert in Forensic Psychology of the Institute of Legal Medicine. (1975 - 1981)
Conversations with Dr. Nicasio Hernández de Armas President of the Criminal Chamber of the Supreme Court
Conversations with Dr. Aramis Taguada Lawyer second leader of the National July 26 in 1953. Lawyer of the Law Firm of Reina Street. Havana.
Political prisoner.
Conversations with the Minister of Justice José Torres Santrail
Opinions of many Prosecutors and Judges of that time.
The War of Blacks against Blacks by Peter Hawthorne

Chapter # 11
The plan to blame the United States for a genocide

These are potential threats to National Security, but in terms of Human Rights in an incomplete and rude way we can know that in Cuba there are some 586 prisons for men, women and children with a prison population of almost half a million people, just as I use it in 1980, they can use this human mass both to export it and to create serious disturbances when they need them.

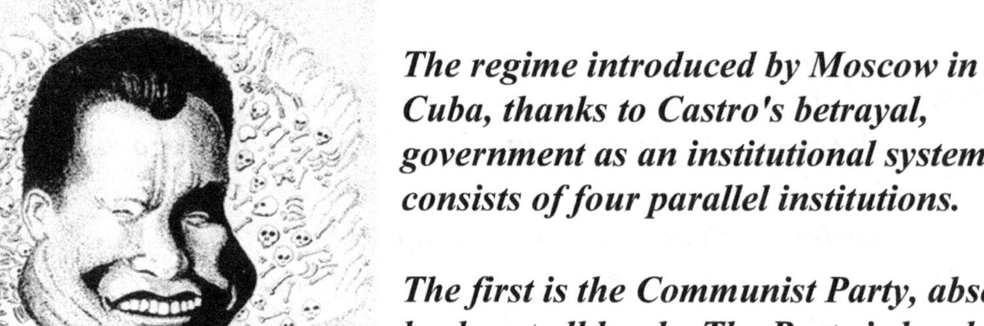

The regime introduced by Moscow in Cuba, thanks to Castro's betrayal, government as an institutional system consists of four parallel institutions.

The first is the Communist Party, absolute leader at all levels. The Party is headed by the "Big Brother" and covers the entire national territory, by province, municipality and by each labor, military or police center.

The party has departments for each type of activity of workers, such as ministries, institutes, etc.

The Council of Ministers headed by the "Great Leader" as the main executive branch. It has three geographical and administrative levels for each ministry, national, provincial, local and each unit has within the Communist Party and Young Communist as public control and oversight of the administration and of each worker.
The National Assembly is a strictly formal or decorative institution that meets in National Assembly twice in years to create and control the legal and administrative activity of the entire country.

You can propose new laws, but the member of parliament, or the delegates of the People's Power to all its instances by itself cannot do any project. The projects are absolute ground of the Party when it is directed to the ministers. The vote is public with the 100% traditional approved for each intelligent idea of Big Brother.

The Control Bodies: This is Against Intelligence, exists by the Ministry of the Interior and by the Armed Forces, the repressor and the controller that work within each civil or military institution in clandestine ways at all levels and only subordinate and execute the information to the head.

The officers have hegemonic power for everything. The who, where, why, when, how many, etc. 100% of the time each file is updated by many different levels and sources.

Less than 2% of the population has the privilege of being a Party Militant. This is the great open door to obtain privileges of social and political position. The militancy is a condition to be a boss in any case, obtain a university degree, accommodation, transportation, fly abroad, special consideration and privilege in their work, but also absolute impunity.

But everyone is obliged to be an active member of the "Organization of the masses" such as the Defense Committee in their neighborhood, union member in each worker center, member of the Student Association, Federation of Cuban Women, Pioneer of children and girls up to 14 years old. Militia or Territorial Troops, etc. Being a member means receiving orders to do jobs such as guards, cleaning the streets, painting the building, collecting waste, volunteering at the farm, meeting, reading the newspaper every morning, reading in groups and giving an opinion on Castro's speeches, two or three for months, etc.

Each activity is evaluated by the militants and sent to different instances as required.

All citizens have a file in the files of the Department of State Security associated with the algorithmic number of their Identity Card, which requires the Law to be permanently ported, if the Police Authority requires it and does not carry it, the prison goes

This identification number is an arithmetic algorithm where the date of birth, starting with the year of birth, the month and the day, its gender: 01 and 02, the century of birth, a digit in this serial number that includes everything type of personal and demographic data and the reliable level of each individual on a scale of rank from 1 to 9.

Law # 150 National Security Law imposes massive mobilization in case the risk of destabilization, the danger of the government, this mobilization is related to this ordinal number in the scale, because each citizen level has a type of tunnel where it will be "protected".

The latter is this value of this citizen for the government. They also take note in relation to the family and / or any social relationship. Each time this individual has a systematic evaluation to know what level of confidence can be deposited by the government in each citizen. Every citizen needs a report and receives permission to move or visit his family or friend, and show this RD-3 document in the Defense Revolution Committee, this condition is strictly enforced by law.

• "War of the whole people" or "War against all people"

The legalized path for the extermination of the civilian population in the Russian territory called Cuba.

This Law, in its aspect, hides the teleological purpose with its descriptive content of the participating organizations and, in a very general way, describes the rather bureaucratic participation of the political, military and social institutions involved and the concern of the logistic material base to guarantee the life of the protected.

It is necessary to read it with a critical spirit and to know the scenario where its scope was developed to realize its danger, this is the objective of this Chapter.

The National Defense Law # 150, this drawing made during my stay in prison reflects an insistent thought on this sensitive issue because since 1981, I learned about the mobilization methodology of the FAR, then during the Practical Command Exercise as Reserve Officer in Regiment 117 of Cerro municipality for 4 months, knew how to prepare this deadly trap for our compatriots under the name of War of all the People, which really is the War against the People.

The perfect parallel between the scenes of Cambodia and Cuba explains how the Castro had and have all their military and repressive structure plus the manipulation of the press in order to exterminate the civilian population of Cuba in a silent and justified manner when they understand it necessary.

Original drawing made with urine and black smoke, the "prison ink" to make tattoos. Quivican Prison / 1995

I was able to see the video, considered a State Secret of the Expanded Defense Committee of the State Council when Castro explained to the members of this Committee how to do mass Mobilization in detail and how to use the National Tunnel System.

I received this video from General José Abrantes, former interior minister to send him abroad, when he was in Guanajay prison, in 1990, shortly before he was killed, with a saline shock. The Department of State was depositary of the video through Mr. Evans of the SINA. (1990). The biggest Florentino Aspillaga DGI also spoke in the United States on this Plan of mass murder, also known by.

Proof of the positive impact of Pol Pot's plans on Fidel Castro, he was awarded in Cuba with the highest distinction of the Council of State of the Republic of Cuba, the Order of the National Hero "José Martí"; Another distinction that the Cambodian monster received has been bestowed by the Guinness Records Record Book, "Pol Pot , the man who has killed more people in less time."

A few months after his visit to Cuba and being the subject of the protocolary attention of the Head of State, this bloodthirsty tyrant carried out the most cruel murder known in history, but immediately these unfortunate events occurred as a result of the absolute faculties that confer the governments of the international communist brotherhood.

The similarity of the conditions of application and the purpose of Law 150, have the experience of what happened in Cambodia, a few days after the overthrow of the Cambodian regime, Vilma Espin de Castro, president of the Federation of Cuban Women, member of the Bureau Politician and Minister of Food and Chemistry by "under the table", visit Non Penh, capital of Cambodia, accompanied by the Lieutenant Colonel of the Directorate General of Intelligence, Western Europe section, Magaly Garcia companion of Vilma Espin to take first-class experience how the Pol Pot Plan had been implemented with the narration of experiences and details of the event in context, then when it was exposed to the Political Bureau, this "inspired" the Commander in Chief, who was very impressed with the efficiency of the method used for his "hero" Pol Pot and Ian Sari.

Immediately Castro gave the order to the MINFAR to elaborate a Law for the National Mobilization Order in a state of war or national emergency and coordinate the use of all means to "preserve the civilian population".

The main objective of this preservation of civil society was to justify the absolute neutralization of the population that could use its potential to rebel against the power of the regime by taking advantage of an attack from abroad or any political event that would endanger the stability of the Soviet / Castro regime. .
As Fidel Castro states in the video, "once in the tunnels the enemy bombs would be responsible for justifying the collapse of the tunnels and the death of thousands of civilian refugees."

The National Data Base of the regime, now is updated with new personnel communication like the cell phones, national Internet what can take control about the every email users, FaceBook messagers, all of this elements under Ministery of Information headed by Master Spy Commander Ramiro Valdes, they have in real time the national public opinion and take the repression of any insurrection focus.

Re

f.

Speech taped by Council of Cuba Fidel Castro at the Expanded Military Council, this vido came to my by the General Jose Abrantes and I sent to USA Interest Office in Havana, Cuba

Testimony and Archives of the author

Law # 150 National Defense

Law # 59 Law of Social Hazard

Course on Civil Defense

Visit to the Model Refugee *Tunnels of Havana*

Chapter # 12
Biological Weapons against the United States

Cuba introduces phytosanitary epidemics in the United States
Epidemics to damage agriculture have used diseases such as Citrus

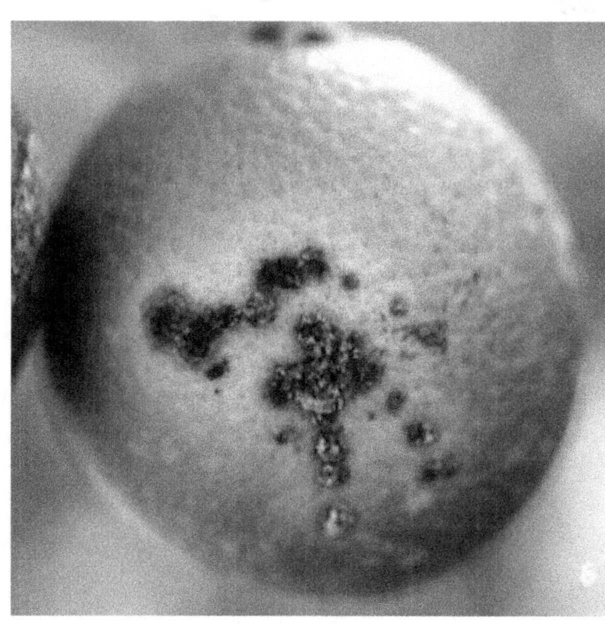

Canker, Spring and
The "Citrus Canker" virus was
activated in Cuba by Agronomist
José Matos of the Citrus
Technological Institute
"Revolución de Octubre" in
Bauta, province of Havana, under
the auspices of the Plant Health
Institute led by Dr. Heliodoro
Martínez- Rush. Every year new
diseases appear in the Citrus of
Florida as shown in this
photograph.
This institute made deliveries to
the United States using migratory

birds as vectors or carriers, once
contaminated with encephalitis and other diseases. Its director was also the
President of the Sociedad Colombófila and Guillermo García presided over
the National Assembly the Commission of Flora and Fauna, which with
the justification of a study on the Migratory Birds from the United States
and Canada which migrate annually in the winter to Cuba, on its return to
the North were infected with different pathogenic viruses. Some birds
continue to the South and have also spread pests throughout the South
American area. The subversive purpose of Russia and Cuba is to sow
problems and difficulties of all kinds and in all countries that can.

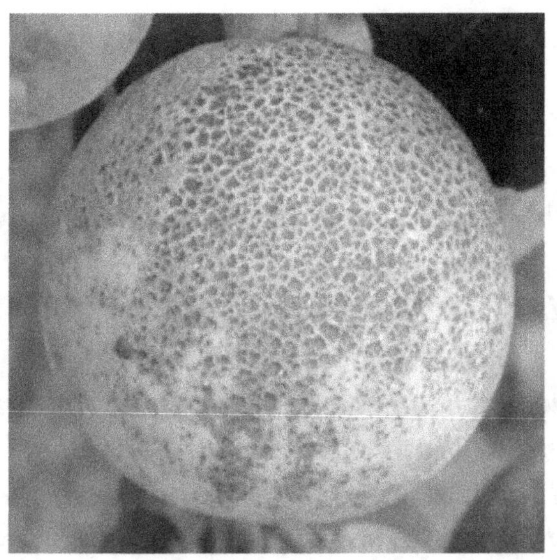

Citrus Cancer began in Florida and moves across the continent. From 1995 to date it has taken the southern half of the continent.

Chemical and biological weapons are produced in Cuba and the Soviets stored large quantities in the province of Camagüey in a complex of large proportions where some R-12 missiles were also hidden inside the tunnels, which due to contamination have killed many

soldiers radioactive contamination, including Colonel Desiderio Melendrez de Cascorro, Camagüey and many floodgates have been walled up. It is known that the Biotechnology industry in Cuba has been a front to produce weapons of mass extermination.

The Giant African Snail, (Scientific name: The Achatina Fulica never seen before in the American continent only known in Hawaii introduced by Japan before the attack on Pearl Harbor.

This snail destroys the plant at night only by contact and returns to the deep subsoil before dawn, being almost impossible to detect it, these actions have created bi-million dollar losses in the Citrus Industry in the States of Florida. These outbreaks are almost impossible to eradicate after of years have been declared endemic.

The great factory of chemical fertilizers of Cienfuegos bought in England was canceled the contract when discovering on the part of the English that the objective of the factory, was not the fertilizers but the Soviets were interested in copying the technology and producing in Cuba, elements chemicals to produce binary explosives, banned and persecuted by the UN Security Council at the time of Leonid Brehznev.

The "Quimonor" plant in La Paloma, in Matanzas, produces toxic gases for military use and in the Armored Troop Repairs Plant in Wajay, Havana, "Elephants" trucks were designed and assembled to remotely disseminate the toxic gases in the Battlefields, some of these trucks were captured in Saddam Hussein's troops during the last US war against Iraq.

BIOLOGICAL WEAPONS "Made in CUBA"

The first experiments with germs and toxins began in the years 1969 until 1979 by the so-called Biological Front in the West of Havana "Atabey" in the surroundings of the CENIC and the residence of the Minister of the FAR. The first experiments were with toxins from algae and shellfish, such as fly vectors Drossophila Lipsophaga. Also Fidel Castro's order the Porcine African Fever to destroy the most popular meat in Cuba. Killing the private porcine mass.

Many Institutes and Research Centers of the so-called Academy of Sciences of Cuba formally addressed, Dr. Rosa Elena Simeon, member of the Political Bureau of the PCC and President of the Cuban Academy of Sciences, but in turn the so-called Biological Front directed by The Commander in Chief and his subordinate General Guillermo Rodríguez, Head of the Medical Services of the FAR operatively have the capabilities and facilities for collateral investigations in different branches of Biology, Chemistry, Institute of Immune Assay, Institute of Blood Products, Institute of Molecular Biology,
Institute of Tropical Diseases, Institute of Epidemiological Investigations "Carlos J. Finlay" Plant Health Research Institute, Research Institute of Veterinary Sciences and Animal Health, Research Institute Agricultural Sciences, Research Institute Sub. Aquatic, Institute of Animal Production Research, Institute of Military Medicine, Bureau of Scientific Research, Center 3, etc. and others.

The First Plant, properly destined to Bacteriological Weapons, was inaugurated in April, 1994, near the Central Military Hospital, the second began to work in the spring of 1995 near the "Carlos J. Finlay" Hospital in the municipality of Playa, City of Havana. The facade was the construction to expand the Dept. of Pediatrics of the Military Hospital "Carlos J. Finlay".

The First Plant exists less than 1000 meters from the Central Military Hospital "Luis Díaz Soto" in the municipality of Habana del Este, City of Havana (Navy Hospital) using the facilities of said Hospital, on which more accurate data are available.

The residents of the health area are used to validate the products validate the products and without knowledge of the medical staff and of the patients themselves in different ways, they have been administered attenuated virus to know the results and the efficiency levels of the substances created in said installation, this is known as the Validation and Normalization of the Experiments.

Creating epidemics of Optic Neuritis, Meningitis, Peripheral polyneuritis and another virus epidemy, using the prisoner like Guinea Pig. I was victim of this experiment in Quivican prison with Optical Neuritis and Hepatitis I meet with other hundreds of prisoners unable to walk and also open the mouth to eat. Some of the Room H inmate, dead at this time. That thing happened in National Prisoner Hospital in the Havana Combinates Prisons.

he Production of Laboratory Animals, especially the Dalmatian dogs that enjoy a lot of sympathy in the US and are massively raised in the CENPALAB (Laboratory Animal Production Center) located between Santiago de las Vegas and Bejucal, is intended to be used as VECTORS. In other Centers of the Biological Front, among them the old farm of the former President of Cuba, Carlos Prio Socarras, located in Capdevila, municipality of Rancho Boyeros, migratory birds are controlled to use them as host vectors of viruses such as the one known by the East Fever. of the Nile, using mosquitoes as intermediaries between the vector and humans.

They have also tested rodents, reptiles and insects and small containers the size of a medicine bottle in the form of spray to spray it in public meetings such as a sporting event or a large store, in central air conditioners, etc.

Directly also with chemical or biological substances in the pollution of aqueducts, food processing plants for human and animal consumption, etc. In general, the countries that develop Biological Weapons are working or already have this diabolic list of Diseases, according to the Intelligence Agencies of the West, or by scientific organizations concerned with the Non Proliferation of Weapons of Mass Extermination as the Monterrey Institute and by the American Federation of Scientists (FSA) based in Washington, these diseases commonly appear in these listings, which are detailed below.

"Biological warfare agents include living microorganisms (bacteria, protozoa, rickettsia, viruses, and fungi), and toxins (chemicals) produced by microorganisms, plants, or animals. (Some authors classify toxins as a chemical instead of biological agents, but most do not, and they were included within the 1972 Biological Weapons Convention as reflected in its formal title, the Convention on the Prohibition of the Development, Production and Storage of Bacteriological (Biological) and Weapons of the Toxic and its Destruction) .

Environmental Research Base, as a protective mantle but directed by Cuba in Puerto Rico, the Caribbean and the Amazon.

Cuba, under the pretext of studying the Environment and Ecological Systems, infiltrates its agents to investigate the migration of birds and their behavior patterns and then use them as a vector carrying pathogenic viruses to the territory of the United States, such is the case of what is currently They are doing at the "El Paraíso" farm located at Km 10.3 of highway 511 in Ponce, Puerto Rico, and with these studies of the environment in a manipulated manner they raise opinions so that the Puerto Rican people feel threatened by the presence of the Naval aviation on the island of Vieques, however the real reason is to obtain data to use migratory birds as vectors of epidemic viruses. The names of the entire group of Cubans sent by Castro and his positions in the military scientific structure of the regime are well known, as is the United States government.

The so-called Carpenter Bird System for the CIA and Pronto Auxilio for the Military Counter Intelligence of Castro.

But if all this were not enough there is much more, the Russians have a system at the level of the whole planet to modify the weather, this chain of low frequency transmitters to the ionosphere layer causes changes that alter and make unpredictable and more violent hurricanes, torrential rains or prolonged droughts.

This chain of transmitters has locations around the Arctic and the south of the United States, Cuba, the locations are Angarask and Kabarorovsk in Liberia, in Gomel, in Sakhalin Island, in Nikolalaiev, Ukraine, another is Latvia near Irga and could not miss in this diabolical project the authorization of Castro to give a piece of Cuba, these are the antennas located in the area of Quivican, Guira de Melena and Batabanó, in the Castro military circles this area is known as "Pronto Auxilio", for these facilities never lack electricity, to operate this system the Russians have in Cuba about 2,500 technicians who live in the area of Managua, Cast "Sierra Maestra" and "Naroka" in Santiago de las Vegas. In my opinion the number of soviet advisor is much lees, may be around 50-60 specialist.

The transmission antennas are located in an area of southern Havana known as "Pronto Auxilio" linked to the Cable Co Axial with the Lourdes Centers and the Central Command of Armed Forces Post.

This same system of Long-Term Meteorological Blockade was carried out on the Pacific coast from a ship creating droughts and floods in California in the 70s and 80s.

Currently near the Moscow International Airport, there is a small sample or exhibition plant for the international armament market that is well managed by the Russian mafia, before "nomeklatura" top leaders.

According to information, China has delivered medium-range missiles of type MB-15 during 1990. The explosive charges were landed by the port of Mariel, according to Pentagon sources, by that date.

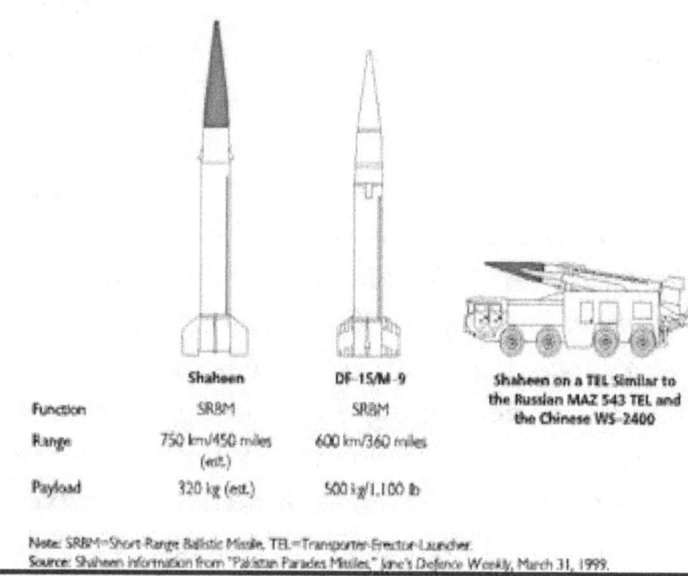

The DF-15 is a modern short-range ballistic projectile put into service around 1990-91. It is a solid fuel projectile with an inertial guidance system although it can be updated in the future with GPS. It is estimated to have a range of 600 km.

Its load can be nuclear.

It was initially thought that the DF-15 was a one-phase projectile, however recent reports suggest that it may have a separation warhead with its own miniature propulsion system. Such a system is significant because it would allow to make changes to the trajectory of the term of the warhead, suggesting some form of terminal guidance.

The M-9 (DF-15) is deployed on a mobile erector-platform - the launcher (TEL) vehicle. The warhead is dual capable conventional or nuclear with a 950 kg payload (nuclear performance is unknown but can be approximately 90 KT). The solid fuel of the projectile means that its launch preparation time can be as short as 30 minutes.

Export models of the DF-15 are known as 'M-9s' and it is presumed that they carry only conventional warheads. Several sources suggest that M-9s may have been exported to Syria, Libya, Iran, Cuba and Pakistan. This is the harsh reality that has left us an ambiguous, passive and permissive policy of the United States and the European Community, this last "consort of Castro".

All the advances of the Science and Technology of the Humanity, Castro put them at his disposal to destroy those he considers his enemies.

Testimonials
Author Files
Documentary "Red Alert" by Dr. Ed Palmer, Dr. Ken Alibek and Dr. Ed Prida.
Inspector of the Department of Agriculture of the Citrus Cancer Eradication
Program of the State of Florida from 1998 to 2005 EI # 1460 at the Opa Locka, Plantation, Port Saint Lucy and West Palm Beach Bases
Rolando Barros Prida(my nephew) death working in toxins to be used in Cuba-Angola War in Santiago de las Vegas Veterinarian Laboratory.

THE END
Thanks for your attention!

The Cuba's Attacks by Ed II and Edward Prida III